EFFECTIVE EMPLOYEE RELATIONS

A Guide to Policy and Practice in the Workplace

RICHARD PETTINGER

KOGAN PAGE

First published in 1999

Kogan Page Limited
120 Pentonville Road
London N1 9JN

British Library Cataloguing in Publication Data

A CIP record for this book is available from the British Library.

ISBN 0 7494 2693 4

Typeset by Kogan Page Limited
Printed and bound by Biddles Ltd, Guildford and Kings Lynn

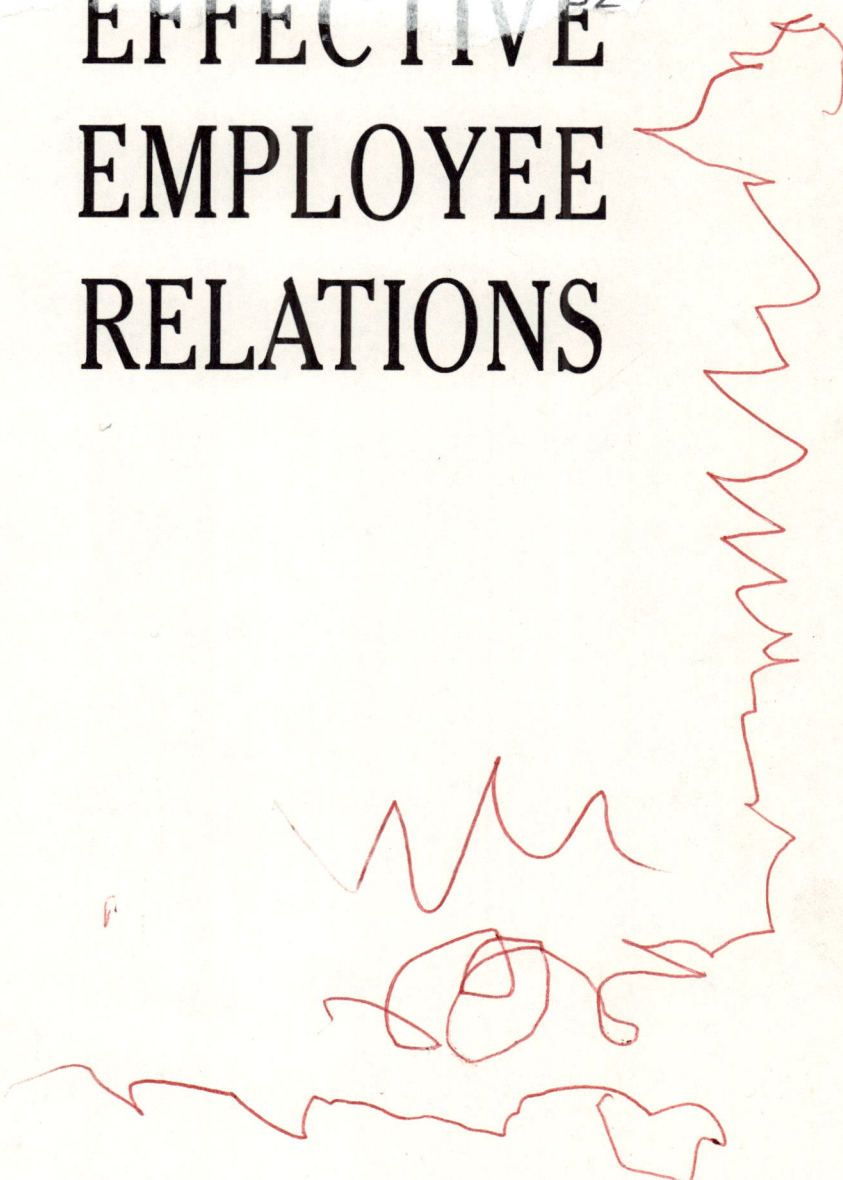

HE

EFFECTIVE

EMPLOYEE

RELATIONS

CONTENTS

PREFACE

Employee relations is the term used to summarize the relationships between employers and their staff, managers and subordinates, within and between different work groups, departments, divisions and functions in organizations. Alternatives have been tried and tested – for example, staff relations; employment relations; or even human relations; and people still continue to refer widely to industrial relations, which was always the term traditionally used. While this last may appear a little archaic at times, people at least understand what it means.

Or do they? Consider the following quote:

> If you stop someone in the street and ask them 'What do you think about employee relations and trade unions?' the chances are that you will get an emotional response which is either strongly for or equally strongly against them. Unfortunately, it is far less likely that you will get an informed response.

These words were written on behalf of the Industrial Society by Julie Baddeley in 1981. In truth, they could have been written at any time in the past two hundred years by anyone expressing a general view of what employee relations means to them. In the UK, employee relations (ER) excites some of the strongest passions and prejudices to be found anywhere in society in general, and workplaces in particular.

The whole subject is shrouded in political perspective and prejudice. Different political parties have used ER in support of their own specific agenda, and differing points of view have been widely written up and reported in the media. Again, the presentation of views in the media is often ill-informed; this has not prevented their proliferation, nor the adoption of these prejudices by sectors of the public at large.

There is no doubt that old images and legends die hard. It is now nearly twenty years since the last public service strike in the UK. This took place in 1979; refuse was piled up in Hyde Park, and bodies remained unburied, because those who carried out these tasks had withdrawn their labour. Yet to certain points of view and vested interests, this remains the outward face of trade unionism in particular, and employee relations overall.

Furthermore, trade unions and the Trades Unions Congress, and employers' associations and the Confederation of British Industry, used to exert great influence on political drives and initiatives; it was an often stated tenet of Conservative government policy of the 1980s and 1990s that this influence – especially that of trade unions – should be reduced.

Moreover, trade unions once had a clear role in the world of work. They sought to deal with the worst excesses of employer practice and to ensure minimum standards of pay, terms and conditions of employment and job security for those in particular occupations. However, it also remains true that the peculiarly British development of trade unions – of a large number of highly specialized unions concerned with precise occupations – has been divisive and ultimately damaging to the interests of those whom they have purported to represent. Industries that were traditional bastions of unionism – ships, docks, steel, coal, engineering – have largely collapsed, and with them has gone the influence of the powerful industrial unions that used to represent those who worked in them. While these industries prospered, their trade union leaders, employer and employer association leaders, were powerful influential public figures whose advice was regularly sought by leading politicians in the formulation and implementation of pay policies and national, industrial, commercial and public service strategies. As those industries collapsed, so their union and employer leaders lost influence also.

The picture was further clouded by adoption of the phrase 'the right to manage' by politicians. Politicians took the view that legislation to remove trade union power and curb what was seen as excesses – lightning strikes, secondary action, restrictive practices, demarcation, restraint of trade – would grant this right to companies and public service organizations. Only when the effects of structural industrial decline, the rising unemployment and the legal framework that was created became engaged did it become widely understood that the right to manage and the capability to manage were very different.

At the beginning of the 1990s, the position of employee relations in the UK had been transformed, from a highly structured, rigid and political influential factor of everyday life into something of a morass. Out of this has emerged a range of legal, social, ethical and political issues, changes in employment practice and organization status and examples of alternative approaches. It therefore becomes essential to seek an alternative term to industrial relations, and so the phrase 'employee relations' is used.

Many of these alternative approaches have come about as the result of inward investment in the UK from overseas companies – especially from the Far East. Meanwhile at home, companies such as Virgin, Marks & Spencer and Body Shop have sought to develop their own distinctive standards of employment practice.

The emergence of alternative industrial relations and employee relations formats from the Far East bear further initial mention. On the one hand, companies such as Sony, Sanyo and Nissan have brought highly conformist and cohesive approaches to the plant and distribution activities and operations that they have established in the West, and these have been reinforced through extensive long-term investment in employees through guarantees (as far as possible) on permanence and continuity of employment, continuous training and development, distinctive standards of management, distinctive standards of product and service quality and output, openness of information and approach and high sectoral pay levels. On the other hand, western companies have located their production activities in deprived and poverty stricken areas of existing low wage economies in the Third World, recycling many of the old industrial revolution practices that were supposed to have been abolished many years ago, and in which trade unions played a key part.

Much of this misses the point in any case. In order to get the informed response indicated above, it is necessary to study the totality of the subject, and each element of which employee relations is composed. The nature and mix of these elements, and the adoption of principles underpinning them, varies between organizations and, at an operational level, is dependent upon the qualities, expertise and attitudes of departmental managers, section heads and supervisors in this field for their effective delivery. In the end therefore, effective employee relations – and the contribution that it makes to organization success, effectiveness and profitability – is dependent upon the importance and priority placed on it in individual situations. This can only be achieved if organizations and their managers first understand the totality of the field.

The purpose of this book is therefore to work through the totality of the employee relations field. Chapter 1 is an introduction and summary of the historic and present situation, and introduces some current lessons and issues. Chapters 2, 3, 4 and 5 concentrate on the legal, managerial, behavioural and operational principles necessary for the creation of an environment in which effective employee relations can take place. Chapters 6 and 7 are concerned with the effective management of conflict, first from an organizational point of view and

(Chapter 7) when problems have to be sorted out through recourse to the law. Chapters 8, 9, 10 and 11 are concerned with the application of the principles of management in the specific field of employee relations – designing and creating policies and institutions (Chapter 8); understanding the motivation and individual and group inter-relations necessary for organizational harmony (Chapter 9); attention to work methods and patterns (Chapter 10); and identifying those managerial qualities necessary (Chapter 11). Finally, Chapter 12 is concerned with the future, identifying likely developments in employee relations, summarizing lessons from elsewhere in the world, especially Japan, and noting the legal, social and operational constraints, within which organizations and their managers will have to work.

The book is of value to all those concerned with effective management of staff. It is also of value to students of management at all levels – undergraduates following business and management studies courses and also those engaged in postgraduate or post-qualification studies. Above all, it is of great value to those following specialist programmes of study, especially those of the Institute of Personnel and Development, and the Institute of Management. It will also be of value to those studying human resource management, staff management, on MBA and other taught Masters programmes, and of key interest to those following postgraduate studies in specialist human resource management areas.

Richard Pettinger

INTRODUCTION

Employee relations (ER) is the system by which workplace activities are regulated, the arrangement by which the owners, managers and staff of organizations come together to engage in productive activity. It concerns setting standards and promoting consensus. It is also about the management of conflict.

Much of this has its roots in the economic and social changes of the industrial revolutions and the urbanization of the 19th century, the inherent conflict between labour and the owners of firms, the formation of collectives (combinations of groups of workers to look after their own interests) and the demarcation lines and restrictive practices that some occupations and trades were able to build up. The influence of these traditions remains extremely strong, particularly in long-established industries such as factory work, transport and mining. However, in recent years there has been a serious attempt to change the attitudes of all concerned in this field, and to generate a more positive and harmonious ethos. Companies and their managers have come to recognize the importance of positive employee relations and the contribution that they make to profitable and effective organizational performance; some trade unions have seen this as an opportunity to secure their future, and to attract new members. Other unions have lost their influence because of the great numbers of jobs that have disappeared in the sectors that they represent.

PERSPECTIVES

It is usual to distinguish three perspectives as follows:

■ **Unitarism** This assumes that the objectives of all involved are the same or compatible, and concerned only with the well-being of the organization and its products, services, clients and customers. The most successful of unitary organizations (eg McDonald's, Virgin, IMG) set very distinctive work, performance and personal standards, to which anyone working in the company must conform. This is also inherent in the Japanese approach to the management of the human resource.

■ **Pluralism** This admits a variety of objectives, not all compatible, among the staff. Recognizing that conflict is therefore present, rules, procedures and systems are established to manage it and limit its influence as far as possible. This is the approach taken especially in public services, local government and many industrial and commercial activities, where diverse interests have to be reconciled in order that productive work may take place.

■ **Radicalism** This is the view that commercial and industrial harmony is impossible until the staff control the means of production, and benefit from the generation of wealth. Until very recently, this was a cornerstone of the philosophy of many trade unions and socialist activists in industry, commerce and public services.

ER STRATEGIES

ER strategies ultimately depend on the industrial or commercial sector concerned, or whether it is public or government serviced. One of the following positions is normally adopted.

■ **Conflict** The basis on which staff are to be dealt with is one of mistrust, divergence, irreconcilable aims and objectives; disparity of location; divergence and complexity of patterns of employment and occupations; professional, technical, skilled and unskilled staff. In such cases as this, the ER strategy will be devised to contain the conflicts, to reconcile differences, and to promote levels of harmony as far as possible. This has been the basis of much UK employee relations in the past; and remains a key influence today.

■ **Conformity** The diversity of staff and technology may be (and often is) as great as in the above scenario, but where the ER strategy rather sets standards of behavioural and operational aims and objectives that in turn require the different groups to rise above their inherent differences. Organizations such as Nissan, Sony, Body Shop and Virgin have all sought to adopt this view.

■ **Consensus** The way of working is devised as a genuine partnership between the organization and its staff and their representatives. Genuine consensus or partnership is very rare.

ER, STAFF AND THE ORGANIZATION

Whichever is adopted, there are common threads. Organizations must understand the nature and strengths of the types of staff that they employ. They must recognize that there are divergences of aims, and different priorities that must be resolved if effective and profitable work is to take place. The nature of ER and related staff management activities will vary accordingly, but at the outset all staff, whatever their occupation, must form an identity with the organization that is both positive and complementary to its purposes. Boundaries of performance and behaviour requirements must be established in order that these purposes are achieved effectively and successfully. Issues to do with the nature and style of workplace regulation and staff representation must be resolved. Above all, ER and staff management must be seen as continuous processes and an area for constant improvement. If designed and conducted effectively by the organization, it will constitute a major return on the investment made in the workforce as a productive entity.

Whichever ER strategy is adopted must therefore be supportive of, and complementary to, the wider aims and objectives of the organization. This will extend in some measure to the capabilities and qualities of the workforce, but ultimately the workforce must be harmonized to the needs of the organization. Effective ER strategies start from this point. They may have regard to staff who, for example, are highly trained or professionalized; however, the overall direction of ER will seek again to match these with organizational requirements. Where staff have a very strong group identity – because of again, their profession, or because of sectoral traditions, or a long history of unionism for example – the organization must work to ensure the harnessing and commitment of this to its own purposes.

The inability of organizations to do this can be seen across the whole range of industry, commerce and public services. In the last of these, major conflicts have arisen between the 'professional' commitment to client groups – teachers to pupils, doctors and nurses to the sick, social workers to the disadvantaged – and the management by organizations of these staff. ER in these situations is largely ineffective because of the inability of organizations to direct their professional staff in ways universally understood as effective, and because of their lack of regard for, or ability in, ER matters. It has been compounded by the perceived conflict of objectives between service managers and service professionals. Finally, at no stage have professional people generated an identity with the service organization that remotely touches that which they have with their profession.

Summary box 1.1   The boundaries of employee relations

ER boundaries are established by organizations as follows:

- organization culture, attitudes and values
- standards of performance that are required
- standards of ethics, behaviour and attitude
- parameters of employee relations activity and where those parameters begin and end
- organizational and managerial approaches to staff management in general
- organizational and managerial approaches to the management of disputes, grievances, discipline and dismissal
- procedures for the management of disputes, grievances, discipline and dismissal
- consultation, participation and communication structures
- the precise forms of workforce representation, including the recognition of trade unions
- the desired aura or climate of workplace staff relations.

Note

The aura or climate is the backdrop or general impression created. This is reflected in the nature and numbers of accidents, disputes and absences at the place of work; it may also be indicated by rates of turnover and labour or problems with particular staff categories.

Whatever standpoint is adopted, it is important that both managers and staff understand it so that they can identify their mutual expectations. Needless disputes are kept to a minimum as long as everyone understands the position of everyone else.

Industrial situations are traditionally no better. ER in coal mining across the world has been so bad that miners have adopted loyalties to anyone other than the mine owners. In the UK, the focus of coal mining is the union, which provides welfare, leisure and recreation facilities, support for families in case of death or injury, representation at disputes, and a lobby for increased investment in safety and technology. Endemic throughout hundreds of years of coal mining, the result has been that the first and only loyalty of the staff has been to the union; at no stage has any managing organization, either private or nationalized, been able to provide an identity equivalent to this (nor is there any real evidence that they have tried). Rather, they have taken the view that conflict is inherent, and have sought to devise 'safety-valve' ER strategies, to ensure as far as possible that when conflict does blow up, it can be contained without serious disruption to the work in hand.

The strategy adopted will be supported by staff handbooks and rule-books, the procedures used and the ways in which these are promulgated, and any formal structures that are devised and put in place. These are, in turn, underlined by the nature of staff representation, induction and orientation programmes, and day-to-day work practices (see Summary boxes 1.2 and 1.3).

THE FRAMEWORK OF EMPLOYEE RELATIONS

The UK tradition: the tripartite system

In the UK, it is usual to regard the framework of employee relations as tripartite. In this view, the parties are government; employees, their representatives and trade unions; and employers, their representatives and associations. Each has distinctive roles (see Figure 1.1).

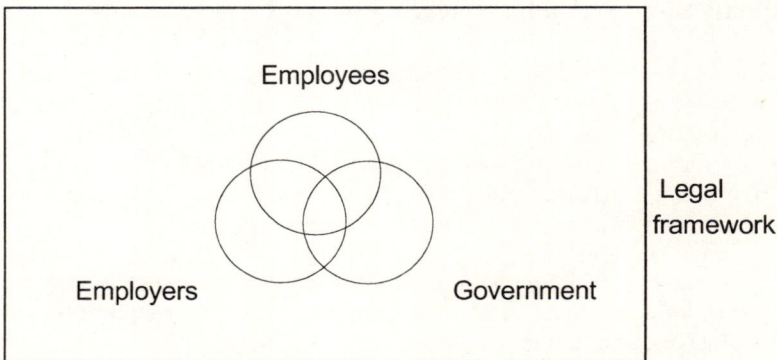

Figure 1.1 *The tripartite system of employee relations*

Summary box 1.2   Other considerations

- **The structure of the workforce**: operational aspects; dispersion; departmentalization and groupings; particular ways of working
- **Staff management aspects**: of core and peripheral work groups; specialist sub-contractors, consultants and advisors; those on fixed term or fixed project contracts
- **Technology**: its usage; its effect on the working environment; the rate at which it changes; the skills and expertise required
- **Patterns of work**: attendance patterns; output patterns; job and work mixes; nature and style of supervision
- **Expertise nature**: the specific nature of the expertise employed; the mix of expertises employed; the nature and style of management approach to that expertise
- **Balancing** and **reconciling** a great mixture of conflicting and divergent elements in the basic interests of organizing and maintaining effective working methods and ensuring fairness and equity to all
- Balancing **harmony** and **contentment** with commitment, drive and organization purpose
- The establishment and provision of **standards** and **sanctions** for the enforcement of rules
- **The capability of managers**: one of the greatest advances in the field has been the recognition of the qualities, aptitudes and attitudes necessary for the promotion and maintenance of effective and harmonious ER, and the training of managers and supervisors in the field.

Summary box 1.3   Problem-solving in employee relations

As well as a strategy and direction for the overall direction and management of ER, a strategic approach to specific ER matters will be adopted by organizations and their managers. As well as briefings for staff and training for managers in ER skills and knowledge, organizations will take an approach to the management of workplace conflicts based on answers to the following six strategic questions:

- What is the likelihood of a dispute occurring? If one does occur, how long might it last? What are the wider consequences to ourselves, and to our staff?
- If a dispute does occur, can we win it? What are the consequences of winning it? What are the consequences of losing it?

- If a dispute does occur, what costs will we incur? As well as financial cost, what of the questions of PR, media coverage and local feelings in our community? Is this a price worth paying?
- What happens when it all settles down? How will we interact and work with the staff afterwards? How long will any bad feeling last? What are the wider implications of this?
- What other ways are there around the matter or dispute in hand? Are we able to use these? What are the pros and cons of going down these alternatives, vis-à-vis a dispute?
- What are the behavioural and psychological aspects that surround this issue? If we win the dispute, what will be the effects on the workforce? And on managers? Are there questions of morale to be considered? If we lose, would loss of face be important? How could we save face, if that were to arise? What would be the response of the workforce and its representatives?

From consideration of the matter in hand in this way, and by establishing the answer to these issues, the answer to the following question is critical:

- Why are we seeking, entering, or preparing to enter, into this dispute?

Government

The government is the single major universal influence on ER everywhere. It is the single largest employer responsible for the pay, terms and conditions of employment of the civil service, the armed forces, the police, the emergency services, local government and services, nationalized industries and utilities and health and social services. As the dominant employer, it sets standards of employment and ER practice that others will be expected to follow; and there is great scope for setting 'model' terms and conditions. Major public activities (especially large hospitals, government functions and nationalized industry premises) are often the dominant employer of a locality, directly affecting what others have to pay to attract staff to work for them.

Governments make employment and employee relations laws, as with everything else, and set the standards and boundaries of practice. They also establish codes of conduct, codes of practice and employment protection and encouragement policies. They may also set contract compliance rules, requiring anyone wishing to tender for government contracts to adhere to particular standards of practice. Governments may also use the military police and emergency services in times of industrial strife to keep essential services open and maintain the general national quality of working life.

Governments codify all aspects of workplace relationships – the rights and limits of trade union activities, the rights of individuals at the workplace, the rights of organizations and their managers, equality of opportunity, the right to strike and the right to work.

Employees

The interests of employees at places of work are looked after by trade unions, staff associations, some professional bodies and the individuals themselves. Over the years, the greatest single influence has been trade unions.

Trade unions were first established to protect the interests and standards of living of persons working in particular sectors. A variety of definitions have therefore grown up, and unions may be classified in the following way:

■ industrial unions: all members are from one industry (eg mineworkers, steelworkers and railway workers)
■ skilled or craft: in which all the members have completed a course of training or apprenticeship (eg electrical or engineering)
■ white collar: for example, the civil service and banking unions
■ local government: as a distinctive sector
■ professional: representing groups such as teachers and nurses
■ technical: representing managerial and research staff
■ general: representing the unskilled and semi-skilled.

In recent years, trade unions in many parts of the world have lost influence and reputation as the source of much of their power and membership, the manufacturing and primary sectors, have declined. New jobs created have been in the assembly, service and retail sectors, where no traditions of unionism exist. Legislation has been enacted to ensure that proper procedures are followed before strike action or other disputes take place. Governments have reduced the national influence and reputation of the unions by setting their own ER agenda, and by covering the widest possible range of employee representative bodies (see Summary box 1.4). Finally, automation and technological advance has eliminated most of the demarcation distinctions between occupations, and the move is now towards multi-skilling and the flexible workforce.

Summary box 1.4   The Donovan Commission

Part of the review of the Royal Commission on Trade Unions and Employers' Associations (the Donovan Commission of 1965–7) was to define for the first time what the real roles of unions were. In summary, the findings were that unions:

- bargain for best possible wages, terms and conditions for members
- lobby for improved share in national wealth for members
- influence government policy and the legal framework on behalf of members
- lobby for social security for all
- lobby for full employment, job security, wage levels and cheap housing for the poor
- bargain nationally, regionally, locally and industrially, for organizations and individuals
- represent members at disputes and grievances and for any other reason for members according to need.

Source: Donovan (1967).

Unions have therefore had to seek new or redefined roles. They have turned from national lobbies to effective action at individual workplaces on behalf of individuals and groups of members. They have engaged in cooperative agreements with organizations, including productivity, training and no-strike arrangements. They have gained benefits for members such as advantageous rates for personal and possessions' insurance, and health care. They have engaged in mergers and membership drives in order to maintain and improve on the levels of influence that they have.

Employers

The third party to the framework is the employer, represented by employer and trade federations and associations, individual companies and organizations. The influence of employers is currently at its highest level, and rising, on the conduct of workplace employee relations, though (as with the unions) the employers' lobby has declined at national level.

The function of the employer in ER is to set standards of staff management, attitudes, behaviour and performance for the organization or company, to set terms and conditions of employment, and pay levels and methods and to act in a fair and reasonable way towards all employees at the workplace. They may take part in national arrangements to set minimum standards for the sector concerned. They may choose to recognize trade unions or not. They will make representations to government on their own behalf, through their associations and federations.

In recent years, the area of ER has become recognized for the first time as an area of profitable and effective activity. Managers are now being trained in the skills of staff relations and problem-solving. Great emphasis is increasingly emerging in the devising of human resource policies, the tone and style of staff handbooks, the attitudes and approaches to staff and workforces.

THE EUROPEAN UNION VIEW: SOCIAL PARTNERS AND THE SOCIAL DIALOGUE

The European Union (EU) of the present day had its origins in the European Coal and Steel Community (ECSC). The ECSC was formed in 1951 by six countries – Belgium, France, West Germany, Italy, Luxembourg and the Netherlands. The purpose was to abolish import duties on cross-border movements of coal and steel within these six countries, while imposing a common external tariff on supplies of these commodities from elsewhere in the world. From an early stage, however, it was much more than a purely economic arrangement. Employers' associations, trade unions and other employee representative bodies were actively and positively encouraged to contribute to the development of coal and steel community policy. The best interests of the ECSC would be served in the long term, it was deemed, if there was workplace harmony, and security and stability of employment.

Since then, the ECSC has developed – first into the European Economic Community (EEC) or Common Market, and subsequently into the European Community (EC), and finally into what is now known as the European Union (EU). At all stages, the institutes governing the European Community and Union have taken the view that there was a much greater legitimate involvement for all those concerned with workplace management and activities, than the narrow economic – and traditional – view adopted in the UK. In the management of organizations therefore, the EU enshrines the concept of social partners. The social partners are deemed to be:

■ the European Community and its institutions, including the European Parliament
■ trade unions and other employee representative bodies and interests
■ employers' associations, other employer representatives and individual organizations
■ other expert, quasi-legal and academic bodies with a legitimate or vested interest or expertise in the direction and management of organizations in particular, and ER at large.

It could be argued that the basis of the social partnership is similar to the tripartite system. However, the approach adopted is fundamentally different. It cites a partnership rather than a set of parts. It gives both employees and employers a legitimate – and legalized – position as organizational stakeholders equivalent to that of shareholders. Moreover, it is reinforced by the content of the European Union Social Charter to which the UK signed up in September 1997 (see Summary box 1.5 and Appendix A).

Summary box 1.5   The European Union Social Charter

The European Union Social Charter enshrines the fundamental rights of all EU citizens, in society at large as well as at places of work (see Appendix A). The Charter covers:

• the freedom of movement for workers and self-employed persons across all countries of the EU
• adequate protections for employment and remuneration
• improvement of living and working conditions
• adequate social protection and social security
• freedom of association – including the right to join trade unions and associations, and the right not to join trade unions and associations
• adequate and continuing vocational and job training
• equality of treatment for men and women
• information, consultation and participation of workers on key workplace issues
• health and safety protection at work
• protection of children and adolescents at work
• the access of elderly persons to labour markets
• the access of disabled persons to labour markets.

EU social – and ER – policy is still being developed. In general, however, all provisions above apply to all employees regardless of their length of service or hours of work. Specific issues concerning employers' responsibilities in continuous job and vocational training, pension rights, job and workplace security, and the maintenance of other social institutions such as the family (eg through parental leave), are still being worked through. At the time of writing, it is clear that organizations and their managers are going to be required to take the broadest possible view of employment, social and human rights.

MULTI-UNIONISM

A large part of traditional ER has been taken up with the reconciliation of differences between trade unions. This has occurred not just between occupational groups within organizations, but also within them. Multi-national corporations, public and health services carry vast, complex and sophisticated employee relations superstructures consisting of committees, sub-groups, working groups and ad hoc groups that all have to be managed and harmonized by the ER managers and departments concerned.

Moreover, they arrive at working practices which the functional managers in the organizations must adopt and respond to.

The complexities of multi-unionism have been compounded in the UK by the tradition of setting nationally agreed terms and conditions, wage levels and trade union policies (see Summary box 1.6). A feature of organizational approaches to ER has been to attempt to reconcile these. A variation of this has occurred (in industry rather than services) where national minima have been agreed across the board and then top-ups offered by employers in relation to their difficulties or otherwise in attracting and retaining staff. This phenomenon is known as drift in wages and conditions and is a key feature of local collective bargaining arrangements.

Summary box 1.6   Multi-union illustrations: UK

- The teaching profession in the UK is served by the following unions: National Union of Teachers, National Association of Schoolmasters and Union of Women Teachers, Assistant Masters and Mistresses Association, Professional Association of Teachers, National Association of Head Teachers and Deputy Heads' Association. Some are more specific than others; however, there is nothing to prevent a head teacher from continuing to belong to one of the generic unions.

- A Registered General Nurse (RGN), may choose to belong or not to any of the public service unions. However, his or her qualification will be endorsed by the Royal College of Nursing, which is a recognized trade union as well as professional body.

Recourse to arbitration

This is open to all those involved at all times in their attempt to resolve disputes at the workplace. Arbitration is available whether these disputes are individual (between a manager and a member of staff) or institutionalized (between an organization and a union or body of employees). Used effectively, it represents a means of resolution that is both considered and subject to internal scrutiny and which may also have the benefit of acceptability on the part of all because a third party has arrived at the conclusion.

Arbitration is not in itself a universal means of problem-solving. It can only be applied where all other approaches have failed, or when there is an issue of presentation concerning the means of delivery of a decision.

It is not an employee relations policy. Regular recourse to arbitration encourages extreme positions on the part of those in conflict so that any middle position recommended by an arbitrator is as favourable as possible. Internal credibility is lost. Continued recourse to arbitration leads to the frustration of those who can, and would, resolve their own problems and this leads to the loss of ER skills, expertise, aptitudes and, therefore, control.

Recourse to arbitration thus becomes an additional tool to be used by managers when the context and situation requires. Its use and value will be pre-evaluated in the light of these situations, the advantages and disadvantages weighed up by managers when they decide on whether or not to go to arbitration on a particular matter.

CONFORMISM AND CONSENSUS

Conformist ER requires the subordination of divergent and conflicting interests at the workplace, in the interests of pursuing common and understood aims. These are set by the organization in advance of any staff agreements. The stance normally taken is that the organization must be successful, effective and profitable, and that the purpose of ER (like all other workplace activities) is to contribute to this.

For the approach to be truly effective, overwhelming obligations rest with the organization and its managers. Standards are preset and prescribed, not the subject of negotiation. Areas of managerial prerogative, matters for consultation, and aspects open to negotiation, are all clearly stated. Conformity leaves much open to consultation, but very little to genuine negotiation.

Procedures are quick and direct. Managers seek to solve problems and promote harmony. Conflicts of interest between groups are kept to a minimum. Disputes (especially those to do with pay and conditions) are resolved within given deadlines. Staff identity with the organization must be strong. The position of trade unions (and any other staff representative bodies such as staff associations) is clearly defined and limited at the outset. The basis of any agreement is set by the organization. The union or representative body is invited to work within it. If it feels unable to do this, it will not be recognized.

The single union agreement

This approach to ER is highly regarded especially by Japanese companies operating in the West. It is a conformist approach. The ER agreement is made between the company and one trade union, along the conformist lines indicated above, with the overriding concern of streamlining and ordering workplace and staff relations, to ensure that their operation is as effective and ordered as any other business activity. Pre-designed and predetermined by the organization, such agreements are normally limited to a single site or operational division.

Invitations to tender for the rights to representation of the staff are issued to a range of trade unions. The unions then normally present the benefits that accrue to the organization dealing with them. The organization will hear all the presentations, and then decide on one union, which it will recognize, and which will then represent all the staff.

It follows that the groundwork for this must be carried out very carefully. There are problems of acceptance on the part of managers, who may not be used to dealing with a particular trade union, and on the part of the staff also, who may have no previous affinity or identity with it. There are also problems of acceptance on the part of highly organized occupational groups for the same reason, and on the part of those unions that are not to be recognized.

To be effective and successful, this strategy for the management of ER must have the following attributes:

- It must mirror the philosophy, ethos, style and values of the organization concerned; there must be commitment to it and a willingness on the part of the organization to resource and underwrite it all.
- Managers and supervisors are trained in the procedures and practices of ER, the ability to manage staff on a basis free from inherent conflict, and the ability to solve rather than institutionalize problems when they occur.
- Wage levels tend to be at the upper end of the sectoral scale, and will also be good in relation to other variables such as regional considerations and the ability to compete for all categories of staff in both the sector of operations and the locality where work takes place. Wage rises are never backdated.
- There is one set of procedures, terms and conditions of employment only, operated by the organization in conjunction with the recognized union. The procedures themselves, together with the rest of the ER policy, are devised and drawn up by the company and the union is invited to participate on preset terms. The ER sphere is not a matter for joint negotiation or agreement.
- The union represents all members of staff at the workplace and there is no other ER format. Staff are encouraged to join the union but are not compelled.
- Disciplinary and grievance practices operate from the standpoint of resolution and prevention of the matters in hand rather than institutionalization. Above all, they are aimed at getting any recalcitrant employee back into productive work in harmony with the rest of the company as quickly as possible. Where recourse to procedures is necessary, these also are designed for maximum and optimum speed of operation. The purpose here is to prevent any issue that may arise from festering and getting out of control. An example of a single union agreement is given at Appendix B.
- The disputes procedure is normally that of binding pendulum arbitration (see page 16) and represents the final solution to the matter in hand. It is only invoked at the point where an official dispute would otherwise take place; there are cultural as well as operational pressures that ensure that this gets used as rarely as possible.

This style of ER is above all designed to be a business-like approach and arrangement, designed as part of the process of ensuring the success, continuity and profitability of the organization. As such, it is integral rather than an adjunct to it.

Single table agreements

The single table agreement is a variation of the single union agreement (see Summary box 1.7). The principles, practices and approach are the same. All staff are on the same basic terms and conditions. Representation is allowed from more than one union, and is conducted from the one central standpoint. The advantage is that, within the broad constraint, it gives a measure of choice to the individual member of staff in the matter of representation.

Summary box 1.7   The basis of the single union or single table agreement

- The standpoint in the first section of any agreement is that of a business venture and the contribution of employee relations to success, continuity and business profitability.
- The parameters of employee relations and the extent and limitations of the union's involvement and influence are clearly defined.
- Consultative and participative meetings are to take place on a regularized and formalized basis; matters for consideration are prescribed (though there is an in-built flexibility).
- The standpoint of grievance and dispute and disciplinary handling is clearly stated. The full operation of procedures for these should be kept to a minimum; where they are necessary, they should normally be fully invoked and the issue resolved after a maximum of two weeks. Rights of representation and appeal are clearly indicated.
- Arbitration procedure is clearly stated.
- The final paragraph reinforces the tone of the agreement in which the necessity for industrial action in any form is precluded and which again restates the business nature of the agreement.

Pendulum arbitration

This is the term given to the instrument most widely used as the alternative to conflicts and disputes. It is invoked only at the point where a strike or other industrial action would otherwise take place.

An arbitrator is appointed by agreement of both sides to the dispute. The arbitrator hears both sides of the dispute, and then decides wholly in favour of one party or the other. Someone therefore always wins (and is seen to win) and someone always loses (and is seen to lose). The concept of pendulum arbitration is based on this – faced with the prospect or possibility of losing a dispute, each party will wish to resort to the negotiating table once again to resolve the differences. In particular, in Japanese companies, there are strong cultural pressures on managers not to get into disputes, and not to lose them if they do.

Pendulum arbitration normally represents the final solution to any dispute, against which there is no appeal; this is clearly stated in handbooks and agreements in which this is the instrument for the resolution of disputes. Those entering into it agree to be bound by the outcome before the arbitrator hears the case.

ER without unions

If employee relations is to be conducted without unions, the reasons why people join unions must be removed. Trade unions grew to prominence in organizations to represent the employees' interests, to serve particular groups, and as a brake on the worst excesses of management that led to a quality of treatment across the whole of the business sphere that by any standards, commercial or ethical, was unacceptable and untenable. If this arises, once unions have been eased out or derecognized (or in a new organization, where there is no intention to have them in the first place) the staff will simply join up again en masse. So an approach to ER that precludes the need for outside representation is essential.

This normally consists of adopting a benevolent, consultative and open mode of general communications, corporate attitudes to the staff and an enlightened general attitude as the cornerstone of the ER and staff management approach. Operation of procedures and practices must be fair, and be perceived as such. Pay, pay rises, working conditions and other operational matters are consulted upon through works councils, organization councils and staff associations.

Responsibility for the style and tone of employee relations rests entirely with the organization. Staff adopt the desired corporate attitudes, values and aspirations.

The single status concept

This concept is based on an ethical stance that all employees should be treated equally, and that the same fundamental terms and conditions of employment are to apply to all. There is, in these situations, a single staff handbook applying to all. Terms and conditions, and elements of the contract of employment, on such matters as holiday accrual, hours of work, the provision of staff facilities, working clothes and safety and protective wear, are the same for all. Participation in such things as profit-related or merit award payment schemes involves everyone.

Behavioural issues reinforce this. Everyone is addressed in the same manner regardless of occupation. The work of each employee is valued and respected. Differentiation between groups and categories of employees is on the basis of work function only; there are no exclusive canteens, or car-parking spaces.

Flexibility

Related to single status is the concept of the 'flexible workforce', where everyone concerned is both trained and available for any work that the organization may require of them. Staff normally will be made to understand, when they first join, that they may be required to undertake duties away from their normal or habitual occupation. In the wider interests of staff motivation, organizations will endeavour to do this on a positive rather than coercive basis. Nevertheless, it is a fundamental departure from traditional specialization, demarcation and restrictive practices.

Implicit in this are obligations on the part of employees to accept continuous training and development as part of their commitment to the organization – and this applies to all categories and occupations.

Works councils

Many organizations have established works councils in recent years. This is akin to having a board of directors looking after the employee (rather than shareholder) interests. Representatives are drawn from all departments, divisions and functions, as well as any recognized trade unions.

The European Works Council Directive 1994 required all companies to establish works councils that came under the following headings:

■ EU Scale Undertakings – with at least 1,000 employees within the EU and at least 150 employees in at least two member states
■ EU Scale Groups of Companies – groups controlled by a single parent company, with at least 1,000 employees within the EU, and owning or controlling at least two undertakings in separate member states, each with at least 150 employees.

The Works Council Directive 1994 is certain to have its scope extended by the EU in the next few years. Since the UK signed up to the EU Social Charter in September 1997, this will apply to all UK undertakings, as well as those within the rest of the member states of the EU.

ER PROCEDURES

These are written and promulgated for the purpose of regulating workplace activities – general employment practices, standards and approaches, general standards of workplace conduct and activity, discipline, grievance, disputes, health and safety, internal opportunities and equality.

They are used by managers in their pursuit of, and operation of, these aspects of work. They are for guidance, and only where something requires precise operation (such as a safety procedure), or there is a legal restraint (such as with discipline), should they be adhered to strictly. Their purpose otherwise is to set standards of behaviour and practice at work; this also has implications for the more general standards of decency, ethics, and staff treatment that are established at the workplace. Procedures also indicate and underpin the required attitudes, and let everyone know where they stand. More generally, they define the scope and limits of the influence of the workplace. Above all, they have to be understood and followed by all concerned; as long as they meet any legal requirements, organizations and their managers must follow what they promulgate.

Procedures should always be in writing, and state to whom they apply, and under what circumstances. They should be written in the language of the receiver, so that they are easily and clearly understood and followed. The best induction programmes will contain both coverage and explanation of them, so that new employees know from the outset where the boundaries lie, and what the expectations and obligations under them, on the part of both themselves and the organization, are.

Procedures should be reviewed and updated regularly, and when they pass from currency, they should be changed to reflect this. Staff groups and any recognized trade unions should always be consulted on the introduction, use and application of procedures and any changes that are made. Ultimate responsibility for both the standards that they set, and their design and implementation, must always remain with the organization.

Summary box 1.8 compares UK employee relations practice with that adopted in the USA and Europe.

Summary box 1.8   Comparative employee relations

It is relevant to draw attention here to the uniqueness of the United Kingdom ER system and its variants from others. This is especially true of the trade union movement. Until 1993, all UK trade unions took at least a collective standpoint and most were overtly socialist, at least in their leadership. The Labour Party was originally founded to represent the interests of the unions in Parliament; the major stakeholders in the Labour Party remained the trade unions. Only now is this relationship being seriously examined for the first time.

The other quirk specific to UK trade unions is their sectoralization and specialization. The titles, such as National Union of Teachers, or Rail and Maritime Trade Union, define spheres of influence and interests. They are drawn from a tradition of demarcation and specialization and, again, this is only being examined for the first time in the last decade of the 20th century where there are moves afoot among certain sectors to refocus their outlook.

This is to be contrasted with unions elsewhere. In the USA, they are professional lobbies. They work in the same way as any other such lobby to promote and defend their interests – through the media, political representatives and on industrial, commercial councils and committees. They are neither as universal nor as institutionalized as in Europe and the UK, neither do they carry the same influence (indeed, they have lost credence and influence in the wake of corruption scandals in recent years).

In the countries of Europe, unions adopt a much wider brief than their British counterparts, representing 'public services' or 'the car industry' for example, rather than a particular occupation or subsection of it. They also adopt a much wider variety of stances and affiliations, ranging from communism and socialism to conservatism, Christian democracy and Roman Catholicism. Finally, they take a much wider view of ER. Some are militant (eg France and Italy); some concentrate as much on welfare benefits as wages (eg Holland); while others adopt the stance that a productive, harmonious and profitable undertaking is good for everyone including their members (eg Sweden and Germany)

CONCLUSIONS

The general level of understanding and appreciation required of the managers if they are to be truly effective in this field is clearly deep and complex. They must create the basis of an harmonious and productive working environment so that effective work can be carried out.

Employee motivation must be maintained. The managers must establish formal, semi-formal and informal chains of communication with workforce representatives (if there are any) and with employees at large.

Managers have to bring a range of skills to bear in the day-to-day handling of staff matters. Negotiations, dealing with disciplinary and grievance matters, handling disputes and other problem-solving activities may have to be undertaken. They may have to balance conflicting demands and may only be able to resolve one issue at the expense of another.

Managers may be fortunate enough to be able to conduct ER in an atmosphere of positivism and industrial harmony. Conversely, they may constantly be working in an atmosphere where mistrust is endemic and outright conflict is just below the surface. In such circumstances, the best strategy may simply be to move from problem to problem if by doing so the manager can at least ensure a modicum of output. The ability to make any progress and shape a more positive and effective future for the staff in such circumstances will stem from an understanding of the status quo in the first place. A general appreciation of the traditions, history and background of ER is also essential if the managers are to understand both the current general state of ER thinking and also that of their own organization in particular. These traditions are underpinned by mythology, legends and folklore that still engender great pride in certain sectors of the population; this mythology has its roots in real grievances, deprivation and a style of entrepreneurship and management that was very often entirely unacceptable by any standard against which any such practice would be measured in the world of today.

This helps in an understanding of the behavioural and procedural niceties of bargaining activities, and also ensures that their importance in the conduct of ER is not underestimated. In traditional, long-standing and public UK institutions, both staff and unions are comfortable with this way of doing things; taking a little time to ensure that the processes and structures are adhered to may repay dividends in the early, ultimate resolution of conflict or negotiations. It also helps in the understanding of the scale and scope that any intended reform of ER practice must address. It is not enough simply to cut out the behavioural and procedural aspects, as these provide the format in which ER practice takes place. If such reform is to be carried out, either globally or at the workplace, in relation to these traditions, an entire new system of ER must be devised and implemented. That way, any uncertainty, mistrust and conflict inherent in piecemeal tinkering with the status quo is avoided.

Finally, this history explains the attraction to organizations of both the single union and non-union approaches. Both have a ready-made model and a set of principles from which to work. Both have been demonstrated, tried and tested elsewhere with a marked degree of success and effectiveness in certain circumstances.

It is necessary to understand this as a basis for the study of effective employee relations. It is next necessary to understand:

■ the legal basis for ER
■ the necessity to establish distinctive organizational standards for ER.

It is to these matters that the next two chapters are devoted.

2

EMPLOYMENT AND ER LAW IN THE UK

INTRODUCTION

It is next necessary to understand the legal framework in which ER takes place. This is founded in a combination of UK and EU legislation, and its application through the tribunal, court and justice system.

THE UK LEGAL FRAMEWORK

In the UK, the sources of employment law are the same as all other legal areas:

- statute law which is defined by Acts of Parliament
- criminal law which consists of offences against the nation or the Crown
- civil law which allows for the resolution of disputes between individuals
- precedent in which a judgment on one case is held to apply to others of a similar nature
- custom and practice in which legal status is accorded to something that has gone on for a period of time
- European law which is the ultimate point of reference for any UK citizen on any legal matter including employment.

Recourse to the law for alleged breaches is the same as all other legal areas – the Courts, Court of Appeal, House of Lords and the European Court of Justice. Employment matters may also be taken to Employment Tribunal. UK employment law also specifies the following factors that must be taken into account when considering workplace situations and issues:

■ fairness and reasonableness
■ natural justice
■ best practice
■ precedent.

Fairness and reasonableness

All organizations are unique and because they vary so greatly the test of what is fair and reasonable in particular sets of circumstances is always applied. Fairness and reasonableness is based on a combination of:

■ the size of the organization, the resources at its command and disposal
■ the nature of business and activities, the technology and equipment used, commercial and operational pressures
■ the nature of people employed, their skills, knowledge, qualities and expertise
■ ways of working, including interpersonal relationships
■ respect, value and esteem for staff and customers, honesty and integrity, and ordinary common decency
■ specific legal standards (eg health and safety, product quality and description, trading standards).

Fairness and reasonableness applies to conduct, behaviour and performance; to both employers and employees; and to employers'and employees' representatives.

Natural justice

Quite apart from any legal obligation, natural justice demands that people are treated equally and fairly and with respect and honesty in all walks of life; and work (or indeed lack of it) plays a significant part in everyone's life.

Best practice

Standards of staff and human resource management set by ACAS, the Department for Education and Employment and expert bodies such as the Institute of Management and the Institute of Personnel and Development establish what is known as best practice. Best practice is a combination of fairness and reasonableness, honesty and integrity and natural justice, together with the operational ways of organizing and directing people in order to optimize organizational performance.

Precedent

Workplace and employment tribunal cases are treated as distinctive and individual and, therefore, on their own merits. Tribunal judgments do not set precedent. Precedent is only set in employment law cases where these are referred on or pursued beyond the Employment Appeal Tribunal and into the mainstream judicial system.

AREAS COVERED BY EMPLOYMENT LAW

Contract of employment

This is the basis of the relationship between employer and employee. Not later than two months after starting work, any employee who works more than eight hours per week must receive a written statement giving:

- the name of the employer and the employee
- the date when the employment began, taking account of any period of employment with a previous employer that counts as continuous with the present
- pay or the method of calculating it, and payment interval
- terms and conditions relating to hours of work, holiday entitlement, other time off including public holidays and holiday pay
- job title or brief description of job
- place or places of work along with the employer's address
- any other specific or stated terms of employment.

This is the principle statement and must be contained in one document. In addition, the following information must also be given or be reasonably accessible to the employee:

- health and safety matters reflecting the employer's duty of care
- terms and conditions relating to sickness, injury and sick pay
- any pension arrangements
- the length of notice the employee must give and receive
- the period of employment, if it is temporary or fixed term
- particulars of any collective agreements by which the employee is to be bound
- any specific conditions that apply when the employee is to work outside the UK for more than one month
- any disciplinary rules applicable to the employee and the person to whom employees can apply if dissatisfied with a disciplinary decision or if they have a grievance about their employment and the procedure to be followed
- any implied terms of employment, and employee obligations.

Information given in job advertisements, job descriptions or other company information may also constitute part of the contract of employment.

Any change to the written particulars must be consulted on and agreed, and notified in writing to employees individually within one month of the change. If there is any dispute about the written statement, either the employer or the employee may refer the matter to an employment tribunal.

Collective agreements

This refers mainly to any trade unions that the employer recognizes and the right of the employee to join or not. It normally constitutes a statement of the specific terms and conditions by which both employer and employees are bound, and the specific procedures that are to be followed.

Discrimination and equality of opportunity

All organizations are required by law to be 'equal opportunity employers'. It is illegal to discriminate between people when offering employment, promotion, pay, training and development or any other opportunity on all of the following grounds:

- racial or ethnic origin and religion
- gender, including pregnancy, marital status and retirement age
- disability (except where the employer's premises do not provide suitable access)
- membership of a trade union, refusal to join a trade union, insistence on joining or not joining a trade union.
- spent convictions for previous offences and misdemeanours (although there are many occupations exempted from this, including teachers, doctors, lawyers, social workers, banking and finance)
- length of service or hours worked.

Discrimination may be either direct or indirect.

Direct discrimination is overt – the straightforward refusal of work or opportunities on any of the grounds indicated above. Indirect discrimination occurs where a condition or restraint is placed, the effect of which is to bar, restrict or jeopardize the opportunities of people from each of the groups indicated above.

Health and safety

An employer may not order or request an employee to carry out work that is hazardous or unsafe without first providing the correct protective equipment, clothing and training where necessary. An employer may not request, order or coerce an employee into carrying out any unsafe or hazardous activity.

It is the duty of employers to provide as far as reasonably practicable a healthy and safe working environment. It is the responsibility and duty of all to ensure that this is maintained and that accidents, hazards and emergencies are notified and rectified immediately.

Maternity

All female employees are entitled to 14 weeks' maternity leave regardless of length of service or hours worked. For those who have more than two years' continuous service the period is 29 weeks.

Pregnant employees are allowed time off with pay for ante-natal care.

On returning from maternity leave, the employee has the right to return to her previous job or (if this has ceased) to suitable alternative work.

Time off

Employers must allow reasonable time off from work for employees to carry out the following:

■ public duties, including Justice of the Peace, members of local authorities, tribunals, health authorities, governorships of schools and colleges, boards of prison visitors, jury service if the employee is called
■ duties connected with the activities of recognized trade unions, including representation of members and training
■ looking for work and attending job interviews, retraining, career and occupational counselling after employees have been declared redundant and before they have left
■ maternity (as above).

Redundancy

Employers may dismiss – make redundant – employees whose work no longer exists or where fewer employees are required to carry out existing levels of work. Where redundancies are declared the employer must disclose the following:

■ the reasons for the redundancies
■ the numbers and descriptions of employees affected
■ the criteria for selection
■ the means and dates on which the dismissals are to be carried out.

Employers must consult with any recognized trade unions as soon as it becomes known that redundancies are to occur. This must happen even if only one employee is to be made redundant.

Alternatives – short time working, short term lay-offs, transfers, redeployments, early retirements and calling for volunteers – must all be considered and rejected as impractical before compulsory redundancies take place.

The minimum consultation periods are as follows:

■ 90 days in the case of 100 or more dismissals in a 90 day period
■ 30 days in the case of ten or more dismissals in a 30 day period.

Otherwise consultation must begin as early as possible.

Employees who are dismissed because of redundancy are normally entitled to a lump sum payment. The amount depends on age, pay and length of service as follows. For each year of continuous employment:

- from age 41–64, 1.5 week's pay
- from age 22–40, 1 week's pay
- from age 18–21, 0.5 week's pay.

In 1998, £240 is the maximum weekly pay that is taken into account and 20 years the maximum service. The maximum redundancy payment possible is therefore £7,200 (ie 20 years' service between 41 and 64 = 30 x £240).

The amount is reduced by one twelfth for each month of service completed over the age of 64 so that at 65 (the statutory retirement age) no payment is due.

The employer must give the employee a written explanation of a redundancy payment.

Transfers of undertakings

The Transfer of Undertakings (Protection of Employment) regulations (TUPE) safeguard employees' rights when there is a change of employer following a change of ownership, takeover, merger or privatization. It also applies where there is a change of status – for example, from public to private sector, from building society to plc.

The effects of the TUPE regulations are:

- the existing contract and terms and conditions of employment are transferred in their entirety to the new employer including continuity of service. The transfer may not take place with the purpose of reducing pay levels and other terms and conditions of employment
- recognition rights of trade unions are transferred if the new body maintains a distinctive identity
- dismissals related directly to the transfer of the business are automatically unfair
- both the old and the new employer must consult and provide advance information to any recognized trade unions and to all employees who are to be affected. This must include the timing of the transfer, the reasons for the transfer and legal, economic and social implications for those affected.

Industrial action

Industrial action may be conducted only in the pursuit of a legitimate trade dispute. A legitimate trade dispute occurs between employer and employees on one or more of the following grounds:

■ terms and conditions of employment
■ the physical conditions in which people are required to work
■ dismissal, termination or suspension of employment of one or more employees
■ allocation of work or duties
■ matters of discipline
■ membership or non-membership of a trade union
■ facilities for officials of trade unions
■ machinery for negotiation or consultation and other procedures relating to any of the above matters, including the recognition by employers or employers' associations of the right of a trade union to represent employees.

Industrial action must be preceded by a postal ballot independently scrutinized (eg by the Electoral Reform Society). Those responsible for conducting a ballot (normally a trade union or staff representative) must give seven days' notice of their intent to hold a ballot. They must notify the employer of the outcome and give seven days' notice of any industrial action intended.

So long as this procedure is followed, trade unions preserve their immunity in law from being sued for damages as the result of losses incurred by the particular employer.

A legitimate trade dispute may take place only at the site where the problem arose. Where the problem has arisen at a multi-site location (eg a transport company), then the dispute may be carried out at each site.

Payment

Payment must be made at the intervals stated in the contract and this must consist of the amounts stipulated.

Itemized pay statements must be issued at each interval. These must show the gross pay; the net pay; and the amount of each and every deduction made.

Individual rights

Individual rights at places of work have been clarified and strengthened over recent years (see Summary box 2.1). This has been partly due to UK government legislation and partly due to the European Union (EU). The main individual rights are:

■ the right to fair and equal treatment regardless of length of service, hours worked or whether designated a full- or part-time employee
■ the right to employment protection (protection from unfair dismissal) after two years' continuous service regardless of hours worked or whether designated a full- or part-time employee
■ the right to join a recognized trade union or to refuse to join it; the right not to be penalized, victimized or harassed for joining or refusing to join
■ the right to adequate and continuous vocational and job training
■ the right to a healthy and safe working environment
■ the right to information, consultation and participation on key workplace issues and other matters of relevance and importance
■ the right of access to personnel files and other information held (whether on paper or database)
■ the right to be represented or accompanied in all dealings with the organization, especially matters of grievance or discipline.

Summary box 2.1 Individual rights

The great majority of applications made to employment tribunals are by individual employees. The orientation of the tribunal is therefore towards the individual. Where there is any doubt over the merits and strengths of the case of applicants and respondents, the tribunal normally orders the case to proceed.

Where there is any question that any of the rights indicated above have either been breached or not upheld, the tribunal will normally order the case to proceed.

It is the employer's duty to uphold the rights of individuals. The onus is therefore placed on the employer to be able to prove or demonstrate to the satisfaction of the tribunal that individual rights were upheld. It is the employer's duty to ensure that all employees are informed of their rights.

Employees may not be induced or coerced to sign away all or part of their statutory rights, nor is any such signature legally binding.

LAWS AND REGULATIONS

The main laws, and their coverage, are as follows:

Equal Pay Act 1970

Equal pay: the right to receive the same pay and other terms of employment as an employee of the opposite sex working for the same or an associated employer if engaged on like work, work rated as equivalent or work of equal value. The question of equal value is supported by the Equal Value Regulations (last amended 1996) which place further onus on employers to ensure that the widest possible view is taken of the equality of the value of the work.

Employment Protection (Consolidation) Act 1978; Employment Rights Act 1996

Pay: the right to receive an itemized pay statement.

Maternity rights: the right not to be unfairly dismissed for reasons connected with pregnancy; the right to paid time off work for ante-natal care; the right to return to work following absence because of pregnancy or confinement.

Medical suspension: the right not to be unfairly dismissed on medical grounds; the right to receive pay for suspension on medical grounds.

Redundancy: the right to be consulted by the employer about proposed redundancies; the right of recognized independent trade unions to be consulted by the employer about proposed redundancies; the right to receive payment when made redundant; the right to receive an itemized statement of redundancy payment; the right to pay and time off in the event of redundancy to look for other work or to make arrangements for training.

Time off for public duties: the right to time off for public duties.

Trade union membership/non-membership rights: the right to pay and time off for trade union duties; the right to time off for trade union activities; the right not to suffer dismissal or action short of dismissal for trade union membership or activities or non-membership; the right not to suffer action short of dismissal to compel union membership; the right not to be unfairly dismissed for trade union membership or activities; the right not to be unfairly dismissed for non-membership of the union; the right not to be chosen for redundancy because of trade union membership or activities, or non-membership of a trade union.

Unfair dismissal: the right not to be unfairly dismissed for any reason; the right to receive a written statement of reasons for dismissal; the right to receive a written statement of terms of employment and any alterations to them.

The right to receive a written statement of terms of employment and any alterations to them.

Race Relations Act 1976

Race relations: the right not to be discriminated against in employment, training and related fields on grounds of colour, race, nationality, ethnic or national origin.

Sex Discrimination Act 1975

Sex discrimination: the right not to be discriminated against in employment, training and related fields on the grounds of sex, marriage or pregnancy.

Transfer of Undertakings (Protection of Employment) Regulations 1981

Transfers: the right of unions to be informed and consulted about the transfer of an undertaking to a new employer; the right not to be dismissed on the transfer of an undertaking to a new employer.

Employment Act 1980

Trade union rights: the right not to be unreasonably excluded or expelled from a trade union.

Employment Act 1988

Trade union rights: the right not to be unjustifiably disciplined by a trade union; the right of recourse to a tribunal if discriminated or disciplined by an employer concerning trade union rights; the right of trade unions to hold secret ballots on employers' premises.

Wages Act 1986

Payment of wages: the right of all staff not to have deductions made from their wages unless allowed by statute by the contract of employment or with the individual's prior written agreement; the right of everyone to an itemized pay statement.

Disability Discrimination Act 1995

Disability: the general right not to be discriminated against in employment because of a registered disability; the duty of employers with 20 or more employees to employ a minimum of 3 per cent of registered disabled people; the right to complain to tribunal if discriminated against or disadvantaged by virtue of disability, including opportunities for promotion, enhancement, training and development. Employers must also take reasonable steps to provide facilities, access and egress, and any specialist equipment necessary.

Rehabilitation of Offenders Act 1974

Spent convictions: job applicants and employees are not under any legal obligation to disclose information about previous convictions; the right to deny a previous offence when the conviction for it is 'spent' – a person has served their punishment and been rehabilitated (there are a large number of occupations that are exempted from this rule – especially working with money, people and property; and working within the legal, law enforcement and emergency services).

Trade Union Reform and Employment Rights Act 1993

Employee rights: the right not to be dismissed for exercising statutory employment rights regardless of length of service or hours of work; the right of women to 14 weeks' maternity leave regardless of length of service or hours of work; the right to healthy and safe working premises and activities regardless of length of service or hours of work.

Transfers of undertakings: the regulations governing business transfers are extended to cover non-commercial undertakings.

Trade unions: individuals are given the right to join the union of their choice; the deduction of union dues from pay must be authorized in writing by the employees every three years; the duty of an employer to inform and consult union representatives about collective redundancies is restated.

Industrial action: strike ballots must be postal and independently scrutinized; unions must give employers seven days' notice of their intention to hold a strike ballot; unions must give employers seven days' notice of the industrial action intended; injunctions may be sought by anybody affected by unlawful or unofficial industrial action to prevent this from taking place.

Summary box 2.2   Case examples

Recent cases that have acquired legal status and set precedent are as follows:

Polkey vs. A E Dayton Ltd

> Organizations must follow procedures when dismissing an employee. (Lords)

The ruling was as follows:

- In a case of incapacity an employee must be given fair warning and a chance to improve.
- In a case of misconduct, investigating fully and fairly and hearing what the employee has to say in explanation or mitigation of their conduct.
- In a case of redundancy, warning and consultation with affected employees and adopting a fair basis for selection and taking reasonable steps to redeploy those affected.

The tribunal that considered Polkey's case held that the employer had breached the correct procedure but that the result would have been the same if the procedure had been followed. This was rejected by the House of Lords. The Lord Chancellor stated:

It is what the employer did that is to be judged, not what he might have done.

Heywood vs. Cammell Laird

> Equal pay means pay and not equivalent benefits. (Lords)

Jean Heywood worked as a cook at Cammell Laird. For this work she was required to have a recognized qualification. She argued that her qualification was of the same level as those of men working elsewhere in the company and that therefore, her work was equivalent to that of those men. She was paid less than those men.

The company acknowledged that they paid Mrs Heywood less, but because she received a free meal every day, this made her total reward package up to a level equivalent to that of the men with whom she was making the comparison.

The House of Lords rejected this and ordered the company to make up her pay to the same level as that of the men.

Brown vs. Stockton-on-Tees Borough Council

> Pregnancy may not be used as a criterion for redundancy. (Lords)

Maria Brown worked for Stockton-on-Tees Borough Council. She worked in a group of four female staff. The council made two members of staff redundant and singled Mrs Brown out as one of them because she was pregnant. If 'last in first out' had been used to determine redundancies, Mrs Brown would not have been made redundant; no other criteria for redundancy were published.

The Lords upheld the view that pregnancy was not a valid ground for redundancy; and that to make someone redundant because of their pregnancy amounted to discrimination. The Lords went on to state that criteria for redundancy must be published in advance of redundancies; failure to do so means that last in first out (lifo) will apply.

Price vs. The Civil Service Commission

> Age constraints must not be indirectly discriminatory on grounds of gender. (Court of Appeal)

Belinda Price worked as a civil servant and, at the age of 36, put in for a promotion to the next grade. The Civil Service Commission turned her down on the grounds that she was too old and that everyone who made the particular grade had to do so by the age of 29.

Ms Price countered this by saying that she could not have achieved this because she was out of the workforce for ten years bringing up children. She was otherwise a good and effective worker; the only thing militating against her promotion was her age, and that because of circumstances, this discriminated indirectly on grounds of gender.

The Court of Appeal upheld this view, stating that the particular age barrier was less favourable to women (and therefore discriminatory) than to men.

Burchell vs. British Home Stores

Burchell was dismissed for misconduct by British Home Stores without being given the opportunity to state his case. The Court of Appeal laid down three guiding principles to ensure that natural justice would be upheld:

- The employer should show that there was a genuine belief that the employee was guilty of the misconduct under consideration.
- The employer must carry out a reasonable and thorough investigation into the case.
- As a result of the investigation, the employer must have reasonable grounds for maintaining the belief.

Each point is now always considered and questioned by tribunals where cases arising from misconduct occur.

EXPERT BODIES

Advisory, Conciliation and Arbitration Service (ACAS)

ACAS is an independent statutory body funded by government grant. It is the recognized national source of expertise, advice, information and guidance on workplace employee relations and staff management. ACAS publishes guidelines and codes of practice on discipline, grievance, dismissal, employment practices and the content and use of procedures (see Summary box 2.3). These are available from offices of ACAS, either free or for a small charge.

The general role of ACAS is to promote workplace harmony, understanding and well-being.

Advice   ACAS may be contacted at any time, either by post or phone on any aspect of workplace, employee relations or staff management for general advice and information. ACAS officials also arrange and carry out briefings and training sessions by agreement.

Conciliation and mediation   ACAS may be contacted at any time to arrange conciliation and mediation in disputes that are likely to become serious if they are not resolved quickly. ACAS searches for common ground and areas where agreement might be reached, and makes proposals for tackling other issues. ACAS also conducts conciliation and mediation in all applications to tribunal as stated above.

Arbitration   ACAS may be contacted at any time to arrange arbitration in disputes where there is no apparent possibility of resolution. Both parties normally agree to be bound by the arbitrator's findings (though this is not required by law). The arbitrator hears both cases and then makes recommendations based on their assessment of the merits. The result may be wholly in favour of one party or a compromise between the two, or some alternative solution.

In all cases that come to hearing, the tribunal normally requires satisfaction that the advice, proposals, recommendations and guidance of ACAS have been followed. Where this has not occurred, good reasons must be shown. Where both parties agree to be bound by the findings of an arbitrator, good reason must be shown if one party then decides not to accept these findings.

Health and Safety Executive (HSE)

The HSE is also an independent body funded by government grant. It is the recognized source of expertise, advice, information and guidance on all matters concerning health and safety at work.

The HSE publishes advice and guidelines on general health and safety matters. It has a statutory right of access to all work premises. It carries out inspections, advises on safety matters and in extreme cases, may close down premises or parts of premises where these are considered to be unsafe or unhealthy. Where a case arises from health and safety matters the tribunal always requires satisfaction that the advice, proposals, recommendations and guidance of the HSE have been followed. If this has not occurred good reason must be shown.

Department for Education and Employment (DEE)

The DEE publishes booklets and leaflets giving advice and information on changes to the law and the implementation of regulations. It is the duty of employers to ensure that they keep themselves up to date with current employment legislation.

A tribunal never accepts ignorance of the law as a defence – whether on the part of applicant or respondent.

Commission for Racial Equality; Equal Opportunities Commission; Placement, Assessment and Counselling Teams (PACTS) for the Disabled

These bodies provide independent advice and guidance, and act as a source of information on employment law and related matters. Their advice and guidance is normally considered to be the highest form of expertise available.

In tribunal cases where the advice and guidance of these bodies has been sought, the tribunal will normally place great emphasis on their recommendations.

Trade unions, employers' associations, professional associations, independent associations

These bodies provide advice and guidance and act as a source of information on employment law and related matters to their members. Their advice and guidance carries no particular presumption of expertise. It is, however, generally of high quality and represents the state of knowledge and information available.

Tribunals may choose to place emphasis on the recommendations, advice and guidance given by these bodies.

Summary box 2.3   Procedures

Procedures exist to set standards of performance, conduct and behaviour at places of work and to ensure that everyone knows what is expected of them and that they conform to this. They ensure fairness and equality of treatment for everyone.

All organizations must have procedures for handling and managing all staff matters, especially discipline, grievance, disputes and dismissal. These have to meet standards prescribed by ACAS and the Department for Education and Employment. They must:

- be in writing
- state to whom they apply
- be applied evenly to everyone concerned regardless of rank or occupation
- be accessible, available for inspection and available for use at any time
- be capable of being understood and followed

- be fair and reasonable
- indicate the nature and range of actions which may be taken in given sets of circumstances
- indicate the levels of management which may take particular actions
- provide for matters to be dealt with quickly.

Discipline and grievance procedures are dealt with in more detail in Chapter 5.

European Union Law

European Union Law is broadly superior to UK Law; any case that reaches the European Court of Justice will be judged by this as the final conclusion to the matter in hand.

The particular concern of European Union Law is the strengthening and upholding of individual rights in all aspects of life, including employment. The main areas of concern are:

- ■ freedom of movement for workers and self-employed persons across the European Union
- ■ protection of employment and remuneration
- ■ adequate vocational training
- ■ freedom of association, especially the right to join trade unions and associations, or not to join trade unions and associations
- ■ information consultation and participation of employees on major workplace issues
- ■ health and safety at work
- ■ specific protection for stated groups of employees, especially children, adolescents, elderly persons, disabled persons
- ■ equal treatment for men and women.

The general principle is that current UK legislation reflects the demands of EU Law and standards. It is especially important to note that any case that reaches the European Court of Justice will be judged from a European perspective (see Summary box 2.4).

Summary box 2.4   The European Court of Justice

The following judgments were issued by the European Court of Justice after they had exhausted the tribunal and UK legal systems.

Swift vs. British Rail

> Retirement age and the opportunity to retire must be the same for all employees regardless of gender.

British Rail vs. National Union of Railwaymen

> Union membership agreements – the closed shop – are illegal and may not be enforced; no one should be forced to join a trade union or any other organization against their will (nor should they be prevented from joining a trade union or any other organization if they so wish.

European Union Law has its basis in the Treaties by which it was created and developed, the Social Charter, the different legal instruments at its disposal and the decisions and judgments of the European Commission, the Council of the European Union and the European Court of Justice.

Treaties

The Treaties by which the European Union was established and developed are as follows:

Treaty of Rome 1957 This gave the European Economic Community a distinct legal personality and set up institutions to administer the system. The position of employees, trade unions and other employee representatives, employers and their representatives as 'social partners' was reinforced through the 'Social Chapter' of the Treaty.

The Single European Act 1987 This was implemented in each of the domestic legislatures of the member states, following agreement across the European Community. Its main provisions were free movement of labour so that people from member nations could obtain employment and live in any member state, and receive unemployment and other social security benefits in their chosen country of residence. The common recognition of the qualifications of workers was also to be advanced.

The Maastricht Treaty 1992 From an ER point of view, the main contribution of the Maastricht Treaty was to formalize the Social Charter as the basis on which all employment (and also wider human) rights would be established within the member states of the EU. The UK negotiated an 'opt-out', because the prevailing political view at the time was that the adoption of the Social Charter would lead to increased labour costs and therefore a lack of competitiveness.

The Amsterdam Treaty 1997 This recognized the problems inherent in the continued high levels of unemployment within the member states of the EU (at the time that it was signed, there were a total of 18 million people out of work within the member states). The Amsterdam Treaty required member states to put the fight against unemployment at the top of Europe's agenda. For the first time, it required governments to coordinate their strategies for creating employment and promoting a skilled, trained and adaptable workforce. It also required the member states to produce an annual report on the employment situation in the EU, detailing the effectiveness of actions taken (see Summary box 2.5).

Summary box 2.5   The Treaty of Amsterdam 1997 and employment rights

The Maastricht Treaty 1992 gave every person holding UK citizenship, citizenship of the European Union. Union citizenship complements national citizenship by giving individuals rights in all member states. It does not replace national citizenship, nor does it impose new obligations.

The Amsterdam Treaty builds on this and gives further prominence to the rights of individuals as follows:

- the Council is permitted to take action by unanimity to combat discrimination based on sex, race or ethnic origin, religion or belief, disability, age and sexual orientation
- it is committed to eliminating inequalities between men and women in matters of pay, opportunities and wider social responsibility
- protection against the misuse of personal data held by the Community institutions and member states
- a commitment taken by the European Commission to consult widely among member states and all those interested parties within member states before proposing legislation. This again clearly reinforces the position of all interested parties in places of work as 'social partners'.

The European Union Social Charter

The European Union Social Charter (see Appendix A) enshrined all of the areas of concern indicated above – freedom of movement, protection of employment and remuneration, vocational training, freedom of association, information, consultation and participation of employees, health and safety at work and specific protection for stated groups of employees (see Summary box 2.6). It also makes specific reference to the following:

■ wage levels: the constitution of 'fair wages' in member states and the introduction of a 'minimum wage' in member states
■ a positive commitment to health, protection and safety at the workplace, including the active involvement of social partners
■ the right of access to information that affects all those at places of work
■ the full integration into working life of disabled people, including access to work premises, availability of special transport and equipment and attention to the design of work stations for disabled people
■ improvements in living and working conditions, including equality of treatment for part-time and temporary workers, controls on night working and requirements for weekly rest periods and paid holidays
■ equality of treatment for men and women, and for all those at places of work.

Summary box 2.6   The UK and the European Union Social Charter

The UK government opted out of signing the Social Charter under the Maastricht Treaty in 1992. In 1997, the UK Labour government signed the Social Charter, at the same time as it signed the Treaty of Amsterdam. In this, it committed itself to the following:

• The introduction of a minimum wage. This principle is now established. However, debate continues on the likely level of that wage, and also the scheduling of its introduction. Employers' associations especially have lobbied hard to be given time to introduce such a measure over a period of years. Under the minimum wage proposal, there are clear implications for both employers and employees and their representatives to take account of pay leagues, payment structures and differentials.
• Working hours. The broad principle of the maximum 48-hour working week was adopted by the UK government under the terms of the

- Health and safety at work. Broadly speaking, the Health and Safety at Work Act 1974 is regarded as model legislation by the European Union. It sets high standards of practice, and then requires that these be enforced at individual places of work according to the particular circumstances. In turn, the Social Charter reinforces the absolute right of all those on work premises to the highest possible standards of health, safety and protection at work.
- Maternity and parental leave. The Trade Union Reform and Employment Rights Act 1993 gave every woman the right to 14 weeks' maternity leave regardless of length of service or hours worked; this was in accordance with the adoption of the Social Charter and European Union Law. The principle of paternal leave is also enshrined – at present, however, this is at the discretion of individual organizations.

European Union social and employment policy, under the provisions of the Social Charter, are not fully developed. There are certain to be further developments – especially in the areas of access for the disabled, the protection of children, access to work for the elderly and responsibilities for providing pensions.

The legal instruments of the European Union

These are as follows:

- Treaty Articles. These are binding on all member states and employers immediately.
- Regulations and Statutes. These laws apply immediately and equally in all member states.
- Directives. These are binding on public sector employers immediately, and binding on other employers when enacted by the particular government of the member state in question.
- Decisions of the European Court of Justice. These set precedent and therefore have the same effect as Regulations and Directives.
- Decisions of the European Commission. These also set precedent and become binding immediately.
- Recommendations of the European Commission. These are not legally binding but detail the Commission's views and opinions about how specific issues should be dealt with.

■ Codes of Practice and Guidance. These are issued by the European Commission and its Directorate-General (its administrative establishment).

Note

The Subsidiarity Principle: The view adopted by the EU is that enforcement of particular matters should take place at the most local level possible. Therefore, the enforcement of much European Union legislation is left in the hands of the employment tribunal and courts systems of the UK (see Figure 2.1). Only when there is a specific gap in the laws or regulations of a particular member state is the European Union view enforced at a higher level.

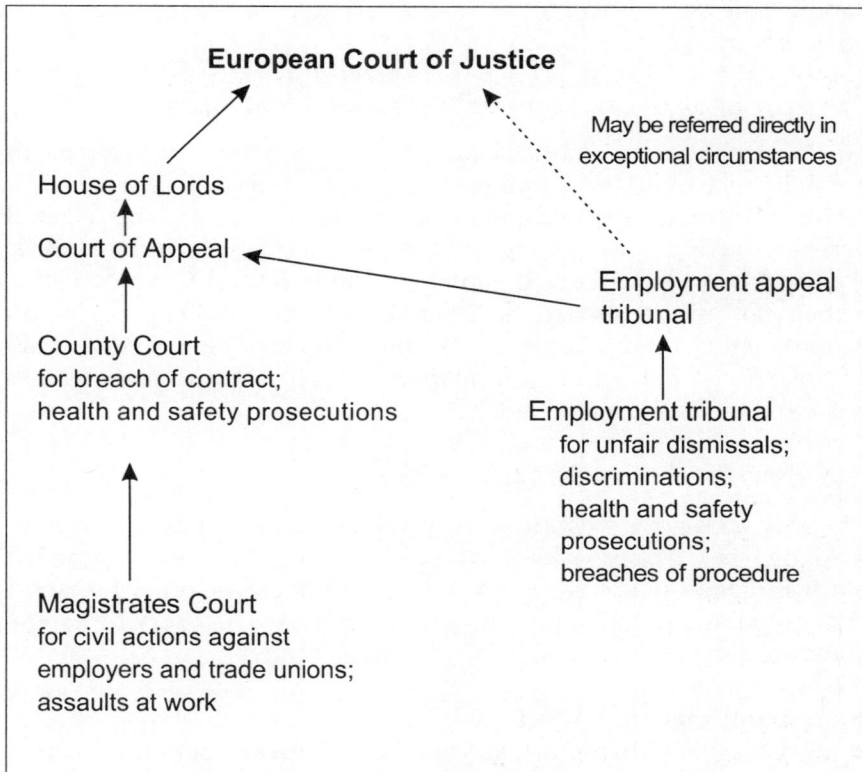

Figure 2.1 *The relationship between UK and European employment law. Routes through the system are indicated by arrows*

Employee relations and European Union Directives

In this context the main EU Directives to note are as follows:

The Acquired Rights Directive 1977 (amended 1997)

The Acquired Rights Directive 1977 ensures the right of all staff to full employment protection, including fairness and equality of treatment, the right to continuity of employment, the right to security of wage payments, and the right to benefits provided by the organization in question, regardless of length of service or hours worked. It also protects employees from dismissal, downgrading or loss of material benefits in the event of the organization's change of status (eg from nationalized to privatized) or in the event of a merger, takeover, demerger or sale.

The European Works Council Directive 1994

The European Works Council Directive 1994 enshrines the principle of pre-eminence of all those at a particular organization. In particular, it requires adequate representation on organizational and managerial decision-making from all sectors of the staff. At present, works councils are required only in those organizations indicated in Chapter 1. It is certain, however, that the requirement to constitute works councils will be broadened, and where this is not possible (eg in very small organizations), the right to information, consultation and participation will nevertheless be enshrined.

The Working Hours Directive 1994

As stated above, this enshrines the principle of the maximum 48-hour working week. It does make allowances for those whose work is carried out in irregular patterns – for example, airline crews, other transport sectors, public security and emergency services. The Working Hours Directive also enshrines the principles of:

■ the entitlement to rest periods at work
■ the entitlement to minimum rest periods between periods of work
■ the right to paid holidays – at present there is no statutory minimum requirement for paid holidays for organizations working out of the UK.

Underpinning all this is the concept of 'the humanization of work' – the recognition that work is to be carried out from the point of view of mutual interest and harmony; that this is only possible in the long term if work is set in the context of the wider spectrum of life, and that people at places of work are to be treated with ordinary decent humanity.

The draft European Company Statute

The proposed European Company Statute recommends the creation of a special form of European organization to be known as a Societas Europeas or SE (if created, the letters SE would replace plc or Ltd at the end of the company name in the UK).

The proposal was first recommended in 1970. However, it has made little progress, because the European Commission continues to insist that SEs have compulsory employee participation in management decisions. Between one third and one half of its board of directors must consist of employee representatives, unless the organization constitutes a works council, which has this form of executive authority and control. It therefore raises the level and influence of staff to that of shareholders.

Employees would also have to be consulted about acquisitions, mergers and takeovers and about any disposal of a part of the business valued at more than 5 per cent of the SE's share capital.

If implemented, SEs will be governed by a set of fresh rules and regulations applicable throughout the EU, rather than by the laws of member states. Such organizations will, however, be able to offset profits and losses between activities in various member countries and this will apply also to subsidiaries. If implemented, therefore, those hitherto responsible only for employment relations would also be required to take much greater account of strategic, operational and commercial issues when devising and implementing human resource management and ER policies.

CONCLUSIONS

The purpose of this chapter has been to indicate the legal basis and framework that exists for the regulation of employee relations in the UK. The importance of the European dimension cannot at present be understated. It is essential that all of those involved in the devising and implementing of ER strategies, formats, standards, procedures and manuals understand this as the framework within which they must work. Only then can adequate, effective and successful ER activity be contemplated.

3

ORGANIZATIONAL STANDARDS IN EMPLOYEE RELATIONS

INTRODUCTION

In the direction and management of organizational and workplace employee relations it is necessary to translate both the background and the legal framework indicated in the first two chapters into a precise basis for effective ER operations and activities. This means:

■ understanding the culture and background of the staff and their locality and environment
■ understanding the perspective or perspectives by which work in general, and in ER in particular, has been conducted in the past and, therefore, understanding the basis of the prevailing expectations and attitudes to work
■ understanding the legal requirements, both in broad terms and also their specific application to the particular organization, and the operation of its sector or sectors overall.

This must then be related to:

■ the desired attitude, approach, standpoint and aura by which ER is to be conducted

- the ethics, standards, attitudes, values and beliefs necessary for its effective conduct
- the composition, style and approach of ER and staff management handbooks, manuals and procedures
- the specific attitude and standpoint from which organization discipline is to be established and implemented
- specific organizational and operational management issues arising from the composition and mix of the workforce, the nature and location of the sector or sectors in which activities are carried out, technology used, and the ways in which work is parcelled up into jobs, activities and occupations
- specific sectoral operational issues such as volatility, seasonality, risk and threat of entry, undercutting, substitution and withdrawal
- specific sectoral psychological issues, especially reputation, respect and esteem
- specific sectoral preconceptions, prejudices and behavioural, prejudicial and psychological barriers (see Summary box 3.1).

Summary box 3.1   Behavioural and psychological issues: some initial examples

British dockers are the best in the world.

Docker's shop steward, 1977 – resisting containerization of the Port of London

We pretend to work, and they pretend to pay us.

Hungarian Diplomat, 1992

It is impossible to print newspapers without printers.

Print Union Father of Chapel, 1981 – during dispute at NewsCorpInternational over the introduction of computer technology

My father got on his bike and looked for work.

Norman Tebbitt MP, 1981 – on his father's attitude to unemployment (speaking at the Conservative Party Conference)

If you don't want this job, there are plenty others who do.

Apocryphal, reflective of many of the prevailing managerial attitudes in the UK of the 1970s and 1980s

Each of these statements represents an easy, quick – and wrong – answer to all of the employee relations and workplace problems in the world. None addresses the fundamental issues that have to be understood if effective employee relations is to be achieved. The factors common to all of the quotes are as follows:

- They all show a complete lack of respect, value and regard for everybody involved (or who may be involved) in the particular situation.
- The attitudes and prejudices expressed form no basis for anything except mutual and enduring hostility and conflict.
- Each is pronounced as a truth by which the world should live, and this flies in the face of the turbulent and changing nature of the business sphere.

There is an equally pithy antidote:

> There is not a protective barrier high enough, that will save organizations from their own incompetence in the management of the human resource.

Tom Peters, 1985 – address to the Royal Society of Arts.

CULTURE

Both the organization form adopted (the structure) and the collective beliefs, values and ethics (the culture) must match the overall purpose of the organization in ways that ensure the best possible return on investment, the most effective relationship possible with markets, customers, clients and the environment, organizational performance, responsiveness and adaptability (see Summary box 3.2).

It is necessary to recognize that no two organizations are exactly alike. Whatever the similarity in output, product or service, ways of working, shared values, management style, attitudes and approaches and the relationship with markets may differ widely.

All organizations are therefore different. They have different methods of operation and working, different ways of doing things, different values, attitudes, beliefs and norms – different personalities, in fact. They are as different from each other as people.

Having said that, it is possible to define a set of features on which organization culture is based:

Age and history of the organization: the degree of prominence that it has established, its traditions, its reputation and how this has arisen, its image, its standing in its markets and communities. Young organizations spend time and resources generating these matters for themselves, while those of long standing will have these elements well established. In all cases, the history, traditions and reputation require managerial understanding and activity to develop them further and, where necessary, to take remedial action.

The size of the organization: and related elements of spans of control, degrees of centralization and decentralization, departmentalization and divisionalization, balance of primary and support functions, the nature and style of all activities. It is also necessary to consider information systems, other control mechanisms, reporting relationships and systems for the monitoring and evaluation of performance.

The nature of work: the mix of skills, knowledge, expertise, professionalism, technical capability and other activities. People who are highly professionalized or trained bring distinctive sets of values with them, which may rub against those of the organization. Particular approaches are required, therefore, to generate organizational and operational harmony. Potential differences must be recognized at an early stage. Highly ordered and regulated tasks and series of tasks are normally mirrored in the organization of people to carry them out. At the other extreme, projects, pioneering and innovation work often require little formal direction, leaving much to the self-motivation and self-organization of those involved.

Technology: the relationship between culture, structure and technology is a critical feature of the operational aspects of ER management. Small scale activities require a lower and more flexible organization than do those with large scale, permanent or semi-permanent and mass output methods. In large complex organizations, economies of scale and the ER implications have to be considered, alongside questions of production and work group organization and departmentalization. From this, there are implications concerning alienation, dysfunction, and organized labour and representation.

The speed at which technology changes or becomes obsolete must also be considered. Organizations cannot seek permanence or stability in an era of rapid technological change or innovation, and even where a particular technology is deemed to have a degree of permanence, this may easily be called into question through the invention of a substitute, or substitute method of working, for the activity in question.

The investment made in technology by organizations also has implications for the culture (and therefore the management of ER).

Organizations that regularly update their technology must also regularly update their expertise and capability to exploit it to its full potential.

Location: the ability to work in harmony with the prevailing local customs and traditions. This includes religious and ethical, as well as social, pressures. It is certain to include legal constraints. There are also population size and mixes, access to services, age and composition of the local workforce. There will be standards set by other employers in the area (especially large employers) that have implications for all those working close by.

The environment: the relationship between the organization, its markets, customers and clients, its competitors and its broader environment. This includes confidence, expansion, contraction, economic and social factors. It includes local reputation as an employer.

States of environmental flux, change, diversity and complexity require organizations that can cope with them, respond to them and exist in harmony with them. It is also necessary to note the degree of stability of the environment. This includes threats and dangers of organization collapse, expansion, contraction and takeover, loss of markets or the gaining of new markets and gains and losses in standing and confidence. The overall ability of the organization to survive and prosper in relation to its environment, and to fight battles with it when necessary, must be considered.

People factors: this constitutes a broad understanding of those who come to work for the organization. As well as degrees of professional and technical expertise, relationships can be drawn between personal characteristics and attributes of status, ambiguity, stability and identity, and their appropriateness to the form of organization in question. For example, the person having a high desire for a senior sounding title will not get this in a small flexible organization. Nor will he or she gain the same measure of order and stability from this organization as from a public service, government, or multinational establishment. Persons of high quality, energy, enthusiasm and ability are more likely to be frustrated in slow moving, highly formalized organizations, than in those which are flexible and dynamic.

Organization purpose: the extent to which this is clear, articulated, understood and accepted by all concerned, and the simplicity or complexity of goals. There are also likely to be subordinate aims and objectives, which may, on the face of it, conflict with the main or stated purpose.

It is also necessary to recognize that organizations change their purposes and directions. This occurs for a variety of reasons – shifts in talents, qualities and technologies, new opportunities, market changes and technological advance.

Shared values: a clear positive set of values or direction given by the organization to its people, with which they can all identify. The adoption of shared values is central to the generation of high levels of commitment and motivation among staff. Recognizing that people bring a diverse range of qualities, and their own attitudes, values and beliefs, is essential. Giving them a clear corporate purpose that is both above individual aspirations and capable of accommodating them, is a key feature of effective ER management. It gives a clear indication of the prevailing ethics and morality of the organization.

Management style: there is a close interrelationship between management style, the work that is carried out and the way in which it is organized and directed. It is affected by the size, complexity, scale and scope of the organization. In turn, it is also affected by hierarchical considerations, nature and degrees of conformity, alienation, the nature and mix of work, the commitment, qualities, capabilities and attitudes of the staff carrying out the work and the expertise and capacities of the managers and supervisors.

Summary box 3.2   Archetype cultures and structures

Handy (1994) and Harrison (1987) defined four archetypes:

Power culture

This is to be found in small pioneering organizations, some political institutions and trade unions, project groups and operational and activity centres remote from head office. The key relationship in a power culture is between the staff and the centre or source of power. Power cultures work best when the organization is very young, when everyone is committed to the same direction and (in longer-established organizations) the direction of activities can safely be left in the hands of a single figure who can act with both autonomy and integrity in the best interests of all concerned.

However, powerful figures will always fill a vacuum. Particular managers, supervisors and employee representatives (including shop stewards), gain an undue amount of influence where there is a lack of direction or purpose given from elsewhere. This is normally the basis on which pressure groups, cliques and other factions emerge. They are invariably extremely disruptive both to the management of organizations in general, and to ER in particular.

People/person culture

This exists for its people, where a group has decided that it is in their own overriding interests to band together and to produce an organization for their benefit. It is to be found in certain research groups, university departments, music, rock and jazz groups, family firms, and companies started by groups of friends. In practice, the most effective and enduring people cultures have a figurehead. For example, Keith Richard is the 'leader' of the Rolling Stones; and academic and research departments have a named individual who acts on their behalf in the context of the establishment as a whole.

In ER terms, the emergence of people cultures – especially people subcultures – is to be resisted at all costs. Again, these occur where there is no broader or accepted organization direction. People form strong common bonds between themselves, and this invariably causes conflict with the broader organization. These subcultures emerge as canteen cultures, professional cliques and, again, as lobbies and vested interest groups. It may also occur, for example, that the members of a safety committee or joint negotiating committee form strong personal bonds, and the consequence of this is that the remit of these groups becomes the most important priority to their members and, again, acts as a diversion from the organization's key purposes.

Task culture

Task cultures are found in project teams, marketing groups and market and customer oriented organizations. The emphases are on getting the job completed to the customer's satisfaction, maintaining levels of customer and client satisfaction and responding to, and identifying, new market opportunities. At their best, task cultures are flexible, dynamic, adaptable and responsive. They accommodate the movements of staff necessary to ensure effective project and development teams and continued innovation, and require a degree of personal, as well as professional, commitment in the pursuit of customer satisfaction.

In the management of ER, task cultures are prone to conflicts caused by confusion where (often with the best will in the world) people have duplicated efforts, or strayed into someone else's territory. More serious conflicts may be caused when some people are known, believed or perceived to have gained rewards above and beyond those merited by their contribution, or where the group is known to be carrying 'passengers'. Conflicts may also be caused where a group or groups know, believe or perceive themselves to be 'elites' and from this they infer that they are carrying the rest of the organization, with all its inefficiencies, on their backs.

Role culture

Role cultures are found where organizations have gained a combination of size, permanence and departmentalization, and where the ordering of activities, preservation of knowledge and experience and stability, are important. Roles are defined, described and ordered. The role culture reflects the bureaucratic concept of hierarchy and permanence. Role cultures operate most effectively where the wider environment is steady and a degree of permanence is envisaged and where the demand for products and services is known (in so far as such a thing is possible) to be relatively permanent and certain.

Role cultures are governed by procedures and rule books. Conflicts and disputes arise, in ER terms, when there are breaches (or perceived breaches) of the rules or procedures. When conflicts do arise, each step of the way is governed by procedures that must be adhered to. At their best, these forms of ER are orderly and proceduralized; at their worst, they institutionalize and prolong conflict, which leads to frustration and alienation on the part of those involved.

Culture design

Whatever is done must be positive and not simply allowed to emerge by default. The values, aspirations and direction of the organization must be conveyed to all those who come to work, so that they clearly understand the attitudes, values and beliefs of the organization. Concerning some staff, this may involve a mutual rejection – organizations accommodate dissenting staff to the extent that dissents can be harmonized or made productive; to go further requires a dilution of core purpose and values. Other organizations take the view that, however expert an individual may be in their chosen field, their way of working would not harmonize with the particular requirements of the situation. This remains true even in the pluralist perspective – at no stage does this require organizations to be 'all things to all people'.

Organizational priorities also affect culture and structure and these must, therefore, be clearly and accurately articulated. It follows from this that the relationship between subsystems and support systems must also be clear. This includes the interrelationship and interaction between different departments and functions, production or primary, and support functions, its marketing, research and development and the systems and procedures that are introduced to facilitate their coordination. It also has effects on the nature, style and delivery of

Culture is not rigid. The design of organizations and their cultures is not the equivalent of designing buildings. Flexibility, fluidity, responsiveness and initiative are all essential components of the establishment of, and ordering of, the culture – and structure – of organizations. Stability also is an essential element, but this is not the equivalent of rigidity. Rather, it is the acquisition of those elements that will give a true permanence and continuity in a turbulent and changing environment – commitment, motivation, identity, harmony and, where necessary, the management of conflict when it arises (see Summary box 3.3).

Summary box 3.3   Organization culture and employee relations

In the management of ER, particular attention must be paid to the following features of organization culture:

climate or aura: the general prevailing cultural and organizational attitude and approach to employee relations and the perceptions of employee relations held by employees and managers

ethics and morality: the totality of organizational attitudes, values and beliefs, the ways in which these are applied, with particular emphasis on equality and fairness of treatment, conduct of disputes and grievances, and the attitudes of management to staff (and vice versa)

openness and integrity: in general dealings across the organization, in dealings between departments, divisions and functions, in dealings between members of particular groups, between management and other staff

rules and regulations: the evenness of application, variations in their application, their currency and effectiveness

distance: the physical distance between members, departments, divisions and functions of the organization, psychological distance based on status, trappings, occupational differentials, forms of address, dress codes, access and communications

lay-out: the design of the physical working environment, constraints caused by technology, constraints provided by status and 'importance', the effects of this on the nature and quality of personal and professional interactions

organizational climate: the overall feeling of the organization – whether this is (for example) based on fear, hope, expectation, positivism, commitment or alienation.

PERSPECTIVES

Identification of the desired perspective is the foundation stone for the employee relations style and strategy to be adopted once the organizational and cultural format is established. Identification of the prevailing perspective in existing organizations is the basis for assessing the strengths and weaknesses of that which currently exists, and for devising strategies to make changes and improvements where necessary.

As we saw in Chapter 1, there are three distinctive perspectives: unitary, pluralist and radical. Setting standards and devising employee relations strategies, policies, organizational approaches and procedures is only effective if the following are acknowledged.

Unitary

Common interests and shared values to which people can and do aspire must be present (see Summary box 3.4). This means knowing and understanding those matters to which people will aspire. These may be divided up under the following headings:

- principles: clear and unambiguous
- direction: clear and unambiguous also, reflecting and summarizing the purpose of the organization, and its ways of working
- terms and conditions: based on adequate and stable wage levels, fairness and equality of work practice, managerial openness and transparency, universal access to information, regular high quality consultation, integrity of operations and activities
- behaviour and attitudes: positive, with the view to create harmony and remove the causes of conflict, based on high moral and ethical standards, based on fairness, equality, respect, value and esteem
- interest and commitment: strategies for generating identity, loyalty and a mutuality of interest
- work composition: including the ability of everybody to progress and achieve their potential, acknowledging limitations in work division and occupational definitions, giving a universality of the principle of opportunity.

Summary box 3.4   Employee relations perspectives and the aspirations of people

Those responsible for workplace management have consistently mistaken the aspirations of their people.

Early in the 20th century, F W Taylor and the Scientific Management School (1947) proposed that, provided that they were paid well, workers would gladly carry out the most mundane, repetitive and boring of tasks. This became the basis for the design of production line work – and as a consequence, organizations and their managers consistently tried to resolve ER issues with increased wages, rather than paying attention to the quality of the working environment also.

The experiments carried out by Elton Mayo (1943) at the Hawthorne Works of the General Electric Company, USA, in the 1930s and 1940s, found that staff responded to the interest being taken in them.

The initial purpose of the research was to examine the effects of different levels of lighting on industrial performance; this was found to be of minor importance only. Indeed, when the lighting levels were turned down to 'eye-strain' levels, productivity still went up, because staff were at the centre of attention and, therefore, perceived themselves as important.

The Affluent Worker studies carried out in Luton, Bedfordshire, in the 1950s and 1960s, found similar results (Goldthorpe *et al.*, 1968). Studies – carried out on production lines at Vauxhall, Skefco and Laporte – found that, while wage levels remained consistently high for those involved, motivation, identity and commitment to the organization was negligible. Moreover, while all staff belonged to the recognized trade unions, identity with these was extremely low – because ultimately the unions involved were perceived to be a part of the status quo and, therefore, perpetuating it, rather than alleviating the boredom and misery of the working environment.

By contrast, when Nissan established in the UK in the 1980s, the company paid attention to all aspects of the working environment. They maintained high wage levels. They also provided an excellent working environment, job mobility and rotation, full flexibility of working, staff development and training for all, together with the opportunity to visit the Nissan Head Office in Japan. They therefore paid attention to both the behavioural and the economic aspects of employee relations.

Pluralist

In the pluralist perspective, a divergence of loyalties, commitments, ambitions and expectations is admitted. This means knowing and understanding what these are and why they exist. The pluralist perspective consequently recognizes the inherent nature of conflict – between different groups of staff, between functions, and within groups of staff. It also admits divided loyalties – an individual for example, may have professional, occupational, work group, trade union or professional body loyalties as well as those to their organization. Very often, this is reinforced where there has been a strong trade union presence, a recent history of conflict of objectives, or where the profession exerts a strong influence on work standards and practice (see Summary box 3.5).

Summary box 3.5 The pluralist perspective and divided loyalties: examples

The doctor

Doctors are required to take a Hippocratic oath – to preserve and improve life to the best of their capability. There is therefore an instant division of loyalty when they are asked by their employer to take decisions based on matters other than the preservation of life – especially economic factors. Doctors also have distinctive and understood loyalties to their professional body, their patients, their reputation and their potential patients. In some cases, the loyalty is divided still further – for example, through trade union membership, in different categories of patients or in different sources of patients.

The sales representative

As well as loyalties to trade unions and professional bodies, customers and clients, the problem may be exacerbated by the following:

- priority clients and customers
- departmental or divisional (rather than organizational) loyalty
- belief in the product/lack of belief in the product
- a stepping stone to a more senior position
- a stepping stone to a higher prestige organization
- determination to make a name for themselves.

All of these may be in the organization's interests, or they may not. There may also be problems concerning their ability to sell the product, and the inability of the organization to service the orders.

The trade union

Sharp divisions of loyalty and identity have very often been encountered where an individual becomes an organizational trade union representative. As well as the loyalties indicated above, the individual is required to serve the organization, the trade union itself, and the local membership, to the best of their abilities.

Example

In 1998, a merger was proposed between Smith-Kline Beecham and Burroughs Wellcome that, if successful, would have produced the fourth largest company in the world. It fell through because those in charge of ensuring that the merger was successful could not agree on what job each would hold in the new merged organization.

In general, work groups expect the markings, trappings and symbols that emphasize their differences, in addition to the fact of their designated professions and occupations (see Summary box 3.6). Rules and frameworks regulating these matters have to be clearly drawn, understood and accepted by all those to whom they apply. They are a key feature of role cultures where everything is expected to progress in a steady and orderly fashion. As a consequence, serious ER problems arise when such rules and procedures are changed, and when promotion and progression paths are streamlined – in other words, when previous expectations are not met. The key to effective pluralist employee relations lies in understanding the range and complexity of these issues, and in acknowledging the extent of their importance to job holders. The potential range of problems, and their nature, is therefore assessed in advance and forms a key part of the basis of effective pluralist ER management.

Summary box 3.6   Markings, trappings and symbols in pluralist situations

In pluralist situations, the main factors to be aware of are as follows:

- Promotion boards: the regularity and frequency of these, eligibility, the nature of the promotions on offer, the regulation of the promotions on offer, histories and traditions by which people have progressed.

- Perks and benefits: company cars, including eligibility, reasons for their being issued, the make and model of the car in question, regularity and frequency of upgrade; holidays, including differentiated holidays, earning additional holidays through extra attendance at work or longevity of service, any holiday subsidy – for example, the ability to combine holidays with business trips; health care – eligibility, extent of coverage (individual or family), range of health services on offer; pension – contributory or non-contributory, eligibility to join the scheme; share schemes – nature of shares, conditions of offer, eligibility, price and volume of shares.
- Job titles: their importance to the individuals concerned; factors of esteem, respect and value; differentiating factors – for example, principle, senior, director, assistant, junior; functional description – for example, marketing, personnel, production, project; non-jobs and euphemisms – for example, 'Director of Corporate Affairs', 'Highways Operative', 'Customer Care Assistant'.
- Differentiated facilities: for example, cars, canteens and restaurants, health care, style and quality of office and other accommodation.

Note

The concern here is understanding, rather than the inherent 'rightness' or 'wrongness' of the situation. If this is what is offered to people at the outset of their employment, and if it is what is important to people, then it must either be fulfilled, or else conflict expected.

Radical

The radical perspective arises from the Marxist premise that efficient and effective industrial activity could only be successful if the workers owned and controlled the means of production. On the face of it, therefore, the approach is both ideologically and commercially discredited (see Summary box 3.7).

However, there are some useful points to note, and substantial lessons in the management of ER to learn.

■ The promotion of employee share ownership schemes and profit-related pay schemes take the point of view that by giving the employee this form of stake in the organization, it helps to gain a positive mutual identity, and that the employee's commitment is gained because they themselves share in the risks and rewards.

■ The promotion of the partnership concept (akin to the EU social partnership) ideally means that ER (as with all other activities) is conducted on the basis of high quality, mutually understood, freely available information. There is a much greater chance of arriving at consensus or agreement on this basis, than where information is not fully or freely available.

■ The radical perspective is very conformist, taking an absolute view of the only possible basis for effective ER. Without necessarily adopting the whole viewpoint, many organizations conduct extremely effective ER from a conformist perspective. Both the Japanese, and also the best forms of ER conducted without trade unions, do so by setting standards to which people are required to conform.

Summary box 3.7   ER and democracy

Some proponents of radical ER state that the only way to achieve this is through pure industrial democracy. Democracy is by and large not favoured by organizations and their managers for the following reasons:

- If consensus is agreed through voting, the majority vote is not always right for the organization.
- The use of a vote is often seen as the abdication of responsibility – the justification for a decision that turned out to be wrong is 'Well, it was put to the vote.'
- Narrow majorities invariably cause as much trouble as they resolve in any case.
- Voting, especially on contentious issues, tends to line up behind pressure groups and factions in favour of differing points of view, and the problem is especially exacerbated when there are more than two points of view, for, in these situations, a 40-30-30 split is easily achievable, and it then has to be decided whether a) to accept the largest single vote, even if it was what the majority did not want; b) whether to re-engage the process; or c) what else to do!
- Democracy can be extremely long-winded, and inappropriate when a quick decision is required.

It is a short step from conformism to coercion, and a short step from coercion to bullying, victimization and harassment (see Summary box 3.8), which is one of the most destructive of all ER problems.

Summary box 3.8   Conformism and coercion

This may be considered from two points of view, the formal and the informal.

Formal

Several Japanese companies located in the UK have had grievances raised against them by staff who failed to understand the remit of the conformist approach of the organization. In 1995, a female member of staff sued Nissan, following a request to attend an evening function. The female member of staff was unable to do this. She was accordingly informed by the organization that her career with the company was over. She consequently took her case to employment tribunal, which she duly won. The tribunal found that the request to attend was effectively a workplace instruction, and that this was an unreasonable condition placed on her.

Informal

Informal coercion came to be recognized as 'a head office phenomenon' in the UK during the late 1980s and 1990s. The most common form of this was where it became common knowledge that it would seriously damage an individual's career if they left the office before the most senior manager present. This practice is normally defended by organizations stating that they expect loyalty and commitment from their staff.

The problem became worse in organizations where it was known or clearly understood that promotions, pay rises and bonuses were offered to those who attended the longest hours. This is also widely defended – the line taken in this case is that 'those who attended for the longest must necessarily have the highest output'. However, this is not the way in which the matter is viewed by staff; they rather view promotions, pay rises and bonuses as the result of attendance rather than output – in effect, they are being paid an extreme form of attendance allowance.

The main issue therefore, is that of understanding. The effectiveness of ER depends on the quality of the initial assessment of the situation – of an organization in its environment, of designing an organization that is compatible with this, the adoption of the ER perspective that is compatible in turn, and understanding the obligations that go with this in line with the points indicated above.

This, then, forms the basis for:

- the content of ER activities: what is included and what is not, where managerial prerogative lies, those matters open for consultation, the constitution of committees, groups and other staff relations' bodies
- the remit of ER: its purpose and direction, the fundamental approach and attitude, suitability for organizational purpose
- ER policy: the attitude and approach to key issues – organization discipline, issues concerning discipline and grievances, pay and rewards, improvements in working conditions, management style, managerial attitudes, the expectations of trade unions and/or other employee representative bodies
- pay policy: the management of pay and rewards, the attitudes to pay and rewards, differentials, equality and inequality, factors such as share schemes, profit-related pay and performance-related pay, attitudes to perks and benefits
- conduct of key issues: approaches to problems, the organizational points of view in the management of problems, specific issues concerning pay and rewards, discipline and grievances, health and safety
- ER systems: formal systems, informal systems, systems for the management of specific issues – especially discipline, grievance, pay and reward and health and safety (see Summary box 3.9)
- ER communications: the process of communications, the content of written and formal communications, the content of face-to-face communications, the ebb and flow of communications, organization responsiveness to employee issues
- organization development in ER: attitudes to staff and management training, priorities for staff and management training, approach and content of the training, especially in negotiating skills, problem-solving, health, safety and emergency procedures, communications, attitude to training and development
- decision-making processes: organizational and managerial standards and standpoints, content of decision-making processes, the extent to which these are autocratic, consultative, participative, or democratic (though see Summary box 3.7)
- the conduct of ER: including consultation and participation, collective bargaining, the constitution of committees, the agenda of committees, the remit of committees, the extent of value and importance placed on key issues through these meetings – especially concerning pay and conditions and health and safety.

Summary box 3.9   Formal and informal employee relations

It is usual to distinguish between the formal and informal as follows:

Formal

This is the constitution and operation of handbooks, rule books, procedures and regulations as laid down by the organization as part of its approach to the management of its staff. Each activity is regulated by what is stated and what is implied. Where the formal system is simple, direct and clearly understood by everyone, it tends to work effectively until gaps become apparent; and these can then be remedied as soon as the problem is identified.

Informal

Informal approaches to employee relations take place in all situations. The extent of their importance is as follows.

- Informal meetings take place where the formal system is too complicated or contradictory or controversial to be used to resolve a particular problem. This usually arises from a formal system not being precise enough, or where its operation would take too long in the circumstances. It may also be that the written documentation is sufficiently complicated to be interpreted in complex ways.
- Where there are problems with the quality of management or employee representation, conflict normally arises. Genuine long-term resolution of conflict only takes place in these circumstances where there is a collective will, and it is normally engaged through informal contact.
- Where there is enduring serious employee relations strife and conflict, communication between the warring parties nevertheless has to be maintained. While formally, therefore, employees and management are at loggerheads, informally communications are maintained. Where this works best, it becomes the seeds of an agreement.
- Where there are matters of organization or employee pride at stake, it is usual to use the informal system to agree the form of wording, or the presentation of the agreement (as distinct from the substance) informally.

CONCLUSIONS

Setting organizational standards for the direction and management of ER requires this level of understanding and expertise. The effective management of ER may be summarized as follows:

Strategic management

This means reconciling the purpose, aims and objectives of organizational ER with business policy and direction, and recognizing the style of ER management necessary with the overall organizational direction. It means attention to the approach in terms of perspective, and acceptance of all the implications that this brings – as a precondition of effective organizational ER. ER goals have to be set, and these must be compatible with those of the rest of the organization and each of its departments, divisions and functions (see Summary box 3.10).

Summary box 3.10   ER and strategy

The adoption of an effective strategic view of ER normally means consideration of the financial (direct and indirect) contribution that ER activity makes (positive or negative) to the totality of organization performance. From this point of view, ER may be viewed as one of the following:

- Cost centre: in which the direction and management of ER is viewed as an overhead, an organizational fixed cost, a costed and (often) apportioned charge for each of the departments, divisions and functions of the organization, either spread evenly overall, or else apportioned at each year end according to the actual cost incurred in each department, division or function.
- Investment centre: this is the organizational development view of ER, in which training, development and advancement in all aspects of ER are included as part of the total organizational development programme. This is found overwhelmingly in organizations that adopt 'learning cultures' or 'cultures of continuous development'.
- Profit centre: this takes the view that there is a direct relationship between the effectiveness of ER (and indeed, all traditional support functions) and organizational financial performance. ER activities, training and development, and the direction and policies that drive these, are designed and undertaken from the point of view that they are contributing directly to customer satisfaction, product or service quality and organizational flexibility, responsiveness and dynamism.

Organizational behaviour

This means understanding the broad culture of the environment in which activities are to take place, and do take place, and understanding the nature of the people who are to be, and are being, managed (see Summary box 3.11). It means understanding the nature of the divergent and conflicting pressures, aims and objectives, aspirations and expectations on the part of each member of staff and groups of staff. It means recognizing the extent to which these expectations and aspirations can be met, and where they cannot be met. It means recognizing the extent to which some aspirations and expectations can only be met at the expense of others, and the extent to which they can all be reconciled.

Summary box 3.11   Japanese companies playing away

Japanese companies that have set up operations in the UK, Western Europe and North America have always recognized the importance of cultural understanding as a key to business success. They have consequently brought their own distinctive standards of expertise and performance, and delivered these in such a way as the cultural history, traditions, hopes and aspirations of their western workforces can be reconciled.

This has in turn, been reinforced by their demonstrably high levels of financial investment, their commitment to lifetime employment and the enduringly high levels of reputation of product quality and service.

Behind all this is an understanding of the work history and traditions in the areas in which they have located. Outwardly, this has been demonstrated by the levels of investment in the communities in which they have located. Inwardly, this has been demonstrated by continued attention to investment in training and development, in the advancement of the quality of the working environment, and in job and work improvement programmes. Underlying all this is a work relationship based on high levels of wage in return for high quality work activities, and the fundamental mutual trust, respect and value that is necessary as a consequence.

Operations management

This means reconciling the style of functional and daily management of activities in all areas, with organization direction and cultural factors. It means recognizing the strengths and weaknesses of the nature of operations, and taking steps either to improve the working environment and range of activities in particular jobs, or recognizing the shortcomings as pressure points with the potential for conflict, and having mechanisms in place to deal with this when it arises.

Organization development

This means developing the standards, quality, expertise and environment of human resource management, staff management and ER alongside the development of total expertise and organizational performance. The purpose here is to develop and improve the capacity of all concerned in the field of ER (see Summary box 3.12). Managers and supervisors are trained in problem-solving, communication skills, negotiating skills and staff management, as well as in the total organizational approach to ER. Staff are trained in communication skills, recognizing problems early, recognizing their own hopes, fears and aspirations and taking steps to resolve these so that recourse to disputes and grievances is kept to a minimum.

Summary box 3.12   Staff representatives

Many organizations support the training of shop stewards, safety representatives and other union lay representatives. Where unions are not recognized, organizations also support the training of their staff representatives. The view taken in both cases is that it is better to deal with people who know what they are doing, and who are trained to do it.

The converse point of view is that it is easier – at least in the short term – to deal with people who do not know what they are doing. It remains true that it is easy to gain short-term success in dealings with those who are not adequately trained. In the medium term, this leads to conflict, disharmony, discontent and, in turn, to increases in strikes and grievances. Those being represented grow tired of failure – and take steps to prove the defence of their position, and therefore replace their representatives who are incapable, with those who are expert and trained. Alongside this, an atmosphere of mistrust and disharmony is in any case engendered – and so organizations and their managers not only face (eventually) capable employee representatives, but also these representatives come to them from an initial standpoint of distrust. In the long term, dealing with the ignorant in this way only leads to enduring conflict – and inevitably declining organizational performance.

This is the basis on which organizational standards and direction in the management of ER is established. It is an essential foundation if the management of discipline, grievances, disputes and serious problems is to be contemplated, and if an effective management style and approach to ER is to be generated across the organization.

4

ORGANIZATIONAL AND BEHAVIOURAL ASPECTS OF EMPLOYEE RELATIONS

INTRODUCTION

The purpose of the preceding chapters has been to establish the environmental, legal and contextual background in which ER takes place. It is clear from this that ER is concerned with both human behaviour and organizational performance. The purpose of this chapter, therefore, is to identify and discuss the range and complexity of the behavioural concepts that are a necessary background and prerequisite to ER effectiveness.

It is necessary to have a general level of understanding in these areas as part of the knowledge and expertise background in the effective management of ER. Identity and commonality of purpose can only be achieved if an understanding of the people who work in the particular organization, their wants and needs, hopes, fears, desires and aspirations are first understood.

The aspects discussed are arranged under the following headings:

■ **leadership:** qualities and capabilities, and the roles and functions adopted in ER
■ **communication:** an understanding of the processes, perception, the principles of effective communication
■ **decision-making:** the processes by which effective decisions are achieved, their communication and promulgation, their acceptance

- **power and authority:** sources of power and authority, the use of power and authority in ER situations
- **conflict in organizations:** sources, existence, management and containment.

LEADERSHIP

Leadership is concerned with getting results through people and all that this entails and implies. Each of the other features discussed in this chapter takes, as its source, the quality and style of leadership of the organization, department, division or function. The nature and style of leadership, in the particular field of ER, plays a critical role in the creation of human structures and systems, motivation and direction, the resolution of conflict, the creation of overall vision and direction and recognizing the obligations that go with this, including providing resources.

Studies of leadership have sought to identify the following:

Traits

The basis of trait theories of leadership is that there is a body of traits or characteristics, which are present in successful and effective leaders. The great limitation of this approach is the diversity of characteristics identified across a range of leaders deemed to be 'successful'. The concept of success is wide open to interpretation, meaning different things in different situations. In this context, the traits that are identified most often are intelligence, initiative, self-assurance, the ability to take an overview, good health, enthusiasm, determination, decisiveness, ambition, commitment, energy, drive, integrity and honesty.

Styles

These identify leadership as being somewhere on a style continuum. Styles identified are as follows:

- Autocratic, in which the leader makes all final decisions, there is close supervision, individual members' interests subordinate to the organization and questioning is discouraged. Within this context, an autocrat may either be benevolent or tyrannical. The 'content' of the leadership style does not vary between the two, though the attitude and approach clearly does.

■ Consultative, in which the leader makes decisions after consultation with the group, there is high quality communication between leader and members and questioning and extensive discussion are encouraged.

■ Participative, in which a consensus view is arrived at, there is high quality communication between leader and group members, the leader is visible and accessible and questioning and discussion are encouraged.

■ Democratic, in which the decisions are made by the group – either by consultation, or by vote if necessary. The great advantage of the democratic approach is that all members are bound by the group decision and support it. The great weakness is that a group decision may be 'wrong' (see Chapter 3).

Contingency theories and approaches

The contingency approach relates traits and styles to the situation, the environment, the technology, the work to be done and the matters in hand. It recognizes that this is fluid rather than static. It recognizes that leadership of the situation may vary; and that a variety of styles may be required as particular aspects of the situation come to the fore. It is more concerned with the position of 'leadership' than 'the leader', and by implication, therefore, recognizes that different people will have different expertise which may be required at different times.

The contingency approach was developed further by Handy (1994), using the 'theory of best fit'. This recognizes that no single approach provides a complete picture or answer. It balances the universal elements of the leader, the subordinates, the task, the technology and the environment, recognizing that there are common elements and attributes on which to draw; and recognizing also that as the situation changes, so does the required style of leadership.

In the creation of an effective ER environment, and its management, it is necessary to recognize a) that a wide variety of traits, styles, characteristics and expertise are to be called into play, based on those traits identified above; and b) that the possession of these, without ER expertise on which to draw, and extensive situational knowledge, will not in itself be enough.

In the leadership and direction of ER, it is therefore necessary to consider two further developments.

The 3-D approach

The 3-D approach identifies appropriate–effective leadership and management styles and inappropriate–ineffective leadership and management styles (see Figure 4.1). Related to ER, these are as follows:

Inappropriate–ineffective

■ Relaxed bureaucrats are people who display insufficient interest in task and relationship interface. Relaxed bureaucrats have a tendency towards secrecy and a lack of commitment. ER problems are therefore likely to become institutionalized. While in some cases, problems will therefore go away, or become obsolete, in others long-term decline in organizational or departmental morale, leading to conflict, is likely.

■ Missionaries put harmony and relationships above other considerations. They are ineffective because their desire to be seen as a good person prevents them from risking short-term disruption of relationships in order to resolve problems.

■ Autocrats are people who put the immediate task before all other considerations. Autocrats make it clear that they have no concern for relationships and little confidence in others. They therefore take a prescriptive and directional approach to ER, whether or not this is appropriate to the situation. Those who work for autocrats tend to dislike and fear them, and are thus motivated to work only when threats are applied. Again, this is damaging and destructive to long-term motivation and morale.

■ Compromisers are people who recognize the advantage of being oriented to both task and relationships, but who are incapable or unwilling to make decisions. They tend towards ambivalence and compromise. The main influence in their decision-making is the most recent or heaviest pressure, or that which comes from the source of greatest authority. This form of approach tends to leave an ER vacuum, a fertile breeding ground for larger than life employee representatives.

Appropriate–effective

■ Effective bureaucrats follow rules without due concern for either the task or the relationships. The best effective bureaucrats are skilled at maintaining morale and being effective, through understanding and applying rules and procedures.

■ Developers place implicit trust in people. They see the job as primarily concerned with developing the talents of others, and of providing a work atmosphere conducive to maximizing individual satisfaction and motivation. While generally effective in ER terms (in that grievances and disputes are generally kept to a minimum), problems do arise when short-run pressures and emergencies are placed on them.

■ Benevolent autocrats place implicit trust in themselves. They are concerned with both the immediate and the long term. They are effective in that they have skills in inducing others to do what is required of them, without creating such resentment that production and output fall. Serious ER problems are caused when the benevolent autocrat leaves and is replaced by someone who is not a benevolent autocrat. People are so used to working with acceptable direction, and with a high degree of identity with the benevolent autocrat, that a vacuum is created (where the replacement is benevolent but not an autocrat) or conflict is created (where the replacement is an autocrat but not benevolent).

■ Executives see their job as effectively maximizing the effort of others in relation to short- and long-term performance. They set high standards for production and performance, recognizing that because of individual differences and expectations, everybody must be treated differently. Their effectiveness is demonstrated by their evident commitment to both task and relationships and by the fact that they obtain their results, and motivation, within the constraints of the environment.

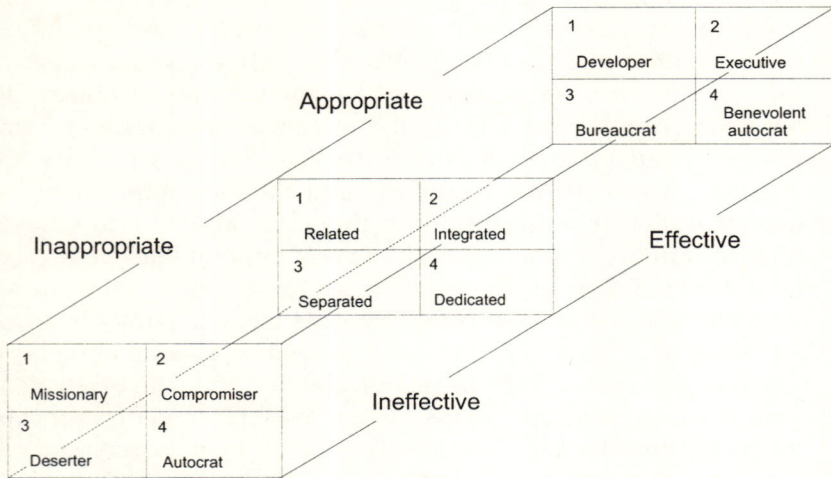

Figure 4.1 *The 3-D approach. The middle set of boxes identifies the four archetype leaders of Reddin's theory. These archetypes may then be translated into appropriate – effective or inappropriate – ineffective personal types* (source: W Reddin (1970))

The managerial grid

Another useful illustration of the leadership and management of ER lies in consideration of the managerial grid (see Figure 4.2).

The managerial grid identifies management styles against two dimensions of managerial concern – concern for people and concern for task, production and output. In ER terms, the following may usefully be defined:

■ 9-1: the country club – production is incidental; concern for the staff and people is everything. ER country clubs occur where negotiating and consultative committees exert too much influence, where they are too high a priority in the working lives of those involved, where no managerial action is taken without extensive consultation with employees' representatives (including trade unions), and where there is an over-proliferation of procedures. ER country clubs also tend to create layers of officials, who then in turn, generate volumes of paperwork and procedure, by which their existence is justified (at least by themselves).

```
  9 │ Country                        Productive
  8 │ Club 9:1                       Team 9:9
    │
  7 │
Concern │
for     6 │
people  5 │              Balance
    │                      5:5
  4 │
    │
  3 │
    │
  2 │
    │
  1 │ Poverty 1:1                    Task 1:9
────┼──────────────────────────────────────────
    │ 1    2    3    4    5    6    7    8    9
```

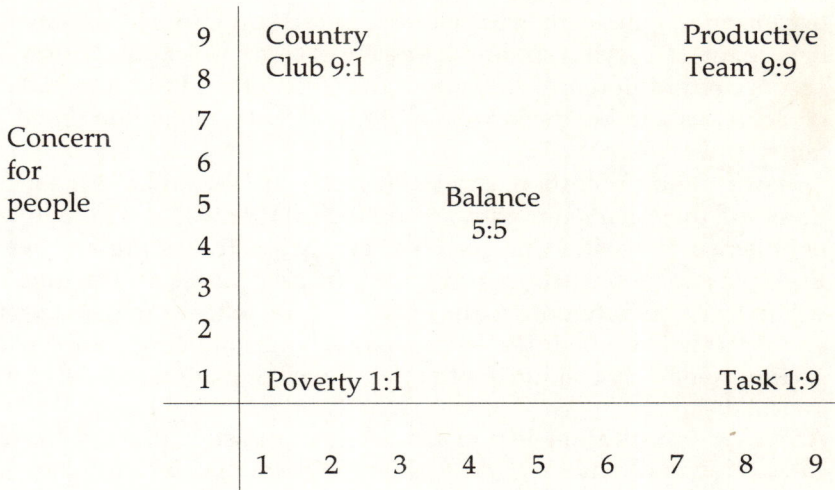

Figure 4.2 *The managerial grid* (source: Blake and Mouton (1986))

■ 1-9: task orientation – where production is everything; concern for the staff is subordinated to production. In these cases, grievances and disputes regularly abound and serious disruption to production occurs when such grievances and disputes get out of hand, or when management mistake their seriousness.
■ 5-5: balance – a medium degree of commitment to people, and commitment to task. This is likely to produce 'adequate' performance – and this is fine as long as it is not disrupted by a serious dispute or grievance.
■ 9-9: the best – in which the organization scores high on both axes. A prerequisite to successful ER in high performance, high concern, situations is complete mutual confidence and understanding, based on high levels and quality of communication, and understanding and acceptance of decision-making processes.

COMMUNICATION

Ultimately, effective ER is based on effective communication. Communication is a process that consists of the following:

- Passive communication, which takes place all the time. In organizations, it is at its worst when it represents a lack of purpose, direction, organization management or method in relation to the information being sent. The style, type and language of communication, through absence or indifference, cause the generation of, and reinforcement of, attitudes and behaviour related to negativity, alienation, uncertainty and anxiety.
- One-way communication, where messages are issued by organizations and their managers without any regard for those at whom they are pitched. It is widely perceived as being directive or prescriptive. Examples are edicts from on high, rules, procedures and manuals written without reference to the needs of those who are to read them and operational schedules that have no chance of being completed on time. One-way communication reinforces alienation and psychological distance.
- Active communication, in which messages are issued that everyone can understand and respond to. Language media and methods of communication are appropriate to both the messages and material concerned, and also to the audiences being addressed. It is the basis for effective work transactions. Organizations set their own modes and styles of communication, rather than allowing these to emerge by default. Staff understand both the wider situation and their own place in it. They are able to question and respond to issues without fear. Strong perceptions can be reinforced, and any strong misperceptions or misunderstandings are quickly cleared up (see Summary box 4.1).

Summary box 4.1   Perception

For those concerned with the creation of effective ER, an understanding of the principles of perception is essential. Perception is affected by the individual's own experiences and knowledge of the world. It is affected also by all forms of socialization – the interaction between individual and society, the interaction between the individual and others with whom they come into contact, and (especially in an ER context) the interaction between the individual and their organization, its structures, systems, culture and procedures. It is also affected by the prevailing influences present in particular situations. It may usefully be summarized as follows:

- **Halo effects** Strong positive or negative characteristics are either apparent or inferred and the rest of the organization's or individual's capabilities are assumed from this. For example, a strong handshake given and received at the point of meeting someone leads to an inference that they are a strong character. Employment with a giant corporation leads to the inference that there is a job for life.
- **First impressions** This is the instant positioning of someone or something on the individual's perceptual map. Initial impressions are very difficult to shift once formed, and this includes both strong positive and strong negative first impressions. Thus for example, strong impressions of an organization formed on the first day at work are very difficult to change. An initial conflict between an individual and a manager may form the impression on the one hand, that the manager is a tyrant and, on the other, that the individual is awkward, and again, this may be very difficult to change.
- **Stereotyping**, in which a set of characteristics is assumed in particular categories of people, and particular categories of people are assumed to have these sets of characteristics. In ER, people use stereotypical phrases and descriptions, for example, the workers, the union, management, white collar workers and blue collar workers.
- **Self-fulfilling prophecy** This is the part of the perception process by which people see only what they wish to see, and hear only what they wish to hear, and edit out the bits that do not fit in with what comes to be a preconceived picture of the world. They therefore come to the logical conclusion that 'all managers are tyrants' or 'all workers are lazy' because characteristics in support of this point of view are picked out, and everything else is edited out.
- **Implicit personality theory** This assumes that particular characteristics go together – such as kindness and gentleness or violence and dishonesty. These are related characteristics with which people may be comfortable. Different approaches are necessary to accommodate the person who is both kind and violent, or gentle and dishonest. As an example, some top film directors and architects are known to be difficult (some would say impossible) to work for. At the same time, those who work for them cite the wonderful experience gained as being more than worthwhile, and rationalize the impossibility of the 'great person' as being a part of their artistic temperament or a consequence of their great expertise.
- **Mythology** This is where people put a largely spurious rationale on the ways in which they organize their information. Again, it is concerned with making the individual comfortable in their particular surroundings or environment. Phrases such as 'you can never trust the trade unions' or 'management are always trying to screw you down' have a strong basis in ER folklore, and become points of comfort for those involved in these situations, especially if they are involved without full knowledge. In ER situations, it can consequently be extremely destructive.

- **Adaptation** This is perception as a continuous process. People's views of the world are influenced directly by the circumstances and surroundings in which they find themselves, and when these circumstances and surroundings change, so does their perception. It is also influenced by priorities – immediate pressures and problems, potential crises, actual crises, or conversely, the absence of these elements. In the management of ER, negative adaptation – the process by which both managers and other members of staff create crises around themselves and then spend their time and energy sorting them out – is extremely destructive.
- **Personal mapping and constructs** This part of perception is concerned with the process by which people's situations, activities, images and impressions are being fitted into the perceived map of the world in ways which can be understood, managed and accommodated. Information gathered is broken down into constructs or characteristics which may be categorized as:

  - physical: assuming or inferring the qualities of people from their appearance, racial group, beauty or ugliness, style, dress, and other visual images
  - behavioural: placing people according to the way in which they act and behave, or the ways in which they are assumed to act and behave
  - role: making assumptions about people because of the variety of roles that they assume, their job titles, their membership of trade unions or professional bodies, the different ways in which they assume these roles, their dominant role or roles, their perceived dominant role or roles, and the trappings that go with them
  - psychological: whereby certain occupations, appearances, manifestations, presentation and images are assumed to be of a higher order of things than others.

This constitutes the bare bones of a means for understanding the ways in which people perceive, edit and organize the information presented to them from their world. This includes the information that comes to them from their world of work. Understanding these principles is essential for all those who seek to conduct effective ER. There are direct implications for all aspects of staff management, and it is important to be able to understand the potential for the disruption of effective staff relations through simple misperception.

Other features of communication

The following should also be noted:

Distortion of the message

This occurs when the message is incomplete, the media used is inappropriate, or the language used is inappropriate. It may also be corrupted by the sender for their own ends.

It is particularly important to recognize this when, for example, using a manager to brief staff with whom they have no particular affinity or identity, or when using a trade union official to convey a particular message. Staff need to have trust and confidence in both messenger and message.

The language used also distorts the message. For example, phrases such as 'as a matter of urgency' or 'as soon as possible', tend to have less effect than 'this needs to be done by Friday night' – in the first two cases, there is no absolute deadline put on the message, while in the last one there is (see Summary box 4.2).

Summary box 4.2   ER and communication distortion

These are some examples of phrases in which staff normally have no confidence:

> There are no plans for redundancies at present.
> Everyone will receive an adequate pay rise.
> Our staff are our most important asset.
> We simply cannot afford a pay rise this year.
> The staff simply do not understand the broader situation.

Each of these statements is imprecise. Each is capable of all forms of interpretation and, consequently, if not backed up or supported with real, direct, precise, unambiguous information, is certain to be interpreted in a variety of ways – not only by those with a vested interest to do so, but also by all those involved, in their own way.

Communication content

Both oral and written communication should always be undertaken with the audience in mind. Accurate, relevant, precise and persuasive information are all important in different situations. There are skills inherent in this that require identification and development.

In ER terms, oral communication is required for conducting discussions and briefings with staff, conducting negotiations and consultations, effective interviews (especially grievance, dispute and discipline), conducting effective performance appraisal and handling staff and organizational problems.

Written communications should always be produced from the point of view of the reader. They should be as brief as possible; if they do have to be long, summaries should be included. While different formats are both required and expected for the minutes of meetings, briefings, papers for consultation, participation and negotiating meetings, and ER policy initiatives, the information contained, together with what is expected and required of all those affected, should be clearly stated.

Non-verbal communication

This either gives an impression of ourselves to someone else without our saying anything, or else it reinforces what we are saying. The main components are as follows:

■ Appearance, which may be broken down into age, gender, hair, face, body shape and size, bearing, national and racial characteristics and clothing. Each of these items on its own, and the combined effects, has great implications for creating impressions, presentation, attitudes and approaches to problems – especially employee relations problems.
■ Manner, which indicates behaviour, attitude, emotional range, levels of confidence, certainty and sureness.
■ Facial expression becomes the focus of attention, and people tend to concentrate most of their attention upon it.
■ Eye contact, which if used regularly, demonstrates interest, trust, concern, integrity and sympathy.
■ Pose, whether static or active, has great effects on the total message.
■ Props and settings – in ER situations, the most common are tables and chairs. Settings are designed to ensure that whatever happens in particular situations, it does so to the greatest possible advantage of the instigator. In ER terms, they are used by those in charge of particular situations either to put someone at their ease, or to put someone in the position desired by the setting director (often at a disadvantage).

Listening, hearing and understanding

Listening, hearing and understanding only takes place when the message is effectively delivered. However simple, direct and unambiguous the language used, the message will only be listened to, heard and understood if it is reinforced with integrity and honesty. It is especially hard to generate the confidence, as well as the understanding, of workforces where there is a history of bad employee relations. Historically, managers have tended to the view that trade unions are disruptive because their members tend to listen to them rather than to the organization's own people; invariably, this is as a result of the fact that, when the staff have listened to the organization's own people, they have subsequently been let down. The reverse is also true – that where employees have known that they have been exploited by their trade union, in the pursuit of trade union interest as distinct from employee interests, they have withdrawn their membership. The skills of listening, hearing and understanding are developed through the commitment, motivation and integrity of a total situation, and of those participating in it, and also through the development of effective two-way communication processes and procedures that are known, believed and perceived to work.

DECISION-MAKING

Three models of decision-making are shown in Figure 4.3.

The purpose of Model 1 is to draw the distinction between the two elements of progression and process. The former is a schematic approach; the latter is that from which the former arises, and which refines it into its final format. Effective and successful decision-making requires the confidence that is generated by continued operation of the process.

Model 2 shows a managerial approach for introducing a major or contentious issue. This should be used for strategic, directional, operational, technological and locational changes, behavioural and human relations issues, solving problems and the introduction of no smoking, uniform, appraisal and representation policies.

Model 3 shows the autocratic–participative range, illustrating the range available in organizational and managerial decision-making. It also provides a sound basis for forethought. Certain types of decision will be better understood, and accepted, if they are delivered in particular ways.

1. Progression

2. Process

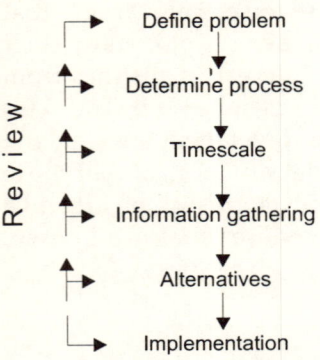
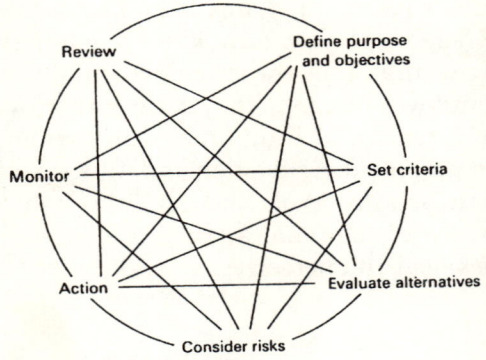

Figure 4.3a

<u>Model</u>

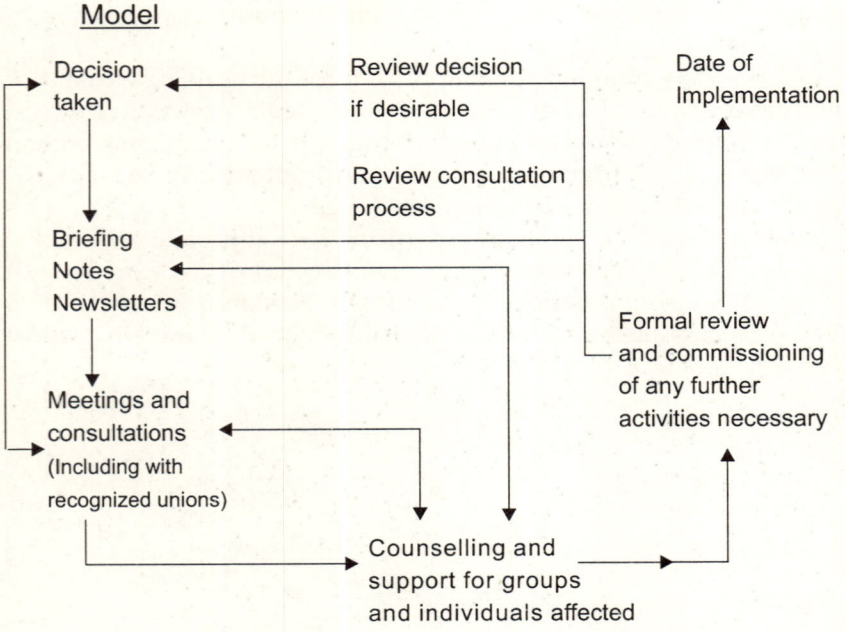

Figure 4.3b

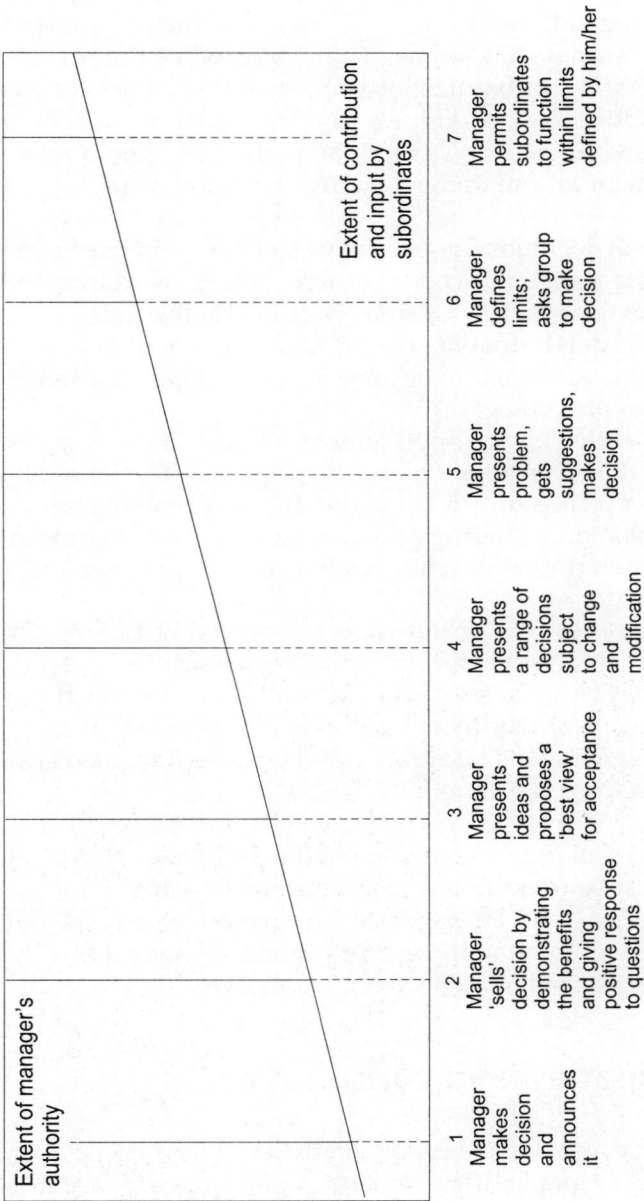

Extent of manager's authority

Extent of contribution and input by subordinates

1 Manager makes decision and announces it

2 Manager 'sells' decision by demonstrating the benefits and giving positive response to questions

3 Manager presents ideas and proposes a 'best view' for acceptance

4 Manager presents a range of decisions subject to change and modification

5 Manager presents problem, gets suggestions, makes decision

6 Manager defines limits; asks group to make decision

7 Manager permits subordinates to function within limits defined by him/her

Figure 4.3c

The key feature in all effective decision-making is communication. However good, sound or 'rational' a particular decision may be (whether in pure ER terms, or for the good of the organization as a whole), it will only be effectively implemented if the reasons why it was taken, and the necessity for the particular course of action, are understood by all concerned and affected. The process requires commitment to, and understanding of, the following:

- **Problem definition** This may appear obvious, but the effects and consequences of particular courses of action will not be fully understood if the issue in question is not accurately defined at the outset.
- **Process determination** This includes the extent of consultation and participation that is to be allowed in the determination of particular courses of action.
- **Time-scale** This has implications for trade-offs between information, evaluation, consultation and participation. The longer it is possible to leave a decision, the better the chances of gaining full acceptance.
- **Information gathering** An effort must be made to concentrate especially on the quality of information and the purpose for which it is to be used.
- **Alternatives** This includes the choice of doing nothing. Once consultation and information gathering processes are engaged, the problem may either be seen to be different from that which was originally envisaged, or worthy of a different course of action.
- **Implementation** Here the support (or at least acquiescence) of everyone concerned is required.

The general objective of anyone in the position of having to take decisions must be to minimize risks and uncertainties, minimize negative consequences, and to maximize the chances of success and effectiveness. In order to stand the greatest chance of success therefore, participation and consultation need to be considered.

Participation and consultation

This can be most effective particularly when adverse decisions are to be taken. For example, if redundancies are proposed, a package agreed between management and workforce is likely to be more acceptable than a package imposed by management alone. The purpose of consultation and participation must be therefore:

- to gain the commitment of the staff – this is only achievable if the proposal is communicated via all means at the disposal of the organization and if adequate and full briefings, meetings and discussions are held

■ to ensure that everyone understands and values the necessity of what is being done (even if this is negative) – this must include coverage of the reasons, together with the timescale and progression for activities

■ to address the needs of groups of staff and individuals – this includes matters concerning relocation, redeployment, retraining, redundancy, changes in operational or behavioural patterns, and changes in organizational expectations

■ to use the period between the taking of the decision and the date of its implementation to best operational and behavioural advantage so that on the day when whatever it is that is proposed comes into being, the transition is made as smoothly as possible.

Consultation and participation are, therefore, concerned with implementation and understanding. They should not be allowed to dilute or affect what is to be done, unless the process itself throws up operational barriers.

It may impact on all aspects of work, from major redundancy or relocation exercises to the introduction of smoking bans, or the implementation of small job changes on the part of individuals.

Consultation in particular must be fair and reasonable. Normally such a period will be for at least four weeks. This minimum will relate to relatively minor and individual changes. For a major exercise – a relocation for example – a period of up to a year may be necessary. For redundancies, there are specific legal constraints. A true balance must be struck between the pressures on the organization and the needs of its staff.

Consultation and participation are active processes, to be led and directed by the organization. It is not enough simply to give a period of notice of changes that are to happen. Responsibility for gaining the understanding, commitment and support of staff in such matters is an obligation placed on the organization's top managers; they must direct it and ensure that it happens in the ways indicated.

Decision-making in its environment

It is also necessary to take the following into account:

■ Limitation of laws and government direction, representing wider, national, local and social constraints and restraints.

- Public interest, which is likely to become of ever-increasing importance in ER, as the EU social partnership model gains ever-greater influence. It is likely in the future that there will be a legitimate public interest in matters concerning redundancy, redeployment, pensions arrangements and the style of organizational management.
- Lobbies and vested interest groups, including trade unions, employers' associations, professional and occupational cluster groups, departmental, divisional and functional interest groups. It may be necessary to recognize at the outset, that in dealings with these groups, some groups may have legitimacy but no influence while others may have influence but no legitimacy. Nevertheless, each has to be dealt with if they are to gain their true measure of influence and, where the group has influence but no legitimacy, to ensure that the point of view that they are raising is dealt with, so that their influence is diluted.
- Organizational adjustment is the part of the decision-making process whereby the organization alters or adjusts its activities in the light of information and experience gathered during the consultation process. It is inevitable that this happens. Even where all that the consultation process, and decision-making process have done is to reinforce the correctness of the organization's chosen direction, confidence and certainty are nevertheless increased on the part of all concerned.

POWER AND AUTHORITY

It is first useful to distinguish between power and authority.

Authority is the recognition of the right to restrict freedom to act (recognition is the key factor, ie the existence of authority is dependent upon shared values between those involved). Authority also refers to the establishment of accepted rules and norms of behaviour that limit conflict.

Power is the ability to influence the attitudes and behaviour of others or, more strongly, the ability of A to get B to do something that B would not otherwise do.

Authority is thus a relationship; power is a resource.

Types of power and authority

In order to understand the behaviour of people in organizations more fully, it is useful to examine the different types of power and authority that exist. Weber (1986) defined three categories of authority:

■ **Charismatic** This refers to a special aspect of a leader's personality. This is the ability to dominate and lead others to an unusual degree. In the fields of staff management and employee relations well-known examples are Margaret Thatcher, Arthur Scargill and John Monks. In most organizations, however, many examples exist at organizational and departmental levels. Many union and other staff representatives, and many managers, supervisors and section heads, exhibit a measure of charisma as the result of the ways in which they carry out their responsibilities.

■ **Traditional** This refers to kinship as the basis for allocating power – typically, son follows father. It is increasingly rare in organizations, although it is still possible to find 'organization dynasties' (such as used to be found in the UK dockyards) or 'trade union dynasties' (where child follows parent into the trade union 'industry').

■ **Legal rational** Here, rules and norms, legitimized by law and custom, provide the justification for the possession of power by certain persons. The rules may apply to committee processes, the constitution of negotiating and consultation fora, or they may apply to selection processes used to make appointments within a hierarchy. Organization rule books, terms and conditions of employment, and procedures are drawn up in this way. All formalized hierarchical organizations are based on this. The formalized ER machinery is also derived from this source.

French and Raven (in Cartwright, 1959) have distinguished five categories of power:

■ **Reward power**, where persons have the ability to give or withhold rewards. These may vary from matters of pay to words of praise.

■ **Physical power** is the use and threatened use of physical force. It is the least acceptable form of power. It should never be formally used in organizations. It is a factor however, in the behaviour of some physically powerful managers and employees. It is present in such activities as strikes, lock-outs and picketing to a greater or lesser extent.

■ **Expert power**, in which knowledge is power. Greater knowledge gives greater power. In ER terms, the capability to conduct effective negotiations gives a clear advantage, as does legal knowledge and understanding in the definition and application of rules, rule books and procedures.

■ **Referent power** is based on personal friendships and contacts of superiors and subordinates and, in ER terms, of managers and employees' representatives. It is a key feature of the 'informal' system of employee relations that is present in all organizations to a greater or lesser extent.

■ **Legitimate power** is present through legal power – the capacity enshrined by law to act in particular ways, and belief – the acceptance of a superior–subordinate relationship.

Etzioni (1964) defined three power resources:

■ **Coercive:** the ability to order or force someone to do something that the other would not otherwise do.
■ **Remunerative:** the ability to influence someone's standards and style of living.
■ **Normative:** the ability to set standards and types of behaviour that enable ways in which people act and react to be predicted with a good degree of certainty.

In terms of the organization and management of ER, it is necessary to understand the following:

■ Power and influence reside in the hands of managers because of the confidence in which they are held, as well as the expertise that they hold.
■ Power and influence reside in the hands of shop stewards and employees' representatives because of the extent of the support that they command; this is reinforced by past track records of success.
■ Power and influence lie in the hands of staff to change or remove their representatives; because of this, a professional distinction has to be maintained between the role of the employee representative, and any personal relationship with the managers with whom they are dealing.
■ It is essential to understand the extent of reward power present in particular situations – especially the capability of organizations and their managers to deliver things that have been agreed.
■ Authority and influence have strong behavioural connotations. As well as legitimized positions in hierarchies, or vested by means of job titles, there has to be a measure of confidence and belief in the individuals in the first place.
■ Understanding of the Etzioni approach concerning remunerative and normative power resources is most important, because it indicates the presence of mutual and universal interests – the improvements of standards of living and the ability to predict people's behaviour in given situations and in response to given circumstances. It is therefore possible to engage people's interest by offering a pay rise. It is also possible, by organizing and designing the means of consultation, to set a regularity and orderliness for decision-making. Conversely, it is also

possible to anticipate and understand people's reactions if adverse or negative ER decisions have to be taken.

CONFLICT IN ORGANIZATIONS

The potential for conflict exists in all human situations, and organizations are no different. In ER – and broad staff management also – it is useful to define the potential for organization conflict as conflict between:

■ individuals within the organization
■ an individual and group or groups within the organization
■ the organization and its staff
■ individuals with vested interests (eg manager, shop steward, staff representative).

It is also useful to identify conflict based on:

■ ideology – where the argument is about what is known, believed or perceived to be fundamentally right or wrong
■ objectives – where those involved in the conflict have fundamentally different objectives, or where they have the same or similar objectives, but fundamentally different ideas as to how to achieve them
■ territory – where conflict is based on the fact, belief or perception that somebody is operating outside their agreed, understood, stated or implied remit.

It is also useful to note the following when assessing the potential for conflict in particular work situations:

■ nature of work, any professional or technical context, training or expertise present
■ the structure of work, the division of work and tasks into jobs, preferred tasks and jobs, least preferred tasks and jobs
■ individuals and their personality, personal objectives
■ personal and professional ethics, standards, attitudes, values and beliefs
■ organizational ethics, standards, attitudes, values, beliefs and expectations
■ organization structure and culture, its ways of organizing its work and the procedures that enable it to function

- the traditions of the sector, company or organization in question, past triumphs and defeats, past successes and failure, current successes and failure, triumphs and defeats
- organizational mythology – larger than life stories, which have their foundation in fact, but which have grown out of all proportion to their actual factual basis, while nevertheless retaining a vital position in organization folklore
- past attitudes and approaches to staff management and employee relations
- present approaches, attitudes, values, knowledge, beliefs and perceptions concerning the precise operation of employee relations
- proposals for the future of employee relations.

Conflict and the behaviour of organizations

A study of conflict as an aspect of behaviour in organizations is concerned with providing a basic conceptual framework and a language that will enable persons in organizations to develop a fuller understanding of its nature. Most importantly for those concerned with employee relations, it concludes with proposals for using conflict as positively and beneficially as possible.

There are four aspects:

The parties to the conflict

The simplest form of conflict involves only two parties. Much organizational conflict concerns more, and often many more, than two parties. One of the problems facing those concerned with the effective management of ER is the capability to define clearly the parties to a conflict, and their purposes for engaging. Differences of perception and communication problems at different levels of an organization can cause difficulties in this connection.

Understanding the objectives of the parties to a conflict is compounded when there are subgroups present on each side of the main divide – for example, when there are several trade unions involved in negotiations with management; or where a management team has been constituted, each of whom nevertheless has their own separate agenda.

The issues

The second aspect of conflict as part of organizational behaviour is to do with the issues themselves. These may be:

- the topics or subjects in dispute
- the perceptions of the parties to the dispute as to what the topics actually are
- the interests of those concerned and involved, especially the interests in resolving the issue (or not), and the basis on which this resolution is acceptable and workable to each party concerned
- whether there is a hierarchy of contentious issues and matters to be resolved and whether each party involved in the dispute has the same hierarchy or priority order of contentious issues and matters to be resolved.

The dynamics of the conflict

In this aspect the following must be considered:

- the factors that brought the conflict out into the open
- the factors that continue to fuel it and keep it alive
- the extent to which the situation has remained the same, or the extent to which it has moved on, and the reasons for this
- the extent to which it is institutional, structural, professional, departmental, personalized or a power struggle
- the length of time that it has been going on, the attitudes of the different players in the conflict, any changes in attitudes that have occurred as the result of its longevity
- the conflicting interests of those concerned, and the extent to which these may be harmonized or reconciled
- the extent to which it is possible to predict certain developments or outcomes, and the extent to which those developments or outcomes are going to be changed or influenced depending upon different courses of action
- the range of possible outcomes, both positive and negative
- the extent to which the problems, as stated, are the actual problems or contentious issues at stake
- the position and influence of any vested interests, lobbies, or other influence groups
- the power and influence of key players to make or break the situation
- the extent and prevalence of any negative influences, especially the capability to block progress.

Where specialist employee relations departments and officials can make a key contribution to organizational effectiveness is in the analysis of the potential for, and reality of, conflict in their organizations. This is carried out using these (or equivalent) criteria and points of entry, so that the true extent and prevalence – and depth – of conflict may be analysed. It is then incumbent upon these officials to go on and propose a range of solutions, from which those with executive authority can make their choice. This is their key contribution to the management of organizations.

The management of conflict

This form of approach at least indicates the extent, prevalence and depth of conflict. Management's first priority is to understand this. It can then in turn, propose strategies for its control or ordering. Uncontrolled conflict is a symptom of an uncontrolled organization (see Summary box 4.3). ER management can then set itself objectives in dealing with the conflict as follows:

■ institutionalizing the conflict, so that at least when it does occur, it can be conducted through procedures and processes that enable orderly resolution, and at least mutual understanding and acceptance of these processes
■ Containing and controlling the conflict by isolating and tackling the most destructive elements
■ ultimately, removing the causes of conflict.

Summary box 4.3   The management of conflict: benign neglect

Benign neglect was a favourite strategy of large public and private corporations and their managers – and their trade unions – during the 1960s and 1970s. It took the form of applying the dictum 'a problem deferred is a problem half solved'.

It is quite true that some problems went away as a result; it is also true that it helped to keep serious confrontation to a minimum. However, it also avoided legitimate professional confrontation of both ER and wider organizational behavioural problems (and also operational issues to the extent that when such problems did arise, and when there were serious competitive questions to be addressed (eg as the result of incursions of Japanese and other far eastern companies into manufacturing industries and products in the UK) organizations no longer had the capability to tackle these.

Neglect – benign or otherwise – can be used only as a temporary measure while more information is being gathered, or a more structured approach is being formulated.

From this, it is possible to:

■ develop and improve rules, procedures, processes and precedents to minimize the emergence of conflict
■ develop and improve the channels and quality of communications
■ separate and isolate sources of potential conflict
■ establish conciliation and arbitration machinery to which all those in the organization can agree
■ use confrontation to try and bring participants to the conflict together in an attempt to get them to resolve matters on a face-to-face basis
■ undertake broader advances in managerial qualities and expertise, alongside the process of conflict management, in order to reduce the risk and prevalence of conflict, and to ensure that managers are able to tackle it more quickly and effectively than in the past.

Early warnings of conflict

These are as follows. Every manager and staff representative must be aware of them, and respond to them when they start to occur.

■ **Declining organizational performance** This is the most important functional and practical symptom. Declining performance trends in a section or department often accompany the growth of conflict.
■ **Declining morale** This is indicated by rising rates of labour turnover, sickness and absence and rising accident rates. Conflict aggravates these problems.

This is a joint venture, especially in organizations that have both formal and informal joint negotiating and consultation processes. It is a key feature of the social partnership approach to industry favoured by the EU, in which responsibility for organizational well-being is shared between all those involved. While it is true that ultimate responsibility for the organization rests with its directors and top managers, there is, nevertheless, an active requirement on the part of all members of staff to raise issues that they believe to be of legitimate concern. It also leads to a much greater universal understanding of the general extent and nature of organizational well-being. This in itself is a key contribution to the effective management of organizations at large, and effective employee relations in particular.

CONCLUSIONS

In summary, the key features outlined in this chapter – leadership, communication, decision-making, power and conflict – are essential prerequisites to the understanding of the totality of ER. It is essential to remember that all ER is founded on the interactions of people, and therefore on their behaviour and approaches in different situations. In principle, it is essential to understand that all organization activities – of which ER is one – are dependent upon effective leadership, communication and decision-making. Absence of these causes ER problems, in exactly the same way as they cause production output and sales problems.

Beyond this, it is essential to recognize the function of leadership, and the need for firm direction and authority in the management of ER, and the potential for conflict and dysfunction that exists in all human situations.

Only when the behavioural aspects of ER are recognized, can an effective approach to the establishment and management of organization discipline, conflict and motivation be contemplated, and the establishment of effective institutions for the conduct of both strategic and operational ER be considered.

5

ORGANIZATIONAL DISCIPLINE

INTRODUCTION

Organization discipline is concerned with standards of attitudes, behaviour and performance. It derives from the total approach to ER that is adopted, especially from the perspective, culture and behaviour of the organization as a whole and the style of operations management adopted. It is developed through the principles of organization development, and the effectiveness of operations and actions in the field of organization discipline are reflected in the priority and quality of management and supervisory staff training in the field, as well as the extent, nature and frequency of issues concerning disciplinary actions and grievances raised.

Effective organization discipline therefore reflects the strategic approach and the style of ER adopted in its pursuit. Specific policy issues can then be addressed under the headings of attitudes and behaviour and performance.

Attitudes and behaviour

Organization discipline in relation to attitudes and behaviour can only be established if the required standards are clearly understood and accepted by all (see Summary box 5.1). They are concerned with the following policies:

- **Equality and fairness of treatment and opportunity** These are the fundamental principles by which the contribution of everybody at the place of work is valued, organizational attitudes where inequality and unfairness are discovered, institutional approaches to victimization, bullying and harassment.

■ **Establishment of shared and accepted norms and values** These arise from the perspective adopted. They include attention to rank, job title, modes of address, dress codes, terms and conditions of employment, wage differentials, questions of status and prestige as well as performance, perks and benefits and opportunities. So long as these are clearly understood, and accepted by all, disciplinary issues and grievances arising can be kept to a minimum.

■ **Positive and negative** This is concerned with the overall approach to problems and other issues – whether there is an organizational will to resolve these as quickly as possible, whether the preferred policy is to institutionalize them, the extent to which they are given priority when they do arise, management and supervisory training in problem-solving and discipline and grievance management.

■ **Responsibilities** In terms of organization discipline, this means establishing the boundaries and requirements of organizational responsibility and the approach to this, professional and occupational responsibility, group division and departmental responsibility and self-responsibility in terms of attitudes and behaviour. It includes indicating responsibilities for product and service quality, and remedy of operational faults. It indicates wider responsibilities including those concerned with the future improvement, enhancement and prosperity of the organization. The converse is clearly apparent also. Organizations have absolute responsibilities in terms of commitments to wages, salaries and the other rewards and benefits due to staff; and to delivering what is stated or implied in the rest of the contract of employment. Responsibility for attitudes and behaviour is therefore clearly shared (see Figure 5.1). Though the overall standards are set by the organization, they must be applied by everyone.

■ **Shared values** Similarly, values determined and adopted by the organization must be capable of acceptance by everyone. There needs to be universal acceptance of what is right, what is wrong, what is acceptable and what is unacceptable.

■ **Style** In terms of organization discipline, this means understanding why a particular management style has been adopted and acknowledging the responsibilities and commitments that this brings. People may be persuaded to accept overtly harsh or strident discipline, or adversarial management or supervisory styles, provided that they understand the standpoint and necessity from which they derive. On the other hand, people may treat an open and honest style and approach with disdain, if it does not also concentrate on organization performance as well as staff comfort.

Organization perspective

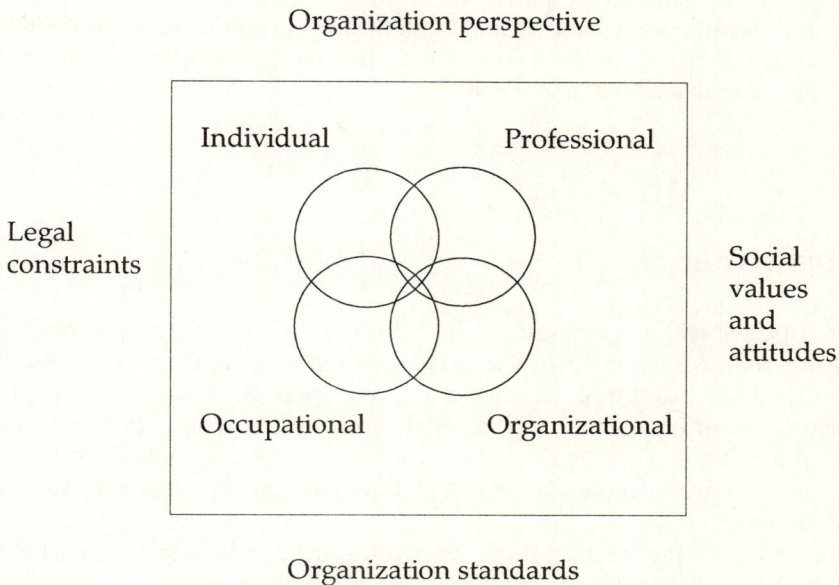

Figure 5.1 *The mix of responsibilities*

Summary box 5.1   Induction and organization discipline

Induction is the process by which employees become settled and productive in their organization and their job or occupation. Much of the induction process is concerned with getting people settled and familiar in their environment.

It is also vital in the establishment and mutual understanding of acceptable and required standards of attitude and behaviour. Initial misconceptions and preconceptions can be nipped in the bud. Precise standards can be indicated.

Many organizations neglect this part of the process. Those that pay attention to it tend to have fewer discipline problems and grievances arising. This part of induction is, for example, a key feature in the removal of the causes of conflict in unitary organizations – both unionized and non-unionized. Japanese organizations working in the UK spend extensive periods of time getting their employees to understand 'the company ways of doing things'. This is also the case with high reputation unitary organizations such as Virgin and Marks & Spencer.

The organization standpoint adopted is that investment at this stage reinforces the respect, value and commitment placed on all employees at the outset of their employment and sets expectations – including attitudes and behaviour – for the duration of their employment. The view is taken that this form of investment at this stage prevents much more serious problems arising later on.

Performance

At one level, organization discipline and the management of performance is straightforward. Departmental, divisional, functional, group and individual performance can each be measured against objectives and targets, and remedial action taken when shortcomings are identified. This again reinforces the need for considered and contextual performance targeting to take place, and the contribution of effective ER.

In practice, it is seldom this straightforward. Underlying causes have to be looked at in the management of inadequate performance in all except isolated cases. Consistently poor departmental performance indicates either supply or output quality problems, or issues concerning the quality of management and supervision, or else factors concerning staff quality, capability or willingness to work. So the key to the effective management of performance from this point of view is attention to the specific issues, and consideration of the broader picture.

The direction and management of organization discipline is devised and defined by senior managers, operated by those with departmental, divisional and functional responsibilities, and accepted by all those who work in and for the organization.

Operationally, it is a process with two key factors:

■ discipline: strategies and activities for the maintenance of standards, and remedial action where necessary
■ grievances: strategies that enable employees to raise questions, issues and problems with the organization, so that these may be resolved.

To complete the picture, it is necessary to consider organization discipline from the point of view of:

■ the stated or explicit: the ways that rules and regulations are laid down, stated standards and levels of performance, the content of discipline and grievance procedures
■ the actual: the ways in which the rules are applied in practice, the ways in which standards and levels of performance are valued, monitored and maintained, and the ways in which discipline and grievance procedures are applied
■ the implicit: wider considerations, especially the aura of ER (as mentioned in Chapter 1), and whether this is positive or negative, based on harmony and progress, or fear and conflict.

This constitutes the basis and context for all organization discipline. It is now necessary to consider in detail the constitution of discipline and grievance procedures and the management of discipline and grievance issues.

DISCIPLINE AND GRIEVANCE PROCEDURES

In the UK, all organizations are deemed to have procedures that cover discipline, grievance, disputes and dismissal. They must be in writing, available for inspection, be understood by all and be followed in all cases.

They must be issued to employees or else be freely and readily available when required. Everyone concerned must understand their general rights and duties and specific rights and obligations under the procedures. In particular, where cases get as far as employment tribunal, the tribunal normally requires to be satisfied that procedures were fully understood and that they were applied and followed.

Disciplinary procedures

All disciplinary procedures must state the circumstances in which they are to be applied. They normally cover the following:

Poor and unsatisfactory performance

This is where for some reason the individual is incapable or unwilling to do the job for which he/she is employed. This requires a clear statement by the manager or supervisor of where and why the performance is falling short, followed by another clear statement of a programme for action to put it right.

This is then subject to regular monitoring, evaluation and review and is concluded with a clear statement to the employee that either performance is now satisfactory or performance is still unsatisfactory, in which case further action is to be taken.

Misconduct

Misconduct includes minor issues and misdemeanours. It also includes negligence, unacceptable behaviour, failure to follow procedures, failure to act in the organization's best interests, insubordination, gratuitous rudeness to colleagues and bad time-keeping. It may include persistent self-certificated absenteeism (though very great care is to be taken with this).

Misconduct may also include victimization, bullying and harassment though ideally, these should all come under the category of gross, or at least serious, misconduct.

Attitudes and demeanour

Attitudes and demeanour are harder to pin down. It is, however, quite legitimate both to make provision for dealing with negative, poor and sloppy attitudes and also those where individuals place their own priorities above those of the organization. Other matters include attitudes to others – for example, where someone engages in a constant or persistent attitude of blame or denigration towards others.

Serious and gross misconduct

The law requires organizations to have and make known to staff what constitutes serious and gross misconduct. The usual form of presentation of this is a list. This list need not be exhaustive. It should give clear and wide-ranging examples. The usual matters covered under this heading are:

■ theft, fraud, sale of confidential information, other dishonesty
■ vandalism, violence, attacks on staff, equipment and premises
■ sexual misconduct
■ serious or gross negligence and inattention to duties and the organization's interests
■ using foul and abusive language, swearing in front of customers and clients
■ overt dishonesty in dealings with staff or customers
■ denigration of the organization to other staff, customers, clients and the public

■ failure to follow safety procedures, endangering life and/or equipment.

Serious and gross misconduct may also arise as the result of persistent misconduct. This includes persistent bad time-keeping, persistent absenteeism, persistent insubordination and rudeness.

All organizations have their own interpretation and variations. There may also be specific operational requirements underpinned by instant recourse to gross misconduct.

General rights

All disciplinary procedures, and the activities that they support, must include the following:

■ the right of the individual to know the case against him/her and to confront the accuser
■ the right of the individual to respond to the case and present his/her own point of view
■ the right to representation at each stage, either by the representative of a recognized trade union or other person of the individual's choice
■ the right to receive in writing a definitive statement of the conclusion and outcome of the case at each stage
■ the right of appeal against the conclusion and outcome at each stage.

Warnings

Minimum standards require a series of at least two warnings (and many organizations have three or four). These may either be written or oral; when oral they are in any case normally confirmed in writing.

The general aim is to ensure that the employee is aware that an aspect of their conduct, behaviour or performance is unacceptable and giving cause for concern. The warning must confirm this and state the remedial action that is necessary.

For poor performance this normally includes retraining or a restatement of the standards of activity that are necessary and acceptable.

For shortfalls in behaviour and conduct, this normally includes a restatement of what the required standards are and why they are necessary.

For both performance and conduct, warnings will normally include a date in the future on which a review of progress is to be carried out.

Recording

Warnings are recorded on the individual's personnel file (or equivalent) for set periods of time. Time periods are stated in the procedure and notified to the individual in each case.

It is normal for warnings for minor offences to be kept on file for periods of between three months and two years. Records of more serious offences may be retained for longer periods. The most serious offences are kept on file for life.

There are no rules governing this. The only requirement is to be fair and reasonable. The organization must balance its need to set and maintain standards with the requirement of individuals not to have their career or their prospects irreparably harmed by relatively minor incidents.

At the end of the stated period, the warning is removed from the file. It may never be used or referred to again.

Serious misconduct

For matters of serious misconduct it is acceptable and legitimate to place individuals on a final warning. This is confirmed to the individual in writing as the result of the hearing and assessment of the case.

Organizations must indicate the kind of offences that constitute serious misconduct (though the list need not be exhaustive). These normally include persistent bad time-keeping, persistent poor performance, rudeness and insubordination.

Gross misconduct

For gross misconduct it is acceptable and legitimate to move straight to dismissal. This is normally called summary dismissal. This is also confirmed to the individual in writing as the result of the hearing and assessment of the case.

Organizations must again indicate the kind of offences that constitute gross misconduct (though the list again need not be exhaustive). These normally include vandalism, violence, arson, sabotage, theft, dishonesty, sexual misconduct, sale and publication of confidential information, other breaches of the criminal law and harassment, persecution and victimization of members of staff.

For both serious misconduct and gross misconduct, procedures must be followed. However serious the alleged offence, the individual is still entitled to hear the case against them, to face their accuser, to respond, to be represented and to appeal against the findings.

Where dismissal does occur the reasons stated for dismissal must be the real reasons for dismissal. This must be notified in writing to the individual and to anyone else who requests the information (eg the Department for Education and Employment).

Suspension

For serious offences it is acceptable and legitimate to suspend employees from work while a full investigation into the matter is held. Suspension is normally on full pay. The reasons for suspension and the date and time from which it becomes effective must be confirmed in writing at the point at which the decision to suspend is made.

Disciplinary hearings

For all disciplinary hearings employees must be informed of the following:

- They must be notified, either orally or in writing, that they are required to attend a disciplinary hearing. The words disciplinary hearing must be used. They must be informed of all the rights indicated above, including the rights to be accompanied and represented.
- They must be informed of the case against them, who has brought it and why. They must be given the opportunity to face their accuser. They must be informed of the nature of the case, whether it potentially constitutes a minor offence, repeat offence, serious misconduct or gross misconduct.
- They must be asked to give their explanation of the events and situation.
- They must be allowed time (but not to excess) to prepare their case. They must be allowed to call witnesses and gain access to documents and papers that affect their case.

Operation of procedures

Warnings

Warnings may be written or oral. The final warning is always written. Any formal warning – whether written or oral – must be confirmed in writing. By law, disciplinary procedures must give at least two warnings before the dismissal stage. In practice, most have three or more (see Summary box 5.2).

For serious misconduct, it is usual to move to the final warning. For gross misconduct, it is usual to move straight to dismissal.

Summary box 5.2   Examples of disciplinary procedures: formats

Two warnings

- **First warning** A formal warning represents the outcome of investigation and discussion into an employee's conduct or performance. If a first warning is issued, the individual concerned will be advised to this effect both verbally and in writing. This will also indicate the duration of the warning, the reasons for the warning and the specific areas for improvement.
- **Second (final) warning** This is issued where there is no significant and sustained improvement in the employee's conduct or performance. When a final warning is issued, the individual concerned will be advised to this effect both verbally and in writing, indicating the duration of the warning, the grounds for the warning and the specific areas for improvement.

If there is no significant and sustained improvement in the employee's conduct or performance during the period of the final warning, the next stage of the procedure will be the dismissal stage.

Three warnings

- **First warning** A formal warning represents the outcome of the investigation and discussion into an employee's conduct or performance. If a first warning is issued, the individual will be advised to this effect both verbally and in writing. This will indicate the duration of the warning, the reasons for the warning and the specific areas for improvement.
- **Second warning** If there is no significant and sustained improvement in the employee's conduct or performance then the next stage of the procedure is the second warning. If a second warning is issued, the individual concerned will be advised to this effect, indicating the duration of the warning, the grounds for the warning and specific areas for improvement.
- **Third (final) warning** If there is no significant and sustained improvement in the employee's conduct or performance then the next stage of the procedure is a final warning. If a final warning is issued, the individual concerned will be advised to this effect indicating the duration of the warning, the grounds for the warning and the specific areas for improvement.

If there is no significant and sustained improvement in the employee's conduct or performance during the period of the final warning, then the next stage of the procedure will be the dismissal stage.

Whatever the number of warnings, it is important that the language used is simple and direct, and not open to misinterpretation.

The onus is placed firmly on managers and those responsible for organization discipline to pay attention to the nature and level of improvement required while people are under warnings.

Procedures must be operated as follows, whatever the level of misconduct alleged and whatever the stage that is being used (see Summary box 5.3):

■ Individuals facing discipline by their organizations must be allowed representation. Where a trade union is recognized and where the individual is a member, representation is normally through that union. Where there is no union or where the employee is not a member, they may be accompanied by a colleague of their choice. This must always be allowed.

■ Individuals must always be told that they are facing discipline in advance of the hearing. This notification may give an indication of the range of outcomes. It must never prejudge the issue.

■ Individuals facing discipline are entitled to hear the charges against them and to face their accuser/accusers in person. They are entitled to respond to the charges and to call witnesses and evidence in support of their case.

■ Individuals who have been disciplined must be afforded the opportunity to appeal. They must be notified of the person/official to whom the appeal should be made, and the deadline by which it should be made.

■ Individuals facing discipline must be notified in writing of the outcome of the case. A copy of this should be placed in their personal file. When a warning is issued, a copy of this should be given to the employee and a copy placed on his/her file. This applies to both oral and written warnings. It should state what the warning was for, any remedial action necessary, what is to happen if there is any repeat and how long it is to remain current.

Summary box 5.3   Disciplinary procedures: other aspects

The following should always be taken into account when considering disciplinary action and provision should always be included in disciplinary procedures:

- **Suspension** This is used quite legitimately in serious and/or contentious cases. Especially in cases of serious and gross misconduct, it is often essential that the individual concerned is removed from the scene while a full investigation is held. If it is decided that there is a case to answer, the individual must then be allowed time to prepare a response.

  Suspension may be with or without pay. It is usual – and best practice – to suspend on full pay. The individual is still on the pay roll. People are also innocent until proven guilty and this, in particular, must be the guiding principle. If charges are found not to have substance, any pay due must always be made up at the point at which innocence is proven.

- **Dismissal** This is the final sanction. It occurs either when an individual persistently refuses to improve their performance, attitude, behaviour or conduct, and as the result of being found to have committed an act of gross or serious misconduct for which dismissal is the penalty.

  Dismissal may either be fair or unfair (see Chapter 2). Even when fair, it is only to be contemplated when procedures have been exhausted, when it is the clear and obvious remedy to the situation, or where the working relationship has been irretrievably damaged.

- **Arbitration** It is both useful and legitimate to make provision for arbitration. It is used most often when an impasse is reached. In these cases, both parties usually agree to the appointment of an arbitrator; and usually agree also to be bound by the arbitrator's findings.

  The arbitrator hears presentations from both parties and then arrives at a preferred or best solution. This may be wholly in favour of one party or the other, a compromise, or a solution not previously considered. Where an arbitration facility exists, this normally presents the final solution to the problem.

  Arbitration is not legally binding. Even where one or both parties have agreed to be bound by the arbitrator's findings and solution, it may then be rejected. However, if the matter then went as far as the courts or an employment tribunal, the onus would be on the party rejecting the arbitrator's findings to demonstrate or prove why these could not be accepted in the circumstances.

  Pendulum arbitration is where the arbitrator hears the views of both parties to the case and is then bound to decide wholly in favour of one party or the other. Someone is therefore seen and known to win and someone is seen and known to lose. Because of the over-emphasis on winning and losing, people avoid recourse to pendulum arbitration wherever possible. Faced with this prospect, they are encouraged to go back and resolve their differences rather than risk a total defeat.

  Pendulum arbitration is very popular with Japanese organizations operating in the West. It is used as a support for single union agreements. Pendulum arbitration is invoked at the point at which a problem cannot be resolved.

Note

Arbitration in any form should only be used as a last resort. It should never become a substitute for strong, effective staff management and employee relations policies. If used too often, it becomes a crutch on which the organization eventually becomes dependent. It also places its capacity, independence and autonomy to resolve issues in the hands of an outside body.

DRAWING UP PROCEDURES

The best procedures are written in simple and direct language capable of being understood by everyone. This leaves little, if any, room for debate, misunderstanding or misinterpretation.

The best procedures set high general standards of conduct rather than trying to cover every eventuality. Where procedures are too complicated, they become an administrative and employee relations nightmare and extremely expensive to support and manage.

The best procedures have two stages only before dismissal and are only used where there are serious misunderstandings, genuine problems or when all else has failed. They should be there to support managers who have first tried to resolve their problems. They should not be invoked because managers and supervisors are incapable of resolving problems.

Having more than the two stages adds to both administrative and employee relations burdens. It also dilutes the effect of the first warning, which becomes less respected and recognized the greater the number of stages that there are.

A three stage procedure is more or less manageable, though again, this adds to the administrative burden. It is also an additional issue for managers and supervisors – especially those with large teams – to be aware of. It does, however, afford the opportunity to those who have made genuine errors to remedy these without the stress of facing a final warning the next time anything goes wrong.

More than three stages should ideally never be considered (though they do exist), as they complicate everything. Managers and supervisors never know where they stand – and neither do the staff. Where lengthy and complex procedures do exist, they are invariably more widely used than where they are kept simple. They become a substitute for genuine problem-solving. They create bureaucracy and expense by their very existence.

The length of time that a warning remains valid is entirely up to the organization, as long as this stands the test of fairness and reasonableness. For example, it is neither fair nor reasonable to dismiss someone for being five minutes late for work on three occasions during ten years of continuous employment.

It is usual to keep warnings for minor misdemeanours on file for between three months and two years; probably the most usual is one year.

It is usual to keep warnings for persistent misdemeanours and misconduct on file for at least five years. This is certain to apply to serious misconduct and also to gross misconduct where, for some reason, dismissal has not happened. In these cases, many organizations keep the warning on file for life.

Best practice states clearly that there should be a single set of standards for the whole organization and that all staff are to be bound by these whatever their occupation, hours of work or length of service. These are varied only for compelling professional and occupational reasons. Under no circumstances are they varied so that different occupations receive different quality of treatment (eg two warnings for junior staff; three warnings for managerial staff), or whereby standards of discipline are relaxed according to levels of seniority.

As well as equality, standards are drawn up with special reference to fairness and reasonableness; solving and not institutionalizing problems and the speed of operation.

Concerning the speed of operation, a balance has to be struck between giving people sufficient time to prepare their case in response and allowing matters to drag on and become institutionalized. There are some general guidelines as follows:

■ Improvements in performance will be timetabled according to the specific case as the result of investigations of poor performance problems.
■ Improvements in behaviour should become apparent immediately, they should be scheduled as such with a short initial review period and followed by continuous review and monitoring.
■ Improvements in demeanour should become apparent immediately through the individual ceasing to demonstrate their bad/negative attitude. Adoption of desired attitudes and values becomes apparent over longer periods of time and should also be monitored and reviewed.
■ Serious and gross misconduct should be dealt with immediately the problem is publicized to staff. It is essential that any issue in these categories is tackled and resolved before it starts to fester and cause serious disruption. It is quite legitimate and often highly desirable

that the individual or the people at the centre of the issue be removed (often suspended) as quickly as possible. This is followed by a full and thorough investigation at the end of which the merits (or otherwise) of the case have become apparent.

The overall aim of disciplinary procedures is always to support the organization's absolute standards of attitude, behaviour and performance. Procedures are never to be used in place of this. They are also concerned with maintaining satisfactory standards of behaviour and correcting unsatisfactory behaviour rather than punishment. Punishment is best used only where all else has failed.

Grievance procedures

Grievance procedures are the formal means by which anyone working in, and for, an organization may raise an issue that concerns them (see Summary box 5.4). This normally occurs only when the matter has first been raised in conversation between the employee and his/her manager with a request that it be resolved and then has not been resolved to the employee's satisfaction.

Grievance procedures must have at least two stages, namely:

■ the employee's right to raise issues with the immediate superior, to have it heard and to receive a response, confirmed in writing giving the employer's view of the matter and the reasons for the decision
■ the employee's right to raise the issue with their superior's immediate superior for review and resolution if they are not satisfied with the outcome of the first stage.

Personnel records

It is essential that complete up-to-date records are maintained constantly. They must include copies of the contract of employment and other terms and conditions. They must also include copies of all formal communications between employer and employee, and especially notes of warnings, conduct, behaviour and performance. Other documentation is also useful – especially general notes, file notes, diary entries, records and minutes of meetings, performance appraisal statements and other general features.

The purpose is to provide an accurate and truthful record of the period of employment. This material is also invariably both useful and required if the employee does at some stage make a complaint at a tribunal.

Summary box 5.4   Grievance procedures: other factors

In the design and content of grievance procedures, the following should also be noted:

- In small organizations and those others where there is only one layer of management, or where grievances are referred directly to the Chair, Chief Executive or Managing Director, the employee has the right to appeal against the decision without prejudice to their future employment.
- In larger organizations, and those where there are many layers of management, it is both legitimate and usual for grievances to be referred onwards up the hierarchy. This helps to ensure that whatever the outcome, this is validated by the organization as a whole rather than subject to the whim of an individual.
- If the person raising the grievance wishes to have a representative or a witness present this must be agreed. This is most likely to occur where serious allegations (eg theft of personal property, discrimination, harassment, victimization or bullying) are made.
- Tests of equity, fairness, reasonableness and natural justice must always be applied and be capable of being sustained when turning down an employee complaint.
- All grievances, minor or major, should be resolved as quickly as possible to prevent real or perceived injustice from being allowed to fester.
- Where serious allegations (eg discrimination, victimization, bullying or harassment) are made, the case must be heard without delay and the problem (if it turns out that there is one) nipped in the bud.
- An employee must never be discriminated against, victimized, bullied or harassed as the result of raising any grievance or complaint whatsoever. If the complaint turns out to have no foundation, the reasons why it first became apparent (usually misunderstanding or misinformation) should be made clear. If the complaint turns out to be malicious, it should then be dealt with through the disciplinary procedure.
- The aim of all grievance procedures must be to support the principle of dealing with problems as quickly as possible. The ideal outcome is always one which is satisfactory to both employer and employee. Where this is not possible, time must be taken to explain clearly to the employee why the matter was refused or turned down and this must be capable of being sustained.

THE MANAGEMENT OF DISCIPLINE AND GRIEVANCE CASES

All cases start when a problem becomes apparent and has to be solved to the satisfaction of all concerned. In all discipline and grievances cases, the onus is placed on managers and supervisors to prove or demonstrate that:

■ they acted fairly and reasonably, and with honesty and integrity
■ they followed procedures, criteria and any recognized standards of best practice
■ the outcome would have been the same for anyone in the same, similar or equivalent set of circumstances
■ alternative courses of action were considered, evaluated and rejected
■ where dismissal has resulted, that the stated reasons for this were the real reasons for dismissal.

The outcome of all cases must be confirmed in writing. This confirmation must state the agreed and actual outcome and not vary either the conclusions or the reasons given.

The outcome of all cases must be based on proof wherever possible. Where absolute proof is not possible, the following should be used:

■ Fairness and reasonableness Any assumptions made must stand the test of what could reasonably be concluded as having occurred.
■ Strong indications This is proof based on their being 'no smoke without a fire', that something has occurred about which the outcome is again a reflection of what is fair and reasonable in the circumstances.
■ Other assumptions This is proof based on the conclusions that a reasonable person could/would arrive at in these or an equivalent set of circumstances.

This is the context in which all discipline and grievance cases are handled.

Discipline

When it becomes apparent that there is to be a disciplinary case, the matter must be investigated as quickly as possible. This involves gathering evidence and witnesses.

Evidence

The evidence required for specific cases is as follows:

Poor performance

Evidence of poor performance is provided by:

- copies of performance appraisals with dates
- details of training and development undertaken with dates
- copies of any previous warnings with dates
- the length of time for which performance has been a concern
- actions taken to remedy this in the past
- actions taken against other employees in similar or equivalent situations.

Bad time-keeping

Evidence of bad time-keeping is provided by:

- copies of clock cards, signing-in registers, print-outs of keyed in or other electronic registers with dates
- copies of warnings with dates
- the length of time for which time-keeping has been a concern
- actions taken to remedy this in the past
- actions taken against other employees in similar or equivalent circumstances.

Absenteeism

Evidence of absenteeism is provided by:

- copies of absence (and where appropriate, sickness) records with dates
- copies of previous warnings with dates
- the length of time for which absenteeism has been a concern
- actions taken to remedy this in the past
- actions taken against other employees in similar or equivalent circumstances
- acceptable and unacceptable levels of absence, the means by which these were promulgated, current standards and levels of attendance
- the organization's general approach to absence.

Misconduct

Evidence of misconduct is provided by:

- dates and times on which the misconduct occurred
- those who saw and/or who were affected by the misconduct

- the effects of misconduct on performance, attitudes and behaviour of the organization and on other people
- any previous warnings for this or similar misconduct
- acceptable and unacceptable standards of conduct, the means by which these are promulgated and enforced.

Bad/negative attitudes
Evidence of bad/negative attitudes is provided by:

- identification of those aspects of behaviour which prove or indicate a bad attitude
- statements from others affected or in contact
- the effects of the bad/negative attitude on others and on organization and individual performance
- any previous warnings and discussions about bad/negative attitude.

In all cases, evidence is acceptable in the following forms:

- copies of letters, memoranda, notes taken from personal, organizational and departmental files
- diary entries, records of meetings, agenda and minutes
- general statements that have some bearing on the case in question
- organizational procedures and practices
- the statements (written and oral) of managers, supervisors, colleagues, peers, subordinates and witnesses.

Witnesses

Witnesses may be asked to give a view on particular matters either by the organization or by the person being disciplined. This request may be either written or oral. The evidence may be either written or oral. In the latter case, a written summary of what was said may be produced and agreed by all concerned.

Natural justice, equity and fairness all demand that an individual be allowed to face his/her accuser and respond to, justify or refute what the accuser has to say. Only in exceptional circumstances will anonymous evidence be allowed and the anonymity of witnesses and accusers be preserved. If the case goes on and gets as far as court or an employment tribunal, witnesses and evidence have to be produced.

Witnesses called by the organization to support a disciplinary case must be allowed to be questioned by the individual concerned. Witnesses called by the individual to support their case must be allowed to attend without prejudice to their future employment or opportunities, and they must be allowed to be questioned by the organization.

Other investigations

Investigations should become a high priority once it becomes apparent that there is a case to answer. Investigations should be conducted as quickly and as thoroughly as possible. For minor cases, this need be no more than a quick trawl through the individual's personal file, or (for time-keeping) through the time-keeping records for the period in question.

For more serious cases, a thorough investigation is essential. Under no circumstances is any manager or supervisor to spoil a strong case against a bad employee because they have not done this part of the job properly.

Neither are conclusions to be arrived at before the full spread of evidence is gathered and available. Carrying out a full investigation enables a complete assessment of all the facts and merits of the case. This enables the disciplinary hearing to be carried out with confidence. It avoids prolonged discussions over areas that have not been fully understood. It enables all areas of doubt to be brought out into the open. Any question that the employee is being victimized is avoided. More generally, it underlines the genuine concern that all managers and supervisors should feel when staff are either not happy or not performing.

The disciplinary hearing

Assuming that there is a case for the individual to answer, once evidence has been collected and witnesses have been arranged, the disciplinary hearing should be conducted as follows.

Beforehand

The individual is notified that there is a case against him/her. The charges should be stated or summarized and the level of discipline indicated. The individual is notified that there is to be a disciplinary hearing. The words 'disciplinary hearing' must be used.

The date, time and place of the hearing should be stated. This should be suitable to all concerned. It takes place as soon as possible. If the individual has compelling reasons why it cannot take place on the proposed date, an alternative should be sought. Compelling reasons are normally:

- insufficient time for the individual to prepare his/her side of the case
- insufficient time to gather specific evidence
- unavailability of key witnesses

■ the individual's unavailability for some substantial reason, normally medical or operational. In the latter case, the organization has to balance the need to clear up the disciplinary matter quickly with its operational priorities and drives.

The hearing must take place within the timescale specified in the procedures. Once there is sufficient evidence that there is a case to be heard, there should be no delay other than for the reasons above.

The individual should be notified of his/her right to be represented and accompanied. Especially for serious cases, many organizations insist that an individual facing disciplinary action does bring a representative or be accompanied.

At the hearing

The manager or supervisor opens the hearing. At some stage, the words 'this is a disciplinary hearing' must be used. The level of seriousness of the matter should be indicated.

The manager or supervisor then summarizes the charges and indicates the range of evidence and witnesses to be brought to support them.

At the end of this summary, the manager or supervisor asks the individual for his/her explanation. The words 'can you give us an explanation?' or their equivalent must be used.

The individual responds to the initial presentation of the case. He/she may withdraw from the hearing to consult with his/her representative or witnesses before responding. The response is normally as follows:

■ Acceptance of the case made: When this happens at this stage, matters move to conclusion.
■ Acceptance of the case made with plea of mitigation: When this happens, the plea of mitigation must be heard, noted and taken into account. Matters then move to conclusion.
■ Disputing/disagreeing with the case made: When this happens, evidence is considered at length, witnesses are called and examined, and any other facts or circumstances brought to light.

Conclusion of the case

The conclusion of the case is based on everything that has been considered. The outcome is one of the following:

■ The case against the individual is proven. The outcome of this is normally either a warning, a final warning or dismissal depending on the circumstances and seriousness of the matter in hand.

■ The case against the individual is proven but with mitigating circumstances. When this occurs, the outcome may still be a warning, a final warning or dismissal, depending on the seriousness of the circumstances. Alternatively, the penalty may be reduced because of the mitigating circumstances, or there may be no penalty.

■ The case is refuted and the individual exonerates him or herself.

Confirmation

Whatever the outcome, it must always be confirmed in writing. This includes the clear statement of the outcome with reasons. Where warnings have been issued, the level of warning must be stated together with the length of its duration and the consequences of any proven repeat performance or behaviour during its currency. Where a period of review is stated, dates on which reviews are to take place must be stated. Any required changes in performance or behaviour must be stated.

Where the individual has been exonerated, this too must be confirmed in writing.

Dismissal

Where dismissal has occurred, this too must be confirmed in writing. This must include the reasons for dismissal, and these must concur with the actual reasons. These same reasons must be those notified to every future employer and also to government bodies such as the Department for Social Security. They must also be used to defend any action that the individual may choose to bring for breach of contract or unfair dismissal.

Appeal

An individual has the right to appeal against the outcome of all disciplinary hearings, including dismissal. This must be notified in writing when the outcome is confirmed. This must state the timescale within which appeals must take place and the name of the person to whom the appeal is to be made.

References

It happens from time to time that employees require references for internal and external job and occupational changes. It is quite legitimate to reveal the individual's disciplinary record provided that:

■ it can be sustained and supported by evidence
■ it is a genuine reflection of their attitude, behaviour and performance during the period of employment
■ it is not presented in a malicious or deliberately detrimental fashion.

Poor performance in one job does not prove that the individual will perform poorly in their next job (just as excellent performance in one job does not prove that they will be excellent in their next either).

Difficult and sensitive cases

Discipline problems become more difficult when they involve directors, senior managers and trade union officials.

In cases where directors and senior managers are disciplining junior members of staff (eg their secretary or personal assistant), great care must be taken to ensure that the staff member gets fair treatment, a fair hearing and that procedures are followed. This can be very daunting for someone who is advising on the conduct of the case, especially where a powerful personality is concerned or where the senior person takes the view that, as they are so senior, they can do what they like and that procedures need not be followed.

The same also applies when a senior manager or director is disciplining their immediate subordinate. It is vital to keep personal and professional issues separate. It is again vital to ensure that the person being disciplined is not being made a scapegoat for a wider organizational or operational malaise.

Where it is a director or senior manager who is being disciplined, this should normally be carried out by the Chair, Chief Executive or Managing Director of the organization. In minor cases, future agreed levels of performance become a matter of agreement between the Chair/Chief Executive/Managing Director and the senior manager in question. In more serious cases, it is both usual and quite legitimate to suspend the director or senior manager under investigation while investigations take place. When this occurs, the matter must be investigated and concluded as quickly as possible; directors and senior managers are usually in charge of extensive functional operations and all the time that they are being investigated, the effectiveness of that function to performance is inevitably impaired.

Suspension

As stated above, it is quite legitimate to suspend an individual pending a full investigation into the particular case – especially where the allegations and problems are contentious or serious (or potentially so).

The individual must be summoned and told that he/she is being suspended. The length (or likely length) of the period of suspension must be notified, together with the allegations and any other reasons why the organization considers this to be the best way to handle the problem.

The individual must be given the chance to defend him/herself and present his/her own version of events if it becomes clear that there is a case to be answered.

Individuals may be suspended with or without pay. This too should be made clear at the point of suspension. It is usual for suspension to be with pay. If suspension is to be without pay, the investigation must be carried out and concluded as a matter of urgency. Suspension without pay should, in any case, only be made in exceptional circumstances – normally where serious breaches of the criminal law are already proven. Where the individual is subsequently exonerated or retained on the organization payroll, back pay must be made up instantly.

Suspension is always confirmed in writing, together with the reasons and duration at the point at which the individual is notified.

Financial penalties

It is quite legitimate for individuals not to receive bonuses, commissions, performance-related and other excellence payments if their performance does not warrant this and there is no hard evidence to support it. When this occurs, the organization must notify the individual of why these payments have not been made. If there is no hard evidence, the individual is entitled to expect that these payments will be made if they are generally forthcoming and have otherwise been earned.

It is illegal to fine employees from their basic wage or salary, or to fail to pay legitimate and earned expenses, overtime or any other allowances (eg shift and disturbance allowances).

Grievances

When an employee raises a grievance, it should be heard and resolved as quickly as possible. This again means that knowledge, information, evidence and (where appropriate) witnesses have to be gathered as quickly as possible.

Equipment

Investigations into grievances concerning equipment should cover:

- an assessment of the equipment
- records of breakages, breakdowns, equipment performance levels and usage
- downtime, maintenance time and breakdown time
- what happened to others working with this equipment

- any financial penalties incurred (especially loss of bonuses) and the extent to which these were outside the employee's control
- any lasting effects on work practices, the working environment and organizational performance.

Personal judgment

Investigations into grievances concerning personal judgment should cover the following:

- attention to the perceptions of those making the complaint
- knowledge and understanding of the particular circumstances under which these have arisen at this time
- knowledge and understanding of any special factors that have led to the reality or perception of uneven or unequal treatment
- knowledge and understanding of any restrictions imposed by organizational rule books, union agreements, working agreements, lines of demarcation or restrictive practices
- knowledge and understanding of any gaps in information that have led those affected to assume that they are receiving less favourable treatment than others (where these occur, the information should always be made good).

Hopes, fears and aspirations

Investigations into grievances concerning hopes, fears and aspirations should cover the following:

- the basis on which the hopes, fears and aspirations were first founded
- anything that has happened to change this basis. For hopes and aspirations, this is likely to include investigations into promises and/or strong indications that were given or led to be expected and into why these have not been fulfilled. Fears, once raised, do not go away but if information is not continually forthcoming, individuals become disoriented, anxious and even traumatized
- where opportunities have been denied, why this has occurred together with a full and adequate explanation
- where the ability to fulfil hopes and aspirations have been negated due to circumstances outside the control of the manager, supervisor or organization.

Power struggles and stand-offs

Investigations into grievances arising from power struggles and stand-offs are likely to cover the following:

■ the real agenda of each protagonist
■ the consequences of being involved or embroiled to those directly affected
■ threats and/or promises made by powerful personalities and over-mighty subjects
■ the particular nature of individual fears of those in the situation
■ the extent of involvement of any other parties (eg trade unions, counsellors, governors on public bodies, senior managers and directors, pressure groups and other vested interests)
■ the prevalence of backing groups. An individual's backing group includes their colleagues, trade unions and professional/occupational clusters. A manager or supervisor's backing group may also include their peers and their superiors. In the latter case, the manager/supervisor handling the grievance may have been told not to give in, to refuse the request at all costs, to find some other way of solving the situation. In all cases, there may be questions of wounded pride and loss of face to be addressed.

Misperception, misinterpretation and misunderstanding

Investigations into grievances brought about through misperception, misinterpretation and misunderstanding are likely to involve the following:

■ why the misperception, misinterpretation or misunderstanding occurred in the first place
■ the extent to which they have occurred before
■ the extent to which they occur elsewhere in the organization
■ gaps in information and communication processes including attention to volume, quality and systems
■ any tainting of the communication processes by, for example, trade union officials, over-mighty subjects, other persons pursuing their own agenda
■ any overriding reasons why there should be gaps in the information (eg confidentiality)
■ reportage and hearsay where organization, professional or personal gossip and rumour has been allowed to get out of hand
■ effects, immediate and lasting, on performance, attitudes, behaviour and demeanour.

Personality clashes

Investigations into grievances brought about through personality clashes are likely to cover the following:

- why the clash has arisen, why it continues, whether it is likely to continue
- its effects on work and output and the working environment
- the extent to which it can in fact be controlled so that an effective working relationship can be achieved
- the hierarchical position of each protagonist
- the attitudes of each protagonist to the other and to their colleagues and work
- the extent to which others are joining one side or the other
- the current state of relationships between the two protagonists and whether these are irretrievably damaged.

Professional clashes

Investigating grievances brought about as the result of professional clashes is likely to cover the following:

- the reasons for holding such diverse points of view
- the extent to which they can or might be reconciled
- the effects on general morale, working relations, the work and the working environment
- any secondary or hidden agenda being pursued by their protagonists
- the subject or core of the clash
- whether the professional clash has affected personal relationships or has actually been brought on by bad interpersonal relationships.

Serious complaints

Serious complaints normally arise as the result of feelings of bullying, discrimination, victimization, harassment or assault. Less frequently, they arise as the result of allegations made by one person about another concerning theft or damage to property. They may also cover specific issues such as unequal pay, differences in general and professional treatment, negative pressurization, denigration and other personal, verbal and physical attacks.

Investigations must cover:

- full knowledge and understanding of the situation
- full knowledge and understanding of the professional, occupational, working and personal relationship
- the length of time for which the offence is alleged to have been going on
- specific incidents mentioned in the allegations
- conversation with the accuser
- conversation with the accused
- conversation with witness(es).

In cases where pay and conditions are overtly unequal, attention must be paid to any operational mitigating circumstances or realities that have either caused this to arise in the first place, or else which make valid the supposed inequality in the particular set of circumstances. No other position is sustainable. In cases of harassment, bullying or victimization, it must be established whether this is psychological, physical, professional, personal or sexual. The matter must then be confronted immediately. No other position is sustainable.

In cases of discrimination, attention must be paid to gathering evidence concerning the employee's performance. No other grounds for discrimination – gender, race or disability – are sustainable.

Serious complaints should be investigated urgently and the protagonists interviewed separately at least, and together if necessary or desirable. Where a serious complaint is upheld, this normally leads to remedial action required of the discriminator, victimizer or bully; and it should lead to serious disciplinary action (the best organizations include this action under gross misconduct). It is unacceptable in any form and it is to be stopped forthwith.

Where a serious complaint is not upheld, a further investigation takes place to ascertain why the complainant thought that there was such a case. The outcome is normally one of the following:

■ genuine misunderstanding of the situation for some reason, and this must be remedied forthwith
■ where criticism of work has been carried out in such a way as to be perceived as a personal attack, and this too should be remedied
■ where the professional and personal approach of the parties involved are genuinely so far apart as to give rise to perceptions of victimization, harassment or discrimination, and this too should be remedied
■ malice on the part of the complainant in which the allegations are false and unfounded.

If the complainant made false allegations, the reasons for this are established. The outcome then is either to refer the complainant to occupational health or professional counselling. Where the allegations were purely malicious, they should lead on to serious disciplinary action (the best organizations cover this form of falsehood under gross misconduct).

Stress and illness

Investigations into stress and illness brought on directly or indirectly as a result of work and employment should cover the following:

- the length of time in the organization
- the length of time in the occupation
- the size, scope and scale of the job
- job and other training received and being received
- specific organization, departmental, occupational, professional and personal pressures
- specific pressures of workload
- managerial and supervisory style and quality
- facts, feelings and perceptions of victimization, bullying and harassment.

These investigations are normally carried out in conjunction with an organization's own occupational health team or permanent health insurance policy. Organizations that do not have these must make arrangements for their staff to be afforded this form of medical treatment when required.

It is important to note that while some people may make a complaint or take out a grievance under this heading, many do not. In this area, the organization has a prime and continuous responsibility for overseeing the good health of its employees.

The grievance hearing

A grievance is deemed to have arisen once the employee makes a formalized complaint. The employee will often use the phrase 'I wish to take out a grievance', though this is not necessary. The complaint may be oral or in writing. It may be made by an individual, or a group directly affected, or through a representative – for example, a spokesperson or trade union representative.

It should be heard initially as soon as possible. The best organizations put a very tight timescale on this – for example, two working days. It should never be allowed to drag on for weeks.

Ideally, most complaints and grievances will be of such a nature that they can be settled to the satisfaction of all concerned at this stage. Ideally also, most managers and supervisors have the authority and responsibility to settle matters at this stage. Where this is not possible the manager or supervisor must first decide whether they do have the knowledge or authority to settle it; if they do not, it is immediately referred onwards to someone who can.

The investigation should now take place. Again, this is carried out as quickly as possible and the best organizations put a time-scale on this (eg a maximum of five working days). If a complaint is serious, it should become the manager or supervisor's top priority.

At this point also, the manager or supervisor should establish what outcome is desired by the complainant(s) and also that which is acceptable to the organization. At the end of the investigation, a full hearing is convened. An individual may choose to have a witness or be represented. A group may choose to attend or send representatives, delegates or spokespersons.

Tackling grievances

Individuals and groups making complaints know their preferred or desired outcome. Managers and supervisors handling complaints and grievances know their preferred or desired outcome; they also know what is possible and acceptable in the circumstances. The greater the coincidence between the two positions, the more likely that the matter will be resolved to the satisfaction of all concerned.

Each party may also take a view on the best outcome, an acceptable outcome and a point below which they are not prepared to settle.

Four general outcomes are possible:

■ win:win – where everyone is happy
■ win:lose – where the complainant gets his/her way after a major concession with which the organization is not happy
■ lose:win – where the organization's view prevails and where the complainant is not happy (this usually leads to the matter being referred onwards up the hierarchy; and to the eventual escalation of the grievance, hardening of positions and the drawing up of battle lines)
■ lose:lose – where both organization and complainant now face a serious stand-off and where major employee relations efforts are required to reach a resolution.

The hearing

The hearing opens with the complainant(s) presenting their position. The manager/supervisor then responds. During the hearing, any evidence necessary will be examined and witnesses may also be called upon if appropriate. Both evidence and witnesses must be made available to both parties no matter who has produced or summoned them in the first place.

Having considered the outcome of the complaint and all the evidence produced, the manager/supervisor then presents a solution (see Summary box 5.5). This may be:

■ full settlement of the complaint to the satisfaction of the complainant
■ partial settlement and partial rejection
■ a full rejection.

In all cases, the decision is confirmed in writing and notified to the complainant. The complainant is entitled to accept the decision, or to appeal, or to refer the matter on to a higher authority. In large organizations, and where matters may be referred onwards, the same full consideration is given to the matter at the next level of the organization (and also at any subsequent progression).

Summary box 5.5   Handling grievances: other managerial considerations

In the management of grievances, the following points should always be considered:

- It is important to treat all complaints with respect and as worthy of consideration. They have, after all, been considered important enough by the individuals who have raised them.
- Managers and supervisors must be able to take a broad view. Each case must be treated on its own merits. It is important that this is so, and that no precedent is set by coming to particular conclusions.
- Where a complaint is being rejected it is important that this is clearly spelt out. Phrases such as 'your grievance is rejected' or 'your complaint is turned down' should always be used and this should be followed by a clear statement of why this is so. It is above all essential when rejecting a complaint by one person about another as this constitutes a key part of the clearing up and rehabilitation of the person about whom the complaint was made.
- Anyone making a complaint must be allowed to do so without prejudice. They must never be subjected to victimization, discrimination, harassment, bullying or coercion by anyone as a result. If it becomes apparent that this is indeed happening, it is to be stamped out immediately, normally through disciplinary action. This also applies to the eventual outcome of the case, whatever that may be.
- The outcome of all cases must be based on organization norms and standards, fairness and reasonableness, equality of treatment and natural justice.
- Existing procedures must always be followed and the opportunities afforded offered to all those who make complaints.
- Desired and acceptable outcomes and undesired and unacceptable outcomes should always be kept in mind. In the end, the onus is on the organization to resolve grievances in ways that are supportive of established standards and practices, and confirm general levels of attitudes, behaviour and performance at the same time as keeping the staff happy, harmonious and productive. This is only possible if a general all-round clarity exists.

Difficult and sensitive cases

Allegations of victimization, harassment, discrimination and bullying clearly always fall into this category. Cases where grievances are brought against senior managers, key staff and trade union officials also always fall into this category. This is especially true where there is prima facie a case to be answered.

These must follow the same principles as other cases. It is also essential that it is both tackled and seen to be tackled. These matters are normally common knowledge on organization grapevines, and confidence and trust are quickly broken and lost if they are allowed to persist or if someone is seen to get away with something simply because of their seniority or other key position.

Anyone taking out a grievance against a senior manager must therefore:

■ put their case in writing
■ be accompanied and represented when the grievance is heard
■ be able to substantiate their case
■ always go through a staff association if there is one, a trade union if there is one and if they are a member, and if all else fails, go to ACAS (see Summary box 5.6)
■ take all steps necessary to identify in advance the person to whom allegations concerning such grievances should be made.

Summary box 5.6   The management of grievances concerning trade union officials

Problems may also be exacerbated when a grievance is taken out against an elected lay official of a recognized union. The point again to remember is that this position gives no special exemption or licence to behave in ways different from those required of everyone else.

When it does happen, the union of which the individual is a lay official must be notified as they will normally be represented by the full-time local official at any subsequent hearing. The individual taking out the grievance is normally represented by an organization official – for example, a personnel or employee relations officer, their supervisor or line manager, or a senior manager.

There are clear absolute responsibilities and duties placed on directors and senior managers in this (see Summary box 5.7). Ideally, they are above reproach as they set the standards for everyone else to follow.

They may not legitimately expect others to follow these standards that they themselves do not keep.

This also is true when allegations are made about highly qualified and expert staff, and persons engaged on key or critical organization tasks and activities. There is often a perception that professional brilliance and high levels of talent somehow explain or excuse behaviour that would not otherwise be tolerated. The first step towards wisdom is to recognize the falsehood of this. The second is recognizing and understanding that no one who behaves in this way towards other members of staff is ever going to be fully effective, however talented they may be. Anyone taking out a grievance against such a person must, therefore:

■ put their case in writing
■ be accompanied and represented when the matter is heard
■ always go through a representative body
■ take all steps necessary to identify the person to whom these allegations should be made.

Summary box 5.7   The management of difficult and sensitive cases

When these cases arise, the following points must always be addressed:

- Difficult and sensitive cases get out of hand most of all when they are not handled swiftly or effectively. There therefore needs to be an organizational resolve that these matters will be addressed in the ways indicated whenever they arise.
- Ensuring that these standards are set and met for senior and key staff and union officials reinforces the expectations and requirements of others. Failure to ensure these standards in sensitive cases always leads to a dilution of overall standards.
- Powerful and dominant (and domineering) personalities use lack of reinforcement to get their own way in all things. It is essential that this is recognized when dealing with grievances. Force of personality can also give rise to genuine misunderstanding (eg one person's directness is another's serious bullying) and if this is the case, the sooner it is recognized the better.
- The advisory, conciliation, mediation and arbitration services of ACAS are available for cases such as these and many organizations find that it is extremely helpful to use them when such matters do arise. If called upon, they will always find any common ground that exists and especially advise organizations and individuals on ways out of situations that are operationally effective, fair and equitable to all concerned.

- Where a senior manager or director is involved, it is normally necessary to get the Chief Executive to handle the case. It may in turn be necessary to convince him/her of the seriousness and merits of the case first.
- Where a senior manager or director is involved, it is essential that the wider interests of the organization are remembered. The genuine interests of the organization are best served in all cases by ensuring that high profile cases are brought to a speedy and fair conclusion.

CONCLUSIONS

The purpose of this chapter is to indicate the basis on which organization discipline is to be built, to provide a basic context and framework for organization discipline and to indicate what must happen when discipline and grievance problems occur. There are clearly right ways of doing this. The drive for all grievance handling is that it is common sense to resolve matters as quickly and effectively as possible, to the satisfaction of all concerned. Where this is not possible, it is essential to explain to the employee why this is so, so that he/she understands the outcome even if he/she does not agree with it. It is also essential to recognize that any grievance that is genuine and is not resolved to the satisfaction of those affected will drag on as it goes through different stages of the organization's hierarchy; and that this leads to a dilution of general performance. Where someone is known or perceived to have been unfairly treated, this harms both the morale and output of the rest of the staff.

Handling discipline effectively is just as critical, though from a different point of view. Again, the emphasis is placed on getting matters resolved as quickly and as effectively as possible. Procedures must always be followed. Representation and appeal must always be allowed. Everything must be confirmed in writing. Failure to observe each or any of these elements always results in any subsequent employment tribunal or court case being found in favour of the employee.

On all sensitive issues, it is essential to realize what matters are classifiable as sensitive and why. The next step is to be aware of the specific vagaries of the particular situation and of any specific difficulties involved. This is, in turn, followed by attention to the personalities, roles and issues involved. These have then to be integrated into the procedures of the organization. Where it is necessary to discipline a senior manager or trade union official, the correct channels, roles and people must be identified. Where a grievance is taken out against a senior manager or trade union official, the precise and correct form for doing this must be identifiable and available to the staff.

All procedures should be kept as simple as possible so that everyone involved understands them. Recourse to discipline and grievance procedures should always be viewed as serious by organizations and their managers. The onus should be placed on managers and supervisors to resolve matters without recourse to procedures. Procedures are best seen as a tool to be used in emergencies, only when all other approaches have failed for some reason.

As well as keeping procedures simple, the language in which they are written should always be positive and direct. This helps to reinforce general positive attitudes and standards of behaviour that the best organizations always require.

A review of procedures based on ensuring that everyone does understand them should form a part of the induction programme of everyone. The outcome of this is that everyone knows where they stand right from the outset, and what their rights, duties and obligations are. This helps to keep problems to a minimum and helps to ensure that when problems do arise, they can be dealt with quickly.

All staff should be briefed in the content of procedures. Managers and supervisors should be trained in their use, value and operation. They should also be trained to ensure that they have a high level of understanding of what organization discipline is in their particular set of circumstances, and where the procedures fit in.

Recourse by managers and supervisors to the use of procedures should always be monitored. Recourse to extreme measures such as suspension, dismissal and arbitration should be reviewed on an individual case basis.

Heavy use of procedures on overtly legitimate grounds invariably means much deeper problems of motivation and morale; this is one of the outcomes of serious levels of employee alienation.

Regular dismissals also affect the morale of those remaining. Again, even where these are legitimate, there are almost certainly other underlying problems – for example, morale (people do not care whether they are dismissed), recruitment (the wrong people are being taken on), training methods (people are not coming up to the mark) or management style (hugely divisive, negative or coercive). Use, evaluation and monitoring of procedures can therefore bring out a whole range of valuable management information and this should always take place.

Ultimately, all that procedures do is to ensure that people receive fair and reasonable treatment. This is no different from procedures that are required in support of the law elsewhere. For example, a policeman making an arrest must always follow a distinctive procedure, otherwise the arrest is unlawful. The policeman's procedure ensures that the person being apprehended understands that they are being apprehended, why they are being apprehended, and what the consequences of this are. Similarly, organizational procedures ensure that employees know what is happening to them and why.

6

EMPLOYEE RELATIONS PROBLEMS

INTRODUCTION

It is clear from the previous chapter that ER in general, and effective organization discipline in particular, are based on a strategic approach, requiring distinctive standards of attitude, behaviour and performance. Effective management of organization discipline and successful use of procedures whenever necessary are dependent upon acceptance of these standards by all concerned and the quality, expertise and attitudes of managers and supervisors.

It is absolutely essential that these standards, qualities and expertise are present for those occasions when serious problems arise. It is in everyone's interest that they are resolved as quickly and as effectively as possible. Not to do so – and not to be able to do so – leads to decline in morale, the rise of factions, over-mighty subjects, departments, divisions and locations. Consequently, operational performance and organization reputation also falter and decline and this leads, in turn, to loss of profits, loss of market share and loss of customer and client confidence. Nobody wishes to be associated with an organization in decline, or one that is constantly beset by conflicts.

The other major contentious area is where staff have to be lost for some reason, either because there is no longer any work for them or because of serious or continuing misdemeanour.

The management of serious ER problems therefore falls into two distinct categories – the management of conflict and the management of dismissal.

THE MANAGEMENT OF CONFLICT

Managerial time, energy and resources devoted to dealing with organizational and ER conflict represent energy not spent producing the output of the organization. It represents a diversion of managerial effort away from achieving the prime purposes of the organization.

On the other hand, as illustrated in Chapter 4, part of the behavioural study of organizations in general, and ER in particular, indicate the inherent presence of conflict. A major reason for adopting a distinctive ER perspective is the recognition of the potential for, and presence of, conflict in workplace situations and acknowledging that strategies have to be adopted for its management.

Sources and causes of conflict in ER

Particular attention must always be paid to the following:

Inappropriate directional and managerial style, approach and attitudes

This has to be seen in the broadest context. It is true that as a general rule about the approachability and visibility of supervisors and managers, the greater the ease of access, the greater the likelihood of fewer problems arising, and these are settled more effectively and quickly when they do arise.

However, where organizations do have operational rules and procedures, and expect their staff to follow them, problems arise also when individuals try to circumvent them or take shortcuts.

Inappropriate managerial groups

This is either where managerial groups do not exist or, where they do, the agenda to which they work is wrong for the situation. The result is usually that departments, divisions and functions try to play each other off. In some cases, this is even encouraged by directors and top managers, in the mistaken belief that they are encouraging their juniors to show their metal or, worse still, taking the view that they are 'dividing and ruling'. In fact what they are doing is wasting organizational resources, and encouraging operational systems based on fear and favour. Known and perceived favouritism and victimization is especially divisive, and a major source of conflict in all but the smallest organizations.

Work technology

Production, information and telecommunications technology is generally excellent for the purpose of output and usage; it is often a major contributor to a bad working environment for those who have to use it. Boredom, repetition, noise, physical and mental fatigue and repetitive strain injuries are all causes of conflict in particular situations. Each relates directly or indirectly to the technology that is used. Traditionally, this was a known factor of production processes above all. It is now a major factor in telephone services, telesales, financial services, database management and operations, and data manipulation and production.

Managerial and supervisory approach, style and attitude

The underlying cause of conflict here is the extent of respect and value that is apparent to the workforce in the style and approach with which they are supervised. Traditionally, this comes out in the extent to which managers and supervisors bully and threaten their people. It is also reflected in the regularity and frequency with which disciplinary warnings are issued, and the reasons for these. It is also usual to note the regularity and frequency with which grievances are raised, against whom, and for what reasons. This is usually symptomatic of a wider organization malaise, stemming from:

■ a lack of managerial expertise and capability at senior levels, which translates down to those in more junior positions
■ a lack of resources necessary to carry out the core business
■ a general lack of commonality of purpose or identity.

Professional and occupational refugees

A major source and cause of conflict is where it is apparent that the first loyalty of particular groups of staff is to their work colleagues, department, division or occupation. This occurs in industrial situations (eg 'maintenance/personnel/the typing pool are a law unto themselves'), in public services (eg 'NHS surgeons are at constant loggerheads with financial controllers and operation theatre managers') and in commercial services (eg 'I work for BA Overseas Division' – with the emphasis on Overseas Division rather than BA). Less prevalent than in the past, but still a major feature in some industries and sectors, is the first loyalty of the staff member to their trade union or professional body.

Lack of mutual trust, identity, respect and loyalty

It is much easier to destroy or damage each of these than to build them up. In many cases, they have been a plain fact of working life for so long that both managers and staff have forgotten, or do not understand, how to build a positive working relationship. Staff get used to looking for hidden messages and agenda in management and organizational communications and, in turn, organizations and their managers draw ever-tighter and more coercive rules and regulations around their staff in order to control them (see Summary box 6.1).

Summary box 6.1   The exception or the rule

A food processing factory in southern England instituted a practice of random searches of its employees. This followed allegations that some staff were pilfering both company products and other equipment.

The problem came to light following an investigation by a night shift production manager. He found that the production totals stated by production teams were always in excess of those accepted by the warehouse. As a consequence, production teams were claiming bonuses to which they were not entitled. The manager identified those involved and handed out notices of impending investigations that may lead to disciplinary action. In line with company procedures, he then placed everything in the hands of the human resource department, fully documented.

The human resource department conducted its own investigation. This confirmed everything that the production manager had found. However, 'the view was taken' that to deal with the problem as stated might be construed as punitive. The system of random searches was therefore initiated.

This caused a strike which led to the loss of £500,000 worth of production. Those staff not involved in the pilfering felt, understandably, that they were being tarred with the same brush as those who had been identified by two separate investigations – and against whom no action was being taken. As well as the loss of production, the company found itself with a collective loss of morale and feeling of grievance based on the view widely held among staff that pilfering did pay after all.

It would have cost nothing for the company to have faced the issue and dealt with the problem with which they were confronted – except a corporate will to engage the positive management of employee relations.

Head office syndrome

Conflicts sourced in head office syndrome occur when it is known, believed or perceived that the head office staff of companies and public services get better salaries, terms and conditions, incentives and opportunities than those who work off-site. It also occurs to a lesser extent where those working away from head office receive directions and instructions from head office that they do not understand, believe in, see the point of or value.

Except where it is a fact that head office staff get better salaries, terms and conditions and opportunities, this is alleviated through attention to the quality of communication and contact between head office staff and others. Where it is a fact, it is a serious problem that is only remedied by organizational activity arising from a corporate will to change. This is because any dispute that does arise is invariably also viewed as a trial of strength between the protagonists.

Tribal warfare

Tribal warfare occurs where one or more department, division or occupational group is known, believed or perceived to be gaining advantages or favours at the expense of others, and for reasons other than operational necessity.

Again, where this is not the case, the issue is remedied through attention to the presentation and style of management. Where it is an issue, it always fuels overall organizational decline as well as employee relations and staff management problems.

Institutional and operational expediency

When it becomes known that problems and issues are resolved in favour of those who raise grievances, and that the organization has a propensity for caving in to demands, staff and their representatives will create issues that are then resolved in this way.

In the short term, there are feelings of individual and collective satisfaction. In the medium to long term, it is seriously disruptive to effective standards and styles of management, and may fuel any other existing propensity for organization decline.

Over-mighty subjects, departments, divisions and functions

Over-mightiness in any form occurs where it is allowed to by senior management. It creates ER problems when attitudes and behaviour are allowed to remain unchecked, when the individual or group is treated with advantage or favour because of the force of their personality or critical nature of their expertise, and when they use this over-mighty position to justify behaviour that would not otherwise be tolerated or acceptable.

Change

Change is a course and source of conflict when it has not been fully thought out, structured and evaluated, where support and understanding (or at least acquiescence) of the staff has not been engaged and when an overt change (eg changes in technology) is being used to bring about other changes (eg reductions in union power or redundancies). People will always accept change provided that they know, believe or understand that it is in their interest to do so. People resist change when they do not know, believe or perceive that it is in their best interests.

A part of ER management therefore consists of presenting change in terms of the benefits that are to accrue to those affected. It is also necessary to be straightforward about problems and drawbacks – especially redundancies and substantial job changes – so that people at least know where they stand at an early stage when change is to take place.

Motivation and morale

The presence of conflict at places of work is always bad for staff motivation and morale. It is true that short-term boosts are given to some parties when they are known, believed or perceived to have won a dispute. It is also true that it is essential to be known to have won disputes when one side is plainly right and the other wrong.

Otherwise, the presence of conflict and long-term enduring disputes cause demotivation and are consequently bad for production, output, customer service and interdepartmental relations. Conflict consumes resources that should be used for core organizational purposes (see Summary box 6.2).

Summary box 6.2   The symptoms of conflict

The major symptoms of conflict, and of loss of motivation and morale, which both lead to conflict and feed off it, are as follows:

- **Increases in customer complaints** When they are wide ranging, they are symptomatic of broad organizational malaise. When they concern a particular product, service, location or department, inquiries should be concentrated in the particular area.

- **Increases in accidents** This is symptomatic of a fall-off in attention to absolute standards of conduct, behaviour and performance.
- **Increases in absenteeism** A key feature of the management of ER is attention to absenteeism. All organizations need their own clear strategies for this aspect of management. They need to know what constitutes acceptable levels of absenteeism – above all, self-certificated absenteeism – and what to do about it if and when it occurs, and if it goes beyond their own clear guidelines and boundaries.
- **Increases in serious illness and injury** This is especially important with reference to stress and industry-specific injuries and illnesses (eg silicosis in mining and quarrying, respiratory diseases in chemicals and paint shop work, eye and back injuries in the data and information sectors and radiation sickness in the nuclear industry).
- **Increases in the numbers of discipline and grievance cases** This should always be followed up by an analysis of the nature of particular cases, leading to a broader evaluation of why these occur.
- **Increases in staff turnover** These have to be set in the wider context of the organization. In some cases, staff turnover is unavoidable, for example, where the organization in question cannot compete on terms, conditions and pay with others in the location; and where it is unable to offer career progression beyond a certain limit. Turnover is a symptom of deeper ER issues when it increases out of this context.
- **Bending the ear** This is where people seek unofficial routes to the organization's main sources of power, influence and resources. It is symptomatic of wider problems when it becomes believed or perceived that this is the way to advantage, as distinct from using formal channels. It is much more serious when this becomes known as an absolute fact.

Specific issues

It is first necessary to recognize the points above as the major sources and causes of conflict. In the effective management of ER and in the creation of a productive and harmonious ER environment, there are specific issues that have to be addressed. These are matters that are extremely damaging to staff relations and organization morale if they are not tackled swiftly and properly when they do occur. On the other hand, if they are handled effectively, they reinforce the absolute standards of attitude, behaviour and performance, which the organization has set for itself.

In the management of conflict, the following specific issues have to be addressed:

- poor performance of senior staff
- poor attitudes and behaviour of senior staff
- vandalism, violence and assault
- fiddles, theft and pilfering
- the management of shop stewards and union representatives
- the management of strikes and industrial action.

Poor performance of senior staff

Poor performance of senior staff is often very hard to pin down, especially when such staff have been given wide-ranging and general job descriptions and key tasks and results remits (see Summary box 6.3). It therefore requires a positive act of will on the part of the top managers of the organization regularly to appraise the performance, activities and outputs of their key people.

Summary box 6.3   Poor performance of senior staff: examples

- The director of a nationalized industry was given a pay-off of £120,000 following his acknowledged poor performance in his part of the transformation of the organization into a plc. Two years later, the same individual was given a £200,000 pay-off following his acknowledged poor performance in the transformation of a national utility into a plc.
- The deputy principal of a further education college was given a pay-off totalling £140,000 when it became apparent that he had made no contribution to its effective running for several years, and was unwilling to take any part in its future activities, or to engage in efforts that would help to secure its future in what was to become a commercialized world.
- The chief executive of a fabrics company was given a pay-off of £1.3 million following a brief period at the helm in which the company's profits fell by 90 per cent.

There are several ER lessons to be learned from these examples. Staff perception is that top people are simply being insured against failure, and that they therefore gain their rewards anyway. Customer, client and shareholder perceptions are along the lines that it is better to give out these sums of money to get rid of someone in these circumstances than to allow them to continue at the organization and do further damage. There is also a view taken by chief executives and shareholder representatives 'there but for fortune' which renders them sympathetic to this form of golden handshake and pay-out.

Overall, each situation needs extremely careful handling. Where someone in such a position is known, perceived or believed as being over-compensated for failure, it is extremely damaging to wider organizational morale if it cannot be rationalized effectively.

Poor attitudes and behaviour of senior staff

For senior staff these are easier to pin down; poor attitudes and behaviour are overt whoever exhibits them (see Summary box 6.4). There is also no reason not to take the same action that would be taken in other cases. Problems arise when senior staff are treated with greater favour than others and, again, where they are seen to be rewarded for their misdemeanours. This also occurs where senior management adopt a stated 'bluff, no nonsense' management style, which is actually a cloak for victimization, harassment and bullying.

Summary box 6.4   Poor attitudes and behaviour of senior staff: examples

Example 1

A vacancy occurred for a managerial post in the human resources office of a County Council Social Services Department. Two persons were short-listed and interviewed – one male, one female. The female was interviewed first.

The interviews were carried out by a senior member of the County Council's Corporate Personnel Services, and two County Councillors from the Social Services Committee. When the man went in to be interviewed, he was staggered to be asked in so many words 'When are you going to give all this up and have babies?'

It subsequently came to light that this was the precise tone in which the Senior Corporate Personnel Officer had asked the question of the female member of staff and so, in the interests of equality, the male member of staff had to be asked the same thing.

In the event, neither applicant got the job; however, promotions and enhancements were found for them both within a very short space of time. The senior member of staff concerned received three promotions in the following twelve months and now enjoys a very high position in the particular County Council.

Example 2

The manager of a project group at a financial services company openly boasted of his bullying management style. He pointed to the high levels of results that his department always achieved and to the success and high regard in which his particular project was held.

Investigations by a team of management consultants revealed that high results were indeed being achieved. However, this was an in-built feature of the nature of the operation – the manager concerned was actually making no contribution to the results. The operations of the project team were governed by computer programs that simply requested the purchase or sale of the commodities with which they were dealing. Moreover, absenteeism in the project team ran at 22 per cent (self-certificated and short-term doctor's note sickness) and motivation and attitude surveys showed that all members of the team, without exception, would find other jobs if they could do so at the same levels of reward. While on the face of it therefore, results remained high, additional costs were being incurred in their achievement.

The particular manager was moved out of the project when this became apparent. He was given a much broader remit – at a 45 per cent increased salary. This was justified by the organization concerned as 'making much better use of his talents'.

The problem is compounded where the organization's top management indulge the protagonist either because they have no confidence in their own ability to deal with him or her, or because he or she is known (or more usually perceived quite without foundation) to get results, or because the person has a key specialism or expertise as well as authority. In these cases, the staff always know that the reason why the senior or key person is getting away with it is because of a lack of will to deal with them. Moreover, staff will simply assume that the person in question is out of control. This, in turn, sends strong negative signals to the rest of the organization, and is very destructive.

Vandalism, violence and assault

The treatment of senior and key staff in these matters should always be exactly the same as for anyone else. When allegations are made, the accused should be removed from the scene immediately and a full investigation carried out. A discipline hearing then takes place according to procedures if sufficient evidence is gathered. If the case is subsequently proven, dismissal will normally follow. There are problems when:

■ the case is not substantiated and is therefore thrown out – this should always be followed up with a much broader investigation into the causes of the allegations
■ the case is substantiated but action short of dismissal is taken – this simply sets a precedent and standard for the rest of the organization
■ senior members of staff are concerned, where they are allowed to resign, or given pay-offs substantially better – in real terms, as well as in proportion – to those from elsewhere in the organization.

Fiddles, theft and pilfering

These may be split into two categories:

From the organization

This is serious because it gives off signals to all staff where it is allowed to persist. Where fiddles and pilfering are known to take place in some quarters, others will establish their own norms for these activities.

Problems again arise when people are dealt with differently according to rank, department, division, occupation or location. They are compounded when it is known, believed or perceived that in some quarters fiddling is tolerated if not actually encouraged, while in others it is hammered in absolute terms (see Summary box 6.5).

Summary box 6.5   The fiddle factor

Lying, deceit and subterfuge are characteristics of some organizations more than others because of the nature of jobs and organizations. Open, non-bureaucratic organizations tend to have less theft than rigid, over-administered organizations. The following attitudes and rationalization techniques are taken to justify fiddling and other forms of criminal and deviant activity:

- minimization: 'it's only a pen; the company can afford it and won't miss it'
- externalization: 'the boss made me do it; I was framed'
- normalization: 'everyone does it; this is what we do round here'
- super-ordination: 'they owed me; it's only fair repayment'.

Another view is to describe those that fiddle in anthropological terms, as follows:

- **Hawks** These are individuals who conduct their own fiddles, maintaining a low profile and high individuality. Hawks simply bend the rules to suit themselves.
- **Wolves** Wolves pilfer according to agreed rules and through a well-defined division of labour. Many wolf packs possess group hierarchical structures, with a distinctive set of orders and rules. Airport baggage handlers, airline and ferry crews, and gangs of dockers fall into this category.
- **Vultures** These operate on their own when they steal but need the support of a group to do it. They are typically in jobs where expense accounts can be stretched, or where commission may be generated.

- **Donkeys** These are people who are constrained by their jobs and are isolated from other workers. Transport workers and supermarket cashiers are both in 'donkey occupations' from this point of view. In these situations, it is possible to create and generate individual fiddles, though it is likely that these fiddles will be as much concerned with providing an element of creativity and imagination in the job, as for long-term steady financial gain.

Source: Livy (1989) and Furnham (1997)

From other members of staff

This is normally more straightforward to deal with because it is from a named individual rather than the impersonal organization. When things vanish from people's desks, lockers, work stations or bags it becomes instantly known that there is a thief about. It needs quick and effective investigation, and the miscreant, when confronted and disciplined, is normally dismissed (see Summary box 6.6).

Summary box 6.6   Dismissal and the criminal law

The Employment Protection (Consolidation) Act 1978 enshrines the principle of 'fairness and reasonableness' in all organizational dealings with their staff. On the face of it, therefore, it is 'fair and reasonable' to dismiss someone if the organization genuinely believes that he/she was responsible for a serious misdemeanour – whether or not this actually is the case. If the individual is dismissed as a result, and if they are subsequently acquitted in any police or crown prosecution, the organization may seek to persist in its view that the action carried out at the time was 'fair and reasonable' because there was an overwhelming belief that this was the case.

One of the UK's largest banks dismissed a member of its staff for being involved in a nightclub brawl. The brawl took place on a Saturday evening at a time when the member of staff was not at work. Overtly, the matter was nothing to do with the employer. However, the bank took the view that, because the case was widely reported in the local press its reputation would be damaged if it was seen to take no action. It therefore dismissed the individual for gross misconduct, citing the fact that, through his actions, the individual had damaged the reputation of the bank.

The individual concerned took the case to employment tribunal. The matter never reached tribunal, but was settled at the conciliation stage through the efforts of ACAS. The bank paid out substantial compensation to the individual, but refused to have him back at work.

The management of shop stewards and union representatives

There is no reason why this should be any more onerous than any other ER activity. It is essential, however, that certain features are clearly understood:

- **Parameters of activity** While union representatives are allowed reasonable time away from their main duties to act on the union's behalf, it is, in turn, perfectly reasonable to define, as far as possible, just what is meant by this. This will often be carried out in consultation with the local trade union full-time official. The precise areas of legitimate union representative involvement are normally stated in staff handbooks and main terms and conditions of employment. Problems occur when the parameters are not clearly defined or not adhered to, or where the representative exceeds their brief, or where the organization and its managers use the representative as a sort of unofficial sounding board or channel of communication. This enhances the representative's position, authority and influence in excess of what is genuinely their remit.
- **Discipline** Union representatives may be disciplined in exactly the same way as anyone else. However, it is usual to inform the local full-time official, and failure to do this normally leads to questions as to why this was not allowed. This is because the local official is effectively acting as the recognized representative for the union's own lay official during the conduct of the matter.
- **Grievances** Union representatives raise grievances in respect of their own working and occupational factors in exactly the same way as everyone else. Further points must be borne in mind, however. It is legitimate for the union representatives to raise grievances on behalf of their members, and to represent their members at hearings, and it is also legitimate for them to raise grievances at organizational level in respect of organization–union relations and factors.
- **Dismissal** Union representatives may be dismissed for exactly the same reason as anyone else at the workplace. Again, however, the local full-time official will normally be involved. It is also necessary to satisfy the legal requirement that the dismissal was for matters of organizational action, behaviour or performance, and not related to trade union activity (for which dismissal is automatically unfair).

The management of strikes and industrial action

Historically, organizations took a wide range of views of strikes and serious industrial action. The only 'logical' reason for strike action is as the result of a serious breakdown in organizational communications.

Historically, however, strikes are also well documented as having taken place for the following reasons:

- They were the result of the activities of communists and other radical subversives working for the overthrow of society.
- They were a useful safety valve, a means by which the monotony, tension and other potential for conflict could be managed from time to time.
- They were called to enhance the reputation of over-mighty individuals and groups, both management and staff.
- They were engendered by managers on career paths who wanted to show just how powerful and influential they were.
- They were engendered by trade union officials seeking to make a reputation for themselves.
- They were a means of breaking the work cycle or a lever for introducing changes in technology or work practices.
- They were used by management to show the workers who was in charge.
- They could be used as a stepping stone on the path to arbitration so that a settlement might be reached that was a) acceptable because it was independent and b) was perceived to absolve the management of any responsibility for it in the eyes of other stakeholders (especially shareholders).

The fundamental flaw in each of these views (except that of serious breakdown) is that it represents a basic lack of willingness to tackle the underlying causes of the issue – inappropriate management style, lack of mutual trust or interest or poor working environment. Each of these views, except serious breakdown, is therefore effectively a conspiracy (to a greater or lesser extent) between two or more groups of stakeholders, at the expense of others. The best that can be said for each is that they can be used in some circumstances to alleviate an immediate problem. In all cases, the fundamental situation is charged with a basic lack of integrity and will remain unchanged until it is itself tackled.

There is also a far greater public awareness of this view of strikes and disputes than previously held. Both customers and investors will be drawn away from dealings with organizations that operate in this way. Suppliers will also look hard at the extent of their dependency on such organizations.

At present in the UK, there are far fewer strikes and disputes than in previous times. Part of this is due to legislation and the removal of trade union immunities except where a strike is officially called. Part of it is due to increased uncertainties about job continuity. Managerial expertise in the field of ER has also greatly improved.

However, it should be noted that legislation has had the effect of ensuring that, when strikes do take place, they have both the commitment and support of those involved. Overwhelmingly, therefore, they now occur only as the result of serious breakdowns in communications, leading to a stand-off between the organization and its staff (or groups of staff).

It is vital that managers understand this. It is also essential that managers understand that because such a breakdown has occurred, it has to be repaired – whatever the eventual outcome of the dispute – if effective and profitable work is to be undertaken afterwards. This remains a factor little understood by both managers and staff groups. It is also compounded by the fact that such disputes are much more self-evidently won and lost, and that one group may have to return to the working situation from a known, believed or perceived point of view of defeat.

When it becomes apparent that there may be a strike or dispute, it is therefore essential that everyone involved recognizes the full potential of the situation. It is only achieved through meetings between the potential protagonists. The problem is compounded in organizations where:

- there is a history of bad working relations
- there are over-mighty subjects, departments, divisions and functions
- there are strong identities with professional and occupational groups as distinct from the organization
- there are strong emergent or canteen cultures.

Nevertheless, this action must be taken and such meetings carried out if the situation is to be retrieved early. It also becomes the vehicle for early recognition of:

- entrenched positions
- secondary or hidden agenda
- underlying issues that may either have been apparent and unsaid, or may not have been apparent in the first place.

The outcome is an initial mutual understanding of the true extent of the dispute, and the real factors that are fuelling it. This will not necessarily prevent it from taking place. It will at least mean that everyone concerned understands why it is to take place – if it does – and the consequences of this in terms of possible outcomes. It should also engage the interest of all those concerned in seeking alternatives to the dispute. It will identify the extent to which the perceived major sticking points are organizational, operational or behavioural and therefore provides a basis either for tackling the issue at source, or for finding alternative solutions, or for at least knowing that one of the protagonists is determined to have a fight.

All of this can then be communicated to those certain and likely to be affected. It is also certain that customers, clients, backers, suppliers and distributors will have their own views. For major organizations, the matter is also certain to be reported in the press and media from a variety of perspectives.

If the dispute is resolved without recourse to industrial action, the majority of stakeholders and interested parties will be happy. There are very few legitimate reasons why disputes take place and anyone who wishes to pursue their own interests or agenda through deliberately generating a conflict can easily be identified. Provided the issue is genuinely and fairly resolved, all parties will either be happy with the outcome, or at least they will understand how and why it was resolved.

Ultimately, all disputes have to be resolved face to face. The decision for all parties is when that resolution is to take place, under what circumstances and whether, in the meantime, the issue is to be drawn out through a long and inevitably divisive and destructive process.

EMPLOYEE RELATIONS AND ORGANIZATION CULTURE

Serious ER problems, including disputes and strikes, are much more likely to occur where:

■ the organization culture is not clear (weak rather than strong, emergent rather than designed)
■ there are strong professional and occupational cliques with which the staff identify first
■ there are canteen cultures at operational levels
■ there are divisions and variations in treatments of terms and conditions of employment according to department, division, location, function or position in the hierarchy.

At the very least, all those involved need to recognize the potential for strikes and disputes that exist in these situations. There can then be taken a long-term view of how matters can be resolved by tackling the problems at source, while in the meantime, dealing with the individual issue when it arises.

Problems are compounded where there is a lack of recognition of the underlying seriousness of the situation (even if there are no actual disputes currently taking place). There is also great potential for trouble when it is generally known that cliques and canteen cultures exist, but a lack of institutional will to do anything about them. When issues do come to the surface in these situations, they always cause enormous trouble and disruption, both in the settlement of the particular matter, and in making organizations and their managers face up to the need to address the underlying causes.

The problem is further compounded where there exists a culture of remoteness or status differential between different levels in organization hierarchies. In these cases, senior management is remote from the daily running and operations of the organization. They are often simply not aware that there are issues to be faced. Trouble then becomes more serious still when they provide 'knee-jerk' responses to the situation, or guess at solutions, rather than going and evaluating the issues for themselves (see Summary box 6.7).

**Summary box 6.7   Remoteness and conflict: food processing in
                            north-western England**

Some years ago, a major industrial multinational had four food processing plants in the Home Counties of England, and one in the north-west, at Skelmersdale in Lancashire. The north-western plant was consistently the worst performer of all. It was regularly told this through company edicts, which were issued from the corporate headquarters in central London. Eventually the factory was told, that if its performance did not improve, it would be closed down.

At first, this threat was greeted with great consternation. Steps were taken by local management, in consultation with recognized trade unions, to improve performance. Improvements were made. However, these were not good enough for the people at corporate headquarters, and so the threat of closure continued.

Eventually the threats of closure ceased to have any effect. People working in the north-west plant eventually came round to the collective view that they were to be closed down anyway.

Indeed, this is what came to pass and the plant was closed in March 1987. At no stage did anyone from the corporate headquarters travel up to the north-west to study the situation for themselves. The matter was decided and judged entirely on preconceptions, prejudices and other perceptions that were centred around a general disparagement of the capability of workers in the particular location, in comparison to those in the Home Counties.

> The company never made any calculation concerning the actual losses that it had incurred commercially as the result of this closure. The dispute between the corporate headquarters and the plant in the north-west was engaged without regard for the service of markets, customers and clients, without regard for the well-being of the staff; and without regard for the genuine effect that this antagonistic approach to the management of conflict had on those who remained within the organization.

DISMISSAL

Individual and collective dismissal may either be fair or unfair. It is fair to dismiss individuals and groups of staff for any of the following reasons:

■ redundancy
■ dismissal and strikes
■ dismissal and discipline
■ dismissal and sickness
■ dismissal and poor performance.

In all cases, however, there are legal boundaries. Consultation must always take place. Rules, procedures and criteria must be published. Everything that is done must be 'fair and reasonable in the circumstances' and adhere to principles of natural justice.

Redundancy

Redundancy occurs where work has ceased, or diminished to the point where it is no longer tenable or viable. To comply with the law, specific consultation periods are required, depending on the numbers of redundancies to be made (see Chapter 2). In the effective management of ER, and in order to preserve the integrity of the organization so that it can continue to operate successfully in the future, this makes sound managerial sense in any case.

Ideally, redundancies are only contemplated when all else fails. Alternatives to redundancy include:

- retraining and redeployment
- pay freezes – these should be applied across the board, and not just to certain groups of staff
- pay cuts – again by agreement, and applied across the board
- early retirement and other severance arrangements
- reduced hours or compulsory holidays
- lay-off periods
- other organizational approaches – especially in the management of finance through the reductions in dividends to shareholders.

Redundancy may be voluntary or compulsory. In the effective management of redundancy, the voluntary approach is the best.

Voluntary redundancy

When it becomes necessary to seek redundancies, people are asked to volunteer. It may also be possible to combine voluntary redundancy with early retirement or other forms of severance. It may also be deemed necessary either to ask for volunteers from a particular group, department, division or function, or to exclude particular groups, departments, divisions and functions from the redundancy exercise (see Summary box 6.8).

Summary box 6.8   Voluntary redundancy: example

In 1980, a large chain of department stores considered that it had to reduce its workforce by 10 per cent. It consequently asked for volunteers for redundancy, as a precursor to a compulsory redundancy exercise.

It was overwhelmed with the response. It was looking for a total of 3,500 redundancies and received 21,500 applications. What was most disturbing to the company was that a very high proportion of its senior staff were volunteering.

As part of the voluntary redundancy package, early retirement was being offered to 'suitable candidates'. One application for early retirement was received from a person of 40. This person had completed 23 years' service with the company, and reasoned that they would be able to retire at 40 on half-pension.

The company withdrew the redundancy exercise. The fall-out from the exercise led to wholesale changes in the directorate and top management in whom the shareholders subsequently passed a motion of no confidence. There was widespread realization that the organization had been directed from a standpoint of remoteness and complacency, and that this would not ensure the long-term prosperous future that everyone expected.

Most of all, however, it was an early corporate lesson in the need to pay attention to the motivation of key and senior staff. In many subsequent voluntary redundancy exercises, organizations have found that it is senior and key staff who are the most eager to leave. Some of this is due to their confidence in their ability to find other work – and therefore to take the redundancy payment as a windfall or bonus. It has also led organizations to question the wisdom of wholesale redundancies – whether from a voluntary or compulsory point of view.

Compulsory redundancy

When the voluntary approach does not produce the numbers required, or operationally, it is not deemed suitable to ask for volunteers or to adopt any of the other approaches indicated, then it becomes necessary that people are notified that they are to lose their job. At the outset, it is important to note the following:

■ There will be an adverse effect on the morale and motivation of those who are to lose their job and this is exacerbated the longer the situation remains unclear or in limbo.
■ There will be an adverse effect on those who are to retain their jobs, if they see that the situation is not handled quickly and effectively. In any case, those who retain their jobs where others are losing theirs, always tend towards feelings of 'there but for the grace of God...'

Whether voluntary or compulsory, all staff affected or likely to be affected, should be informed of the decision immediately it is taken. Procedures and criteria must be published (see Summary box 6.9). The redundancy process must be scheduled so that people know when they are to leave and what support they are to be given during the period of notice. There also needs to be a clear policy on recruitment elsewhere in the organization during periods when redundancies are being made so that those at risk or under threat are able to apply for vacancies when they do arise.

Summary box 6.9   The redundancy process

The following must always be in place:

- **Consultation and information** This must always be provided, on an individual and group basis, and in writing and orally, when redundancies are first considered.

- **Status** All those affected, or who are likely to be affected, must be notified of their status. Their status may be 'redundant' (they are to lose their jobs), 'under threat' (they are likely to lose their jobs) or 'at risk' (they may lose their jobs, and are in the broad frame).
- **Criteria for selection for redundancy** At the point at which redundancies are decided, organizations must determine the criteria on which people are to lose their jobs. This may not be carried out on the basis of gender or hours worked. The principle of 'last in, first out' (lifo) may be deemed to apply in the absence of other published criteria. Where departments, divisions, functions or locations are to be closed down, the reasoning for this course of action must be published. Other criteria must be capable of organizational support, and demonstrably fair and reasonable.
- **Notice periods** There are minimum statutory notice periods (see Chapter 2) depending on the numbers of redundancies involved. Persons made redundant may leave before their notice period expires; however, their notice period must always be paid up in full. It is also invariably unfair to expect people to stay on during the period of their notice if they find themselves another job during the period.
- **Bumping** This occurs where somebody being made redundant finds a volunteer to take their place. So long as this is fair and reasonable in the circumstances, it is acceptable.
- **Redundancy schedule** A timetable or schedule for the redundancy process, including the date or dates on which people are to leave, must be published at the outset. This must take account of any statutory notice periods and must also allow for consultations to take place, and for the adequate provision of information.

Note

European social policy, supported by the Social Charter and the Acquired Rights Directive, is seeking to place ever-greater responsibilities for permanence and continuity of employment on organizations (especially large organizations). This is enshrined in the Amsterdam Treaty 1997, which puts measures for tackling unemployment, and the protection of existing employment, at the head of its agenda.

Dismissal and strikes

If industrial action is not conducted in accordance with the law, especially if procedures on conduct of ballots and notice periods are not followed, then it is lawful to dismiss strikers and sue their unions for losses incurred and damages (see Chapter 2).

In practice, this very rarely happens. Unofficial strikes are now very rare in the UK. They normally arise as the result of a genuine misunderstanding, or else as a 'knee-jerk' response to an organization or management action.

Whatever the cause, to dismiss large sections of the workforce for an unofficial strike simply means that the organization finds itself with a number of vacancies which it first has to fill in order to carry on working. Moreover, those dismissed may simply carry on the dispute anyway (see Summary box 6.10).

Summary box 6.10   Unofficial strikes: Liverpool docks 1993–98

In 1993, the port of Liverpool was privatized. It was taken over by the National Ports Company in 1995. The new owners sought to make large scale redundancies and to reduce substantially the terms and conditions of employment (including the pay) of those who remained.

All those who had previously worked for the company came out on strike. The company engaged temporary, contract and self-employed staff at substantially reduced rates. The previous workforce carried on picketing the employer in order to retain their jobs and in order to gain publicity that would prevent customers and clients from doing business with the employer until the dispute was resolved.

The strike was unofficial because procedures had not been followed – even though it was universal. The employer offered substantial severance terms to those affected, but refused to take them back.

The dispute carried on until January 1998. At this point, the employer made their 'final offer' – a one-off severance payment, applicable to all, of £4,000.

To the amazement of the trade union involved (the Transport and General Workers) the payment was accepted by 80 per cent of the former workforce. After over two years of unofficial strike, and nearly five years of wrangling, the dispute was ended.

To date, nobody has measured the effect on business of the strike or the cost in terms of lost customers and clients, nor have they compared this with the cost of settling the dispute in the early stages.

There is again the question of the effect on the morale of those not involved in the dispute to consider. When unofficial strikers are dismissed, it is very difficult for those remaining to escape the conclusion that this was – wholly or partly – a pretext or founded on expediency.

The management of strikes and other serious ER issues should be undertaken alongside a much more wide-ranging strategic review of ER approaches and policies, and the existing organization perspective, so that the real reasons why the problems arose can be assessed and evaluated.

Dismissal and discipline

It is quite legitimate to dismiss someone for persistent breaches of discipline, including gross misconduct, provided that procedures are followed. If procedures are not followed, dismissal will always be unfair. If it is managed properly, there is nothing contentious about this – indeed, the best employees expect that this will happen, so that their own interests and integrity are protected (see Summary box 6.11).

Problems arise where there is known, believed or perceived unevenness of treatment as follows:

■ where one person has been dismissed and others have not for the same (or very similar) misdemeanours
■ where someone is known, believed or perceived to have profited from their misconduct; this is compounded when it is known that their victim has suffered material or career opportunity losses at the same time
■ where treatment is uneven and dependent on which manager or supervisor, department, division, location or function, is concerned
■ where someone has been dismissed hastily or without due thought, and the organization then sees fit to dress the case up to give it a better presentation at any subsequent employment tribunal case
■ where someone has been dismissed maliciously and spurious or fraudulent grounds are invented to try and justify the dismissal.

All of these issues and the problems that they cause are remedied through the establishment of clear organizational ER standards, and staff and management training in the field.

Summary box 6.11   Discipline and dismissal: examples

Example 1

Operational staff at a plastics factory in the industrial part of north Kent, UK, were required to turn up at work on time. To be late for work was a dismissible offence. This was well known and understood by all. If they were not at their post in order to take over, the machinery would seize up and would cause loss and damage to the value of several hundred thousand pounds.

Over the period 1982–95, the factory dismissed a total of 40 staff for failing to attend on time. Staff who knew that they could not attend for any reason were required to give a minimum two hours' notice that they would not be turning up. This was so that a replacement could be found in order that the machinery would not stop.

In 1995, one member of staff was late for work. On this occasion, the company declined to dismiss the individual. The individual came from an ethnic minority and the manager stated that 'I do not want any racial trouble'.

As a consequence, the company was faced with claims for reinstatement for all those that it had dismissed on previous occasions.

Example 2

In the south-east of England, a senior care worker was dismissed from a special school for maladjusted children. It was alleged that he had struck another member of staff. No one else was present at the time the alleged incident took place.

The head of the school conducted an investigation and decided to dismiss. He called witnesses in support of his action and took evidence from other witnesses which were reproduced in the form of statements, and which were read out at the hearing.

The senior care worker took the case to employment tribunal. A settlement wholly favourable to the senior care worker was worked out at the pre-tribunal stage, under the auspices of ACAS. The senior care worker was able to demonstrate that the incident never took place. Moreover, he was able to cite the fact that, as nobody else was present at the time that the incident was supposed to have taken place, witnesses could neither be called to give evidence, nor to make statements, on the grounds that as they had not been present, they could not have seen what was going on.

Dismissal and sickness

It is quite legitimate to dismiss someone for illness and sickness under the following circumstances:

■ where people have used organizational self-certification sickness procedures to gain additional leave or time off from work, where it can be proven or demonstrated that this has occurred, and where they have been put through the disciplinary procedure in full as the result
■ where a particular condition renders it dangerous or impossible to carry on working and where there is no suitable, possible or agreed alternative to the existing job. In these cases, it is usual to make a severance payment based around the organization redundancy procedure or, in the most serious cases, to arrange early retirement on the grounds of ill health.

There is a clear requirement to treat employees with serious illness or injury with responsibility; and best practice dictates a social and moral, as well as managerial, obligation (see Summary box 6.12). However, there is no obligation to retain ill or injured employees on the pay roll however much they may so wish – this should be agreed through consultation with the employee and their representatives.

Summary box 6.12   Illness, sickness and injury: current issues

Particular managerial attention is required to the following:

• **Stress** No single or universally accepted definition exists for what is known as 'stress'. However, it is incumbent on organizations and their managers to recognize where stress occurs, what causes it and why and, as far as possible, to take remedial action to alleviate its effects. It is particularly prevalent in the public services of the late 1990s – education, health, social work and occupations in the emergency and security services.
• **Repetitive Strain Injury (RSI)** The true extent of RSI is becoming ever more apparent. Continued operation of industrial processes, typewriter and computer keyboards, data screens, and telephone and audio equipment, is widely recognized to cause long-term bodily injury. Again, it is incumbent upon organizations and managers to recognize where this occurs, why it occurs and to take all possible steps to prevent it in the design of jobs, occupations and work stations.

- **HIV/AIDS** No clear guidelines exist for the management of staff who suffer from HIV/AIDS. There is a clear moral obligation to ensure that members of staff with what is after all a fatal disease receive the best quality of life, including all possible employment opportunities, during the onset of the disease. This has clearly to be balanced with operational requirements; it is also necessary to consider the general safety of customers, clients and other members of staff. Neither EU social policy, nor EU or UK employee relations legislation or codes of conduct, is fully developed in this area.

Dismissal and poor performance

It is quite legitimate to dismiss someone for persistent and continuing poor performance provided that they have had their shortcomings pointed out to them and have been offered remedial treatment, training and development in order to improve. It is useful to distinguish the following:

■ Poor performance as the result of the employee's capacity or capability. This may arise for a variety of reasons including:

- promotion to a level of incompetence, away from what the employee does well, and into a job or location in which for some reason he/she cannot function effectively. Such promotion or relocation should always be supported by training and development, induction and orientation into the new job or location. The best ER management in these circumstances will also consider the shortcomings of the selection process that caused the problems to arise
- misperception and misunderstanding at the point of appointment causing unreal expectations on the part of either the employee or the organization, or both. When this occurs, it is best to end the arrangement (often with financial compensation) as soon as possible, by agreement.

■ Poor performance as the result of bad attitude or demeanour which may arise because of the following:

- the employee dislikes the place of work, the job, the manager or the supervisor, or their work colleagues, for some reason
- the employee was given to understand that certain opportunities would be forthcoming, and for some reason these have not materialized

- the employee performs part of their job well but other parts regularly and consistently badly because they dislike those parts for some reason
- the employee is using the job as a stepping stone to go on to other things, and this is exacerbated when the other things fail to materialize for some reason.

Many organizations have disciplinary procedures that relate especially to poor performance and these should be inducted in ways that are indicated in Chapter 5. Procedures must always be followed. If no separate procedure exists for the management of poor performance, then the disciplinary procedure should be engaged, with the reason given as poor performance, and supported by evidence of when and where performance was not up to standard and why, how, when and where it is to be remedied.

CONCLUSIONS

The effective management of serious and contentious ER problems requires a deep level of understanding and expertise – of organizational behaviour, of the roots and causes of conflict, and of the need to understand all aspects of the management of organizations. Failure to do this leads to piecemeal solutions. While this may remove instantly one aspect of trouble, it is likely simply to move the issue on, so that it emerges in another form in another guise.

The best approaches in effective management of ER lie in recognizing how and why conflict is likely to occur, and in the need for evenness of treatment when it does occur. It also requires a genuine understanding of the difficulties and complexities of managing diverse and complex organizations, and of the problems and pitfalls caused by remoteness, lack of genuine empathy, and of a strategic approach to creating an environment in which conflict can be managed, and in fostering the expertise that enables problems to be resolved when they do occur.

7

EMPLOYMENT TRIBUNALS

INTRODUCTION

Employment tribunals were first established under the Industrial Training Act 1964. They deal with a wide range of jurisdictions mostly concerning the individual rights of employees. The majority of cases arise from the unfair dismissal provisions in employment protection legislation. Other cases involve complaints about wage or redundancy payments, sex, race or disability discrimination in the workplace, maternity rights in employment, trade union membership and non-membership rights, and health and safety at work. The 1993 Trade Union Reform and Employment Rights Act has added new aspects to the work of the tribunals – especially in the areas of upholding individual rights. This has been further enhanced by the accession of the UK Labour government in September 1997 to the European Social Charter.

The tribunals' workload has grown substantially in recent years. In 1989 there were approximately 18,000 applications. In 1997 this had grown to 105,000 applications. However, the majority of applications do not come to hearing, being settled or withdrawn often following conciliation via the Advisory Conciliation and Arbitration Service (ACAS).

THE TRIBUNALS

There are separate employment tribunal organizations for England and Wales, and for Scotland, each with their own president.

Tribunals are independent judicial bodies. In England and Wales tribunals are organized on a regional basis, with regional offices, located in principle centres of population. Hearings are also held in a number of other towns. In Scotland hearings take place at the employment tribunals' central office in Glasgow and at centres in other major cities. Hearings may also take place elsewhere according to need.

Each tribunal normally consists of a legally qualified chairman, appointed by the Lord Chancellor in England and Wales and the Lord President of the Court of Session in Scotland, and two lay members, one drawn from a panel of employer members, the other from a panel of employee members. Tribunal chairmen can sit alone in certain cases. Lay members are appointed by the Secretary of State for Education and Employment following consultation with organizations representing employers and employees. The Department for Education and Employment is also responsible for the general administration of the tribunals.

Please note that the term chairman is derived from legislation governing tribunals. It applies equally to men and women.

The parties to the case

Persons (or other bodies such as trade unions) bringing cases to tribunals are known as applicants. Those against whom cases are brought (either organizations or individuals) are known as respondents.

Each party may also call witnesses to support its case. Each party also produces and presents evidence to support its case.

Employment tribunals were set up to provide a straightforward way of settling disputes between employer and employee. Both applicants and respondents may present their case themselves or they may choose to have a representative act on their behalf. For either applicant or respondent, this representative may be a trade union official, barrister, solicitor, human resource management or employee relations expert, or a friend or colleague – indeed, anyone in whom the party has sufficient confidence to place the case.

The case

Tribunal cases are commenced when applicants notify the Department for Education and Employment of their complaint. This is presented on form IT1. This gives the applicant's name and address, the name and address of the respondent, and the grounds on which the complaint is made. This is then passed on to the local office of the employment tribunal.

Time factors

Applicants

Complaints to tribunals normally have to be made within three months of the alleged offence. The period is six months for cases relating to selective re-engagement after a strike or other industrial action. There is no time limit on cases of discrimination or victimization. The three month rule may be waived if it becomes apparent at a later date that an offence had been committed.

Respondents

Once a complaint is made the respondent is sent a copy of the applicant's case by the tribunal office. The respondent is also sent a notice of appearance in which they are asked whether or not they wish to contest the case and if so, to state the grounds for doing so. This should normally be returned within 14 days of receipt, though this may be extended by arrangement with the office of the tribunals if there are good reasons.

Cases are processed as quickly as possible. It normally takes at least three months for a case to come to tribunal. This may be extended due to pressures of work on the local tribunal; in these cases the agreement of applicant and respondent may be sought to have the case heard elsewhere.

Both parties are notified at least 14 days in advance of the proposed date of the hearing. Either party may ask for a postponement provided that a good reason can be shown as to why the proposed date is not suitable.

Summary of proceedings

Once a complaint or application has been made it is notified to the local office of the tribunals. This is then handed on to the offices of ACAS. The following then takes place.

Conciliation through ACAS

With the exception of redundancy payments claims and breaches of contract (where there are absolute legal requirements), ACAS has a statutory duty to become involved in all cases. Their role is to search for the base on which a settlement can be achieved that is satisfactory to both applicant and respondent. Both parties are contacted by a conciliation officer of ACAS for this purpose. The role of ACAS is to mediate, to search for common ground, to establish whether there is a basis for a settlement that is satisfactory to all concerned.

Preliminary hearing

The tribunal dealing with the case may decide to hold a preliminary hearing. This normally happens when it appears that the complaint falls outside its jurisdiction or where the point of view of one party (normally that of the respondent) is that this is the case.

Pre-hearing assessment

The tribunal dealing with the case may decide to hold a pre-hearing assessment or it may be requested to do so by either party. This normally happens when it appears that one party has a case that has no reasonable chance of success.

The pre-hearing assessment normally combines itself to hearing the outline of the case that is considered unlikely to succeed. The other party may attend if they wish.

Tribunals have no power to decide or to dismiss a case at pre-hearing assessment, nor may they order the withdrawal of a case. They may warn parties that they may have to bear some or all of the costs of the other party if they choose to persist with the case and then subsequently lose. However, this decision is taken by the tribunal at the end of the full hearing; it is not decided by the pre-hearing assessment.

The hearing

The procedure is orderly but flexible and informal. The parties give evidence, call their witnesses, question their witnesses and those of the other party. Each party may address the tribunal directly. Each member of the tribunal may question the parties and their witnesses. Each party may represent themselves, or may choose to have any person that they wish to present their case on their behalf.

There is a tribunal clerk available to advise on procedures and to finalize arrangements for the order of proceedings on the day of the case. If necessary, the tribunal itself will advise on procedures during the conduct of the case.

There is no compulsion to attend or to be represented. However, attendance is strongly recommended. The case will be heard and dealt with on the appointed day and on the basis of the evidence, information and representation that is available.

All hearings are public. Anyone may attend and observe the proceedings, including members of the press. The only exception to this is where information disclosed would cause substantial commercial or operational injury to an organization.

The decision

The tribunal announces its decision either at the close of proceedings or else at a later date. In every case, a written statement of the decision together with the reasons for it, are sent to both parties. The statement either gives the reasons in full or else a summary of them. Where a summary only is issued a statement of the reasons in full may be requested by either party.

Review

Tribunals may review their decisions and change or correct them if they are subsequently considered to have been wrong. The most common ground for this is where information that has a direct bearing on the case comes to light after the hearing has been held and where the interests of justice therefore demand a review.

Reviews may also arise as the result of error on the part of the tribunal or where one party did not receive notice of the hearing.

Reviews may be requested by either party on each of these grounds.

Appeal

Appeals are made to Employment Appeal Tribunals (EAT). EATs consist of a judge and one or more lay members drawn from employers' and employees' representatives. A judge may also hear appeals alone.

Appeals to EATs can only be made on a point of law. They must be made within 42 days of receipt of the decision of the tribunal. All appeals must include the decision of the tribunal together with full written reasons (not a summary).

Further proceedings

Either party may seek leave to take the case on into the main court and judicial system. This normally occurs where there is a point of precedent or other potentially major legal issue at stake.

Costs

Normally, each party meets their own expenses. No payments are made from public funds. A tribunal may require one party to meet some or all of the expenses of the other where it decides that the case was frivolous, vexatious, malicious or unreasonable. This only occurs following a warning given to this effect at a pre-hearing assessment. Additionally, a party whose case is considered weak may be required to pay a deposit of up to £150 in advance of the hearing; all or part of this may be forfeit if the case then goes against them.

Preparing and conducting the case

All cases start with the receipt of the application by the employer, who then becomes the respondent. In all cases the onus is placed on the employer to be able to prove or demonstrate to the satisfaction of the tribunal that:

■ they acted fairly and reasonably and with honesty and integrity
■ they followed procedures, criteria and any recognized standards of best practice
■ the outcome would have been the same for anyone in the same, similar or equivalent sets of circumstances
■ any alternative courses of action were considered, evaluated and rejected
■ that the stated reasons for dismissal (if dismissal has occurred) were the real reasons for dismissal
■ that the stated reasons for not appointing (if this has occurred) were the real reasons for not appointing.

If the employer cannot provide proof or satisfaction to the tribunal on each of these points, the case is damaged and may fail.

Part of the employer's case, therefore, clearly consists of proving their honesty, integrity and innocence. There is an initial presumption that there is a case for the employer to answer.

Once an application has been made, all cases normally proceed at least to conciliation and mediation by ACAS and often to a pre-hearing assessment. Both ACAS and the pre-hearing assessment normally seek satisfaction on each of the above points. Only if this is proven or demonstrated to their satisfaction, will they seek to influence the applicant to withdraw their case.

This is the general context of all tribunal cases, and the basis of all effective preparation. In specific cases, effective preparation depends on the following:

■ the nature and content of the allegations, and the nature of redress sought or required by the applicant

- general considerations related to defending and pursuing the case or settling the matter some other way
- investigation into the background to assess the strengths and weaknesses of the case
- assessing the merits of the case, the range of possible outcomes, the desired outcome and the likely outcome
- reasons for proceeding, including a wider consideration of the effects on future working relationships and morale.

Allegations

The allegations on which applications are based usually arise from the following sources:

- There was an unfair dismissal (see Summary box 7.1).
- There was discrimination for reasons of gender, racial or ethnic origin, disability, trade union membership or non-membership.
- Employment was not offered or was refused.
- Promotion was not offered or was refused.
- Training development, project secondments and other opportunities were not offered or were refused.
- Dismissal under the guise of redundancy was made.
- Wages and other terms and conditions were not equal, for equal work, of equal value.
- Lesser pay and other terms and conditions were offered or made in relation to others in the organization.
- There was negativity – where the person was transferred or redeployed because of their gender, racial or ethnic origin, disability, trade union membership or non-membership.
- There was victimization and harassment for reasons of gender, racial or ethnic origin, disability, trade union membership or non-membership or spent convictions.
- A negative or bullying attitude or behaviour was adopted.
- Misconduct took place or could be construed to have taken place.
- The individual was subject to personal, negative or offensive remarks.
- There was racial, sex/gender or disability prejudice on the part of peers, subordinates, managers or supervisors.

Victimization and harassment also occur as the result of:

- a personal dislike or a personality clash – especially between superior and subordinate

- making a complaint against a colleague or a superior
- appearing as a witness at a disciplinary or grievance hearing or employment tribunal.

Summary box 7.1   Unfair dismissal

Unfair dismissal

Allegations of unfair dismissal may arise from facts, beliefs or perceptions of discrimination, victimization or harassment. They also arise from:

- the fact, belief or perception that procedures were not followed, that natural justice was not applied or that the organization did not act with honesty and integrity
- the fact, belief or perception that the applicant has been treated less favourably than others in similar or equivalent circumstances
- the fact, belief or perception that other courses of action were not considered
- the fact, belief or perception that a full investigation did not take place, or that the applicant was not allowed to state or present their case
- unfair selection for redundancy.

Unfair selection for redundancy

Allegations of unfair selection for redundancy arise from discrimination, victimization and harassment as above. They also arise where:

- there is a fact, belief or perception that work has not ceased
- those affected were not consulted, or not fully consulted
- alternatives to redundancy were not explored or offered
- criteria for selection for redundancy were not published and 'last in first out' (lifo) has not been applied
- reasonable time off to look for other jobs was refused or the time given was restricted and inadequate.

In all dismissal cases, employers have to be able to answer allegations made from these points of view.

Health and safety at work

Applications under health and safety regulations and legislation are made under the following circumstances:

- the fact, belief or perception that discrimination, victimization, harassment or dismissal took place because the employee refused to take part in unsafe work or activities without proper equipment, training or supervision
- a perception on the part of the employee that what they were asked to do was construed to be unsafe
- the employee perceived themselves to be placed in an unsafe situation due to lack of adequate supervision, training or explanation
- the employee considered themselves forced, coerced or pressurized into using equipment or adopting practices for which they had not received sufficient or adequate training
- the employee was asked, forced or coerced into carrying out work for which recognized qualifications were required and which they did not have.

These constitute the main sources of applications. They also indicate the nature of response required. All responses must deal in summary detail with the precise nature of the application and the allegations contained. Responses may also include indications of other factors that are considered to be relevant to the case.

General considerations

Whatever the nature of the applications and the merits and strengths of the case, a general consideration of the following is required:

- **Winning the case** This gives the opportunity to prove and demonstrate that the employer acted with fairness, reasonableness and with responsibility and integrity; the converse is that the employer is often seen as a bully (whatever the merits or demerits of the case itself).
- **Losing the case** Here there are consequent losses of credibility, faith and face, and injuries to pride and esteem, as well as to organizational activities and practices.
- **The likelihood of the case coming to tribunal** If it does, it must be considered when and where this is to occur, and the length of time (ie the number of days or weeks) that it is likely to last.

■ The cost and resource implications and consequences of tying people up in case preparation, of having people away from work as representatives and witnesses and hiring, briefing and engaging any expert or external representation that is desired must be considered.

■ **The public relations implications and consequences** This includes media coverage, internal organizational coverage and gossip and feelings in the local community.

■ **The effects on the morale of the rest of the staff** This includes particular staff groups, the need and ability to be able to work effectively and cooperatively in the future after the case is closed and the nature and duration of any lasting effects, especially bad feeling.

Alternatives

Alternative solutions to the problem (normally involving reaching a settlement satisfactory to both applicant and respondent) and the implications of this should be considered. This should include any internal precedent that this might set or indicate and also the pros and cons of the alternatives relative to having to conduct a tribunal case (see Summary box 7.2).

Summary box 7.2   Alternatives to tribunal proceedings

There are alternatives possible for the speedy resolution of issues. They normally arise only when there is a genuine dispute over the merits of the case or else, where the employer (the respondent) has made a mistake.

Recourse to arbitration

Arbitration is where an external referee – or arbitrator – is called in with the agreement of both or all parties to the dispute. Everyone involved normally agrees at the outset to be bound by the arbitrator's findings. Recommendations produced by arbitrators do not carry the force of law, but their content would be taken into account if the case subsequently went to tribunal.

Making a settlement

Settlements normally include one or more of the following: a cash payment, an apology, an agreed reference (for dismissed employees), redeployment or offering other opportunities or jobs within the organization (often in different departments, divisions or locations). Settlements do not carry the force of law, but their content would be taken into account if the case subsequently went to tribunal.

Conciliation agreements

Conciliation agreements are arrived at following conciliation by ACAS. They are drawn up by the conciliation officer on ACAS headed notepaper or forms. They constitute an agreement satisfactory to both or all parties concerned. The agreement is signed by all those concerned, and witnessed by ACAS. Conciliation agreements normally result in settling all matters of dispute and remove the need for the case to proceed to tribunal. Again, they normally constitute one or more of a cash payment, an apology, an agreed reference, redeployment or offering other opportunities.

Compromise agreements

Under a compromise agreement complaints may be settled without going before an employment tribunal. Complaints capable of being settled by a compromise agreement are those regarding termination of employment, sex or racial discrimination and complaints about payments. A compromise agreement has to be in writing and relate to a specific complaint. The employee must have had independent legal advice on its terms and content. The employer must have an insurance policy that specifically covers the risk of a claim by the employee for loss resulting from the advice.

Investigation

A full investigation is undertaken as soon as the complaint or application is received. It covers all aspects indicated in the complaint, the conduct of the parties involved and any wider general or peripheral aspects that may be relevant. It also involves a full consideration of the employer's actions and the reasons for these in relation to the particular application. All relevant documentation and paperwork should be examined. The investigation also involves interviewing all the people involved and a consideration of the context in which they became involved. The application and the reasons given for the application are studied and evaluated on their merits.

This forms the basis of the initial response to the application. This normally forms the basis of the response made on the notice of appearance. The initial investigation also forms a general impression of the merits, strengths and weaknesses of the case.

As well as addressing the complaint or application, the investigation must consider the following:

- the reasons given by the organization for dismissal or for not appointing and whether these are the real reasons
- the parties involved, their occupational, professional and personal relationships, witnesses and other interested or related parties
- the extent to which the application has been treated on the same basis as others in the organization in the same or similar circumstances
- tests of fairness and reasonableness and natural justice
- the application and use of procedures.

Empathy

It is essential to understand the applicant's point of view in bringing the case. For current or previous employees especially, the organization normally has a good knowledge of the applicant. The strength and weaknesses of the case, and the reasons for bringing it can therefore be considered in some detail once the application has been received.

Those who have been refused appointment must have grounds for believing that they have been victimized or discriminated against for an unlawful reason. It is important to understand how they could possibly have arrived at this conclusion.

Frivolous and vexatious

If the application is believed to be frivolous and vexatious or otherwise malicious, the onus is placed on the respondent to prove this. The opportunity to prove or demonstrate this initially arises at either the conciliation or pre-hearing assessment stages. It is also possible and legitimate to pursue this at the tribunal proper (the full hearing) if the matter is not settled beforehand.

Employment Appeal Tribunals have the power to make restriction of proceedings orders. These are requested by employers to prevent individuals from pursuing tribunal and EAT cases on frivolous, vexatious and malicious grounds. Again, the respondent must make the case that the matter is indeed frivolous, vexatious or malicious and incapable of being seen in any other way.

The merits of the case

The result of receiving the application, general considerations, the nature of the allegations and the investigation is that the merits of the case become apparent. These should then be thought of in the following terms:

■ the outcome desired by the respondent
■ the outcome desired by the applicant
■ the range of likely outcomes
■ the most likely outcome.

The reasons for pursuing, defending or settling the case arise from this.

Pursuing the case

Reasons for pursuing or defending the case fall into seven distinctive categories.

Rightness

The organization has behaved and acted correctly and with integrity and the employee has acted wrongly. Dismissal or failure to appoint was the only reasonable course open and this would have been the outcome of any similar or equivalent case. Procedures were followed and natural justice, as well as legal provisions, were applied.

The organization needs to demonstrate publicly that it acted correctly and with integrity as above, and to have this publicly underlined by the successful outcome of the tribunal.

The organization supports its managers and supervisors, who are responsible for upholding its standards of behaviour and performance, and demonstrates and underlines this support in the public arena.

There is a general need to uphold standards of behaviour or performance, and to be seen to do this.

Organizational politics

The organization has behaved improperly or without integrity, yet it still defends the case for some reason. This normally falls into one of the following areas:

■ the need to get someone off the hook, following a mistake or error of judgment

- the need to have an external or independent judgment as an acceptable solution to a difficult or complex situation
- the need for the judgment as a change agent – for example, use of a tribunal defeat as the catalyst and focus for management and supervisory training in staff management skills and knowledge
- a settlement prior to the tribunal may cause an unacceptable organizational precedent to be set.

The balance of probability

This is the basis of the majority of cases. It occurs where there are strengths and weaknesses on both sides or where either party has made a mistake that diminishes but does not destroy their case. In these situations, the range of potential outcomes is both wide and uncertain.

Ignorance

The case goes ahead where:

- the applicant is determined to have their day in tribunal, regardless of the merits or otherwise of their case
- the respondent is determined to defend the case, regardless of the merits (or more usually the demerits) of the case.

Personalities

The case goes ahead because of the personalities involved. The matter has become a trial of strength or showdown between applicant and respondent. Each is equally determined to prove their point.

In these cases the relative merits of the case of either party, the efforts of ACAS, the recommendations and pre-hearing assessment are fruitless. The case proceeds to full hearing and this becomes the ground on which the parties fight out their particular battle.

Pressures

The case goes ahead because of the pressure exerted on either party by their backers. The applicant's backers are normally their work colleagues, friends or trade union. The respondent's backers are normally their own manager, or the organization's upper levels of management.

Partial interest

The case goes ahead because either party or their representative has their own agenda.

For example, a trade union representative may encourage the applicant to pursue their application in order to gain experience of handling cases. A manager or supervisor may encourage the respondent to defend a case in order to enhance their reputation, gain prestige and wider recognition.

Lawyers, trade unions, and professional and expert bodies may also encourage either party to pursue a case in order to clarify a point of law or establish a principle or precedent. They may also do so, again, to enhance their particular reputation.

A key step in the preparation of effective tribunal cases is therefore to know and understand from which of these points of view the decision to pursue and defend the case has been taken.

EVIDENCE

In addition to statements of the initial application and response, the following evidence should always be provided:

■ copies of the contract of employment, other terms and conditions and any other documentation indicative and supportive of the working relationship
■ copies of relevant procedures and staff handbooks
■ copies of all correspondence – letters, memos, reports and file notes – relevant to the case
■ any other documentation considered relevant to the case and supportive of it
■ copies of induction programmes or other evidence of induction and orientation
■ other evidence of how standards of behaviour, conduct and performance were established and promulgated.

The evidence that is to be used should normally be supplied to the other party and to the tribunal in advance of the hearing.

Either party may require the other to provide particular documentation. It should contact the other party with specific requests. If this is not forthcoming, the party affected may apply to the tribunal for an order requesting that this be made available. The application should consist of a list of the documents required, together with a request for permission to make copies. The tribunal may also of its own volition order either party to produce all relevant documents and/or specific items.

Specific evidence

Specific cases normally require the following evidence to be produced:

Dismissal

■ **Dismissal for poor performance** The evidence required consists of copies of performance appraisals with dates, details of training and development undertaken with dates, copies of warnings with dates, the length of time for which performance has been a concern, actions taken to remedy this in the past and actions taken against other employees in similar or equivalent situations.

■ **Dismissal for bad time-keeping** This requires copies of clock cards, signing-in registers, print-outs of keyed in or other electronic registers with dates, copies of warnings with dates, the length of time for which this has been a concern, actions taken to remedy this in the past and actions taken against other employees in similar or equivalent circumstances.

■ **Dismissal for absence** This requires copies of absence and sickness records with dates, copies of warnings with dates, the length of time for which this has been a concern, actions taken to remedy this in the past, actions taken against other employees in similar or equivalent circumstances, acceptable and unacceptable levels of absence, the means by which these were promulgated, current standards and levels of attendance and the organization's general approach to absence.

■ **Dismissal as the result of redundancy** This requires copies of redundancy procedures and the date on which these were published, copies of redundancy criteria and the date on which these were published and distributed, evidence of consultation, evidence of considering other approaches to the matter and why these were rejected, evidence that 'last in first out' (lifo) was applied in the absence of any other published criteria and evidence that whatever the criteria, they were fair and reasonable in the circumstances and were equally and evenly applied.

■ **Dismissal following strike or industrial action** It must be shown whether everyone involved was dismissed and if anyone was subsequently re-engaged or taken back on. Other evidence required consists of the timescales involved (the minimum time-scale is normally six months), selection methods used for re-engagement, new job descriptions and personnel specifications compared with old job descriptions and personnel specifications and the extent and evidence of any wider or more general reorganization.

Failure to appoint

Failure to appoint covers both external appointments from the labour market and internal appointments – promotions, transfers, secondments and other changes:

■ **Criteria for appointment** This requires copies of the job advertisement, job description, personnel specification, skills, knowledge, qualities and expertise requested, choice, purpose and use of selection methods including, where appropriate, interviews, tests, seven-point plans, assessment centres and other structures, nature of previous and current working relationships, references (if appropriate) and any specific conditions or restrictions placed.
■ **Details of the successful candidate** In particular this requires evidence of how he/she measures up to the stated criteria for appointment, how he/she measures up to the qualities of the applicant and other background information and circumstances relevant to their appointment.

Health and safety

The evidence required here is of training and the capabilities and expertise of the employee with dates, evidence that all reasonable steps were taken to minimize the hazard with dates where appropriate, provision of safety clothing and equipment, insistence on using safety clothing and equipment, nature and extent of supervision, including proximity and observation, any advice, guidance or recommendations for the Health and Safety Executive, and the extent to which these were followed, evidence of the general duty of care required and other actions taken to minimize the chance of hazards or accidents occurring.

If the action is being brought arising from an accident or injury, specific evidence is required of the extent, frequency and prevalence of this, or similar or equivalent occurrences in the past and the actions taken to minimize and avoid them.

Discrimination, victimization and harassment

Here the evidence must counter the claim on performance and operational grounds, demonstrating or proving that:

■ in cases of dismissal, the same action has occurred or would have occurred to anyone in similar or equivalent situations
■ in cases of failure to appoint, promote or offer other opportunities, the person was unsuitable because of skills, knowledge and qualities

or that the person or people appointed were more suitable in terms of skills, knowledge and qualities
■ in cases of racial, sexual or other personal harassment, the ability to prove absolutely that this did not take place.

Evidence produced to counter any claim of any form of discrimination, victimization or harassment must concentrate on operational factors. It must be capable of sustaining the position that the applicant was dismissed or not appointed, promoted or offered opportunities solely on operational grounds. The only exceptions are where the person appointed was more suitable or where there is a legal restraint placed that excludes the applicant from having been appointed. No other position is sustainable.

Evidence therefore concentrates on:

■ the skills, qualities, knowledge and attributes required to carry out the given job and the reasons why these are considered essential
■ selection criteria and methods used
■ other information such as performance appraisals with dates, promises made and undertakings given with dates, training and development undertaken with dates
■ any general promises made to the applicant or any other basis on which they were led to expect that they would be appointed.

Documentation produced by respondents concentrates on each of these points. It is also often necessary to produce witnesses capable of sustaining the respondent's case and proving, demonstrating or strongly indicating that the form of discrimination alleged is not present.

The tribunal or the applicant may also ask for a breakdown of the workforce and/or particular parts of it by ethnic origin, gender, disability or union membership (if applicable); if requested, this should be supplied.

Disability victimization and harassment cases are always problematic.

Seeking a settlement with the applicant or failure to defend a case is normally taken to mean that there were sufficient grounds for making the application.

Defending an application and then losing the case normally proves the discrimination, victimization and harassment did in fact take place. Defending and winning a case may not prove that discrimination, victimization and harassment did not take place.

Persistent allegations of discrimination, victimization and harassment are therefore a matter of organization and managerial concern. This should lead to training and retraining, awareness raising, setting and maintaining standards, producing and enforcing policies and disciplining those who breach them.

In all cases of discrimination, victimization and harassment the onus is placed on employers to prove their innocence.

Specific cases

Pregnancy and maternity

The onus is placed entirely on the organization to prove or satisfy the tribunal that discrimination did not take place on grounds of pregnancy or maternity, or reasons related to either. Failure to do so will always result in the tribunal finding in favour of the applicant.

Individual rights

Failure to inform employees of their rights or failure to uphold these, normally results in the tribunal finding in favour of the application. The onus is placed on the employer to prove that they did both inform employees of their rights, and uphold these.

Failure to appear

If either party (or both parties) fail to appear at the hearing, the tribunal normally proceeds with the case anyway. The tribunal will make its decision based on the evidence available – normally the applicant's written statement on form IT1 and the respondent's case set out on their notice to appear. If for any reason the respondent cannot appear or provide representation, they are dependent upon the written evidence – the response to the case and any other written statements and documentation presented in its support.

Breaches of procedure

Breaches of procedures by the employer normally lead to the tribunal finding in favour of the application. This may be contested by the employer on the basis that:

- the breach of procedure did not affect the outcome of the case
- the breach was remedied at a later stage
- the employer has otherwise acted fairly and reasonably in accordance with natural justice and with honesty and integrity.

Again, the onus is placed on the respondent to address the breach of procedure and to produce evidence on each of the points indicated.

Witnesses

Applicants and respondents each call witnesses to support their case. Witnesses may do each or all of the following:

■ make a written statement to the tribunal
■ make an oral statement to the tribunal
■ make their statement via a question and answer routine, conducted by the party whose case they are supporting.

Witnesses must normally attend the hearing so that they can be questioned by the tribunal members.

Witnesses must tell the truth. They must not make false or misleading statements or give false or misleading impressions. They may not be coerced, cajoled, threatened or bullied into placing a particular slant on events. They may confine themselves (or be confined) to specific issues. Witnesses give their evidence on oath.

Witnesses are also normally subject to:

■ questioning by the party whose case they are supporting
■ being cross-examined by the other party (or their representative)
■ questioning by the tribunal members.

If called as a witness, an individual must attend. The only exceptions to this are where they can demonstrate that their evidence has no bearing on the conduct or outcome of the case, or where a written statement is accepted as sufficient by the tribunal.

Witness orders

Where an individual is unwilling to attend or refuses to attend, either party may apply to the tribunal for a witness order. This must then be served (presented or delivered) on the witness in person. The tribunal itself may order witnesses to attend if it believes that they have a substantial or critical contribution or evidence. Applications for witness orders should always give the name and address of the witness and also details of why the witness feels unable or unwilling to attend. An indication of the nature of their evidence and its bearing on the case may also be required.

Failure to attend the tribunal where a witness order has been served normally results in the witness being found to be in contempt of the tribunal. This leads to an initial fine of up to £1,000 and a further order to attend. Persistent refusal may result in imprisonment or a court injunction ordering attendance. The penalties for refusing or ignoring an order are unlimited fines or imprisonment, or both.

Witnesses should be briefed on the reasons why they are required and the areas on which they are to be questioned by the side that calls them. They are also often rehearsed through their evidence.

They should also be briefed on the likely areas on which the other side may examine them and the forms that this questioning may take.

Hearing the case

The main body of work for the case is carried out as indicated above in response to the application following the assessment of the merits of the case. This indicates the nature of the response required.

Structure

All evidence to be presented should be issued to the applicant and to the tribunal in advance, together with a list of witnesses. This gives those responsible for scheduling the case an indication of how long the respondent's presentation is likely to take.

The case is structured with the overall aim of presenting the point of view desired, building on its strengths, acknowledging and explaining any weaknesses, and countering the views of the application.

The general structure remains the same, though its emphasis varies between cases. It should be organized as follows. There should be:

■ an opening statement, setting out clearly a summary of the case, the reasons why this, rather than the applicant's point of view, should prevail, and the reasons for pursuing and defending it
■ an explanation of each of the points raised by the application, together with the necessary evidence and witnesses in support. Questions to one's own witnesses should be organized and structured in advance
■ a presentation of each point that forms the response, together with evidence of witnesses
■ a closing statement, re-summarizing the case and emphasizing the strengths and thrust of the case.

The case is normally best presented by people from within the organization, provided that they are competent and organized, because they will know the general situation better than any outsider.

Those who are to conduct the case must ensure that they have visited a tribunal to observe, note and understand the proceedings.

The case should normally be conducted by at least two people. One should lead, present the case and the evidence, question witnesses and sum up. The other should act as second, observe proceedings, take notes and act as the minder. Their role is to keep the proceedings on track, ensure that the point of the case is not lost, keep aims and objectives in mind, and ensure that any additional matters that become apparent are pursued. This role may be divided if the case is likely to be long and complex.

Use of experts

Experts may be called, either to present the case or to give evidence in support:

■ **Presenting the case** Lawyers, consultants or employers' association representatives are asked to conduct the case where it is complex or heavily dependent on points of law, or where the organization does not have (or perceive itself to have) the necessary expertise.
■ **Evidence** Experts are called where their knowledge, skill or expertise is recognized and acknowledged to be of a high order and/or which represents best practice and which can be shown to have a distinctive and critical bearing on the case.

Note

Experts (especially lawyers asked to conduct the case) are very expensive and the costs and benefits should be carefully weighed. Some tribunal chairmen take the view that the use of lawyers makes the case more orderly and easy to understand; others take the view that the use of lawyers in employment tribunals is not appropriate and that their presence tends to cloud, rather than clarify, issues.

In all cases tribunals are not contests between lawyers. Their purpose is to arrive at the truth of the issue, balance the merits of the case and establish and apply what is fair and reasonable in the circumstances.

The tribunal hearing

The hearing is introduced by the chairman. He or she gives a brief statement acknowledging the parties to the case and the issues. The hearing then proceeds.

As stated in the introduction, the proceedings are flexible and informal. Either party may go first by agreement or by direction of the tribunal. Each party presents their case in accordance with the structure indicated above.

Clarity

The case should be as clearly presented as possible. Misunderstandings, anomalies and ambiguities will always be drawn out and questioned by the tribunal members. In particular, the tribunal will try and establish as early as possible any issues concerning individual rights, the use of procedures, the application of natural justice and other matters concerning fairness and reasonableness.

Questions

Applicants, respondents and witnesses may all be questioned by the other party and by each of the tribunal members. This is informal and each party may pursue as many points as they wish to raise until they receive a satisfactory answer.

Other than questioning witnesses, all statements and remarks are addressed to and through the chairman.

From time to time the chairman may question the relevance of certain evidence or particular lines of questioning. The onus is on the case presenter to be able to give a clear response and indication of why the matter is relevant and should be pursued.

The chairman may also seek to curtail evidence or not to call some of the witnesses if he/she perceives that this is simply a re-statement of ground already covered or if he/she perceives that it has no particular bearing on the case. Again, the onus is on the presenter to show that this is not so.

In all cases, provided a reasonable and clear indication is given, the line of questioning will be allowed, the evidence will be heard, and the witnesses called.

The respondent's witnesses are led through their evidence in support of the case. They are then questioned by the applicant and tribunal members. The respondent may then ask additional questions if required.

The applicant's witnesses are led through their evidence in the same way. From the respondent's point of view, questioning of the applicant's witnesses will concentrate on:

■ any anomalies in their evidence
■ anything that is known or can be demonstrated to be untrue or misleading

■ bringing out any alternative point of view or conclusions from their evidence.

A key role of the minder is to concentrate on the evidence of the applicant and their witnesses, and to pick up the areas indicated.

No legal phraseology is necessary. If the question is not clear or pointed enough, the tribunal chairman will ask for clarification or even rephrase it him/herself.

Aggression

A tribunal chairman is normally extremely hard on anyone who harasses, bullies or pressurizes witnesses – in direct contrast to many court proceedings. Questioning should be forthright and assertive, but never aggressive. If the other party, or their representative, or witnesses become aggressive or adversarial, the tribunal will normally ask them to refrain. The only circumstances where aggression may be allowed to persist is to provide evidence of personality, or other clash or personalization of issues.

Balance of truth

Circumstances arise from time to time where the case hinges on the word of the applicant verses that of the respondent. Where this happens it is essential to stick to the truth and pick out any flaws in the applicant's case. Cases should never be embellished as this calls into question the integrity of the main point. The best course of action always lies in sticking to the merits of the case as presented.

Adjournments and interruptions

Those conducting cases should ask the chairman for adjournments when required. This mostly occurs where a point is raised that had not been previously considered. Adjournments give the opportunity to think the matter through and give a considered response. It is much better than giving an off-the-cuff reply to an awkward and unconsidered point.

Adjournments are also called by the tribunal at suitable points, such as breaks for lunch and tea, and at the end of the day (where the case is to run on).

Adjournments may also be requested by the tribunal at any point for the express purpose of asking the parties to retire to a private place and try and achieve a settlement.

Closure of proceedings

When each side has presented its case and called its evidence and witnesses, the hearing is closed. Each party may choose to make a closing statement. Each party may be asked additional questions by any or all of the tribunal's members. Each party will finally be asked whether there is anything else that they wish to say before the tribunal retires to consider the outcome of the case.

This is the last opportunity to raise points that have hitherto not been made or to emphasize matters that have not been given sufficient merit or consideration.

The tribunal then retires to consider the case. Their deliberations normally take between 15 minutes and two hours. The parties are then called back into the tribunal to hear the outcome and result.

The result of the application

Possible results are as follows.

In favour of the respondent

This means that the application or case has failed and is dismissed or has been withdrawn. It may also occur that the tribunal decides that the matter lies outside its jurisdiction.

In favour of the applicant

This can be either of the following:

■ **Reinstatement** This is ordered where the tribunal decides that the employer was overwhelmingly to blame for the occurrence and orders that the applicant be reinstated to their previous or current position without loss of earnings, prospects, pay, benefits or continuity of employment.
■ **Re-engagement** This is ordered where the tribunal decides that the employer was overwhelmingly to blame as above. Where it is not feasible or practicable to be reinstated to the previous or current position, the employer must find the applicant an equivalent or similar post, again with no loss of earnings, prospects, pay, benefits or continuity of employment.

Orders for reinstatement and re-engagement must be complied with. Failure to do so will lead to an additional compensatory award (see below).

Compensatory awards

Where there is no order for reinstatement or re-engagement the tribunal may award compensation as follows:

- **Basic awards** These are related to length of service and are normally equivalent to the sum the employee would have received if they had been made redundant. The maximum basic award in 1998 is £6,950.
- **Other compensatory and special awards** For unfair dismissal this is calculated on the employee's loss of earnings and other benefits that have been lost as a result of the dismissal up to a maximum of £13,500. For cases arising from racial and sexual discrimination, victimization and harassment, transfers, maternity rights and trade union membership or non-membership issues there is no maximum compensatory award. The tribunal may set whatever figure it deems appropriate to the circumstances (eg the British army has had to pay sums of between £17,000 and £300,000 to female officers who were dismissed due to pregnancy). There is also no maximum for awards made against employers who fail to comply with reinstatement and re-engagement orders (see above). Again, there is no maximum for awards made against employers who have been found guilty of discrimination in making offers of employment to candidates from outside the organization or making offers of promotion, prospects and opportunities from within.

At the time of their application, applicants must state whether they are seeking re-engagement, reinstatement or compensation.

At the hearing, the respondent may plead that it is not feasible or practicable to reinstate or re-engage. When arriving at a decision, the tribunal also takes into account all the employer's circumstances including size, state of activities, profitability (tribunals can ask for accounts, figures, budgets and other financial data to help them assess the case), numbers of employees, turnover and prospects for the future. Awards made against organizations are normally based on their ability to pay – it is not the tribunal's purpose to bankrupt anyone.

Deferral

The tribunal may defer its decision for some reason. This mostly occurs where the members fail to reach a unanimous decision. It may also occur where a point has been raised on which the tribunal is not satisfied and wishes to consider further before arriving at a final decision.

It may also occur for some other reason – especially where a key witness or piece of evidence was not present. In these cases the tribunal is adjourned until such time as they become available.

The tribunal may also widen its consideration to include other matters that become apparent during the hearing. For example, an unfair dismissal case may be broadened if it becomes apparent that there are also matters of discrimination, victimization or harassment present that should be considered.

Notification

The parties to the case receive written confirmation or notification of the result of the tribunal normally within 14 days of the hearing. This includes a formal statement of the decision, together with either a full statement of reasons for the decision, or a summary of the reasons for the decision. Where a summary only is issued, either or both parties may request a full written statement and this is always forthcoming.

CONCLUSIONS

The material contained in this chapter constitutes the basis on which all effective tribunal cases are prepared. It involves understanding the remit and jurisdiction of tribunals, the rights of individuals, the boundaries of employment law and the specific issues that this covers, and investigating and addressing specific complaints and applications. Only if this is all understood, can an effective defence and response be offered.

The material contained also reflects required standards and the highest current levels and approaches to the effective management of people. Understanding the importance of staff management and employee relations as a key to effective work practice is vital. It contributes directly to effective resource usage and therefore to profits; where staff management and employee relations are poor or inadequate these act as a drain on resources and therefore on profits and effectiveness.

Knowing the general state of organization staff management and employee relations and the ways in which managers and supervisors conduct themselves is critical. The attitudes and values of managers and their perceptions of the importance of this aspect of their work must be created and formed in such a way that they adopt these high standards of principles and practice so that tribunal cases are kept to an absolute minimum.

This knowledge also enables proper judgments to be made on all employee relations and staff management issues, whether or not they come before tribunal. Knowledge and understanding are counters to ignorance, received wisdom, prejudice, misunderstandings and problems – and crises and traumas – which otherwise arise.

Individual employment rights must be acknowledged and upheld – especially the rights of individuals to be treated fairly and with dignity and respect in work, as in all other walks of life. This puts pressures on employers in terms of management and supervisory training, design and use of procedures, and the need to consult and provide information. It also means adopting specific professional standards and practices when making appointments and promotions, giving opportunities, setting and maintaining standards of behaviour, conduct and performance, and dismissing staff and terminating employment.

If cases, in spite of all this, do come to tribunal, preparation is everything, however simple or straightforward the matter may appear. Anyone conducting a tribunal case on behalf of their employer must know and understand the material, the background, the reasons why the case arose in the first place and the reasons for its progress to this stage. They must also be fully familiar with the situation and matters of organization politics, the personalities involved and any specific personal, professional or occupational factors that have a bearing on the issue.

A well-ordered case, adequately presented, will always succeed ahead of a haphazard and insubstantial case presented by a great orator or demagogue.

Preparation enables whoever is involved to make an informed initial and continuing judgment on the merits of particular cases. This is vital in all cases; it is critical at the extremes. If the application is frivolous, vexatious or malicious, effective preparation and presentation will quickly demonstrate this to the satisfaction of ACAS at the conciliation stage or a pre-hearing assessment, and the applicant can then be requested to withdraw. If, on the other hand, the organization is being asked to defend a hopeless case, this too becomes apparent sooner rather than later and those concerned at least know what they are up against.

Adequate preparation also enables gaps in knowledge and understanding to be identified. Nobody should ever be afraid to seek help. Assistance is quickly, readily and often freely available, especially from ACAS, the Department for Education and Employment, the Health and Safety Executive, the Commission for Racial Equality, the Equal Opportunities Commission and the Disablement Resettlement Officer. Professional and expert bodies, associations and trade unions are also normally at hand to provide quick and effective advice to their members. Lawyers, consultants and other experts are available on a commercial basis as with all other aspects of working life.

The final point concerns avoidance. All employers and their managers and supervisors should understand the boundaries of the law and the general rights of individuals at work. The adoption of best practice, fairness and reasonableness, honesty and integrity in all dealings with employees enables the chances of having to appear at tribunal to be kept to a minimum. Nobody can prevent an application being made. If these principles have been followed, all applications can be dealt with quickly, effectively and successfully.

8

EMPLOYEE RELATIONS MANAGEMENT: THE DESIGN OF ORGANIZATIONAL ER

INTRODUCTION

As with all organizational activities, ER has to be designed. A clear commitment to purpose has to be determined, a broad, yet specific, direction decided upon, and frameworks and institutions put in place to ensure that it is carried out effectively.

Organizations and their managers design ER to suit their own particular purposes. This stems from their understanding and analysis of their organization in its environment, bearing in mind the nature, size, scale, scope and complexity of their operations. Design requires adopting the desired perspective and understanding the approaches necessary for successful implementation, organization, direction and development of ER.

EMPLOYEE RELATIONS DESIGN

Effective and successful ER design consists of the following:

- **Policy and standpoint** This is the cornerstone of the approach, and is clearly and unambiguously presented at the head of every ER agreement, so that everybody involved knows why the agreement has been made, and what it is to achieve for the staff, and for the organization as a whole.

■ **Recognition** Fundamental rights, duties, obligations and commitments are stated and confirmed. 'Recognition' also refers to any recognized trade unions by name or, where unions are not recognized, it refers to staff representatives, staff consultative committees or the equivalent.

■ **Boundaries** The best ER designs state clearly what is covered in the particular situation, and – either overtly or by omission – what is not covered. The best designs also state clearly overall standards of performance, attitudes and behaviour required and expected. They also make specific reference to fundamental principles of equality and fairness in all aspects of activity.

■ **Coverage** In general, all ER is concerned with organization discipline and strategies for the management of conflict. It also includes health and safety, pay bargaining, meetings with unions and staff representatives, committee structures, participation and consultation machinery and the management of disputes and grievances.

■ **Context** This is the way in which each aspect of the coverage is set out. The purpose is to define the approach to each of the areas covered, which matters are genuinely negotiable, which areas are matters for consultation, discussion and other means of exchanging general information, which areas are the sole remit of management, what matters may be raised by unions and/or staff representatives, and under what headings, when, where and how.

■ **Aura** This is a summary of the overall approach and design. It becomes apparent from the reading of organizational documentation, and of ER in practice at the workplace (see Summary box 8.1).

■ **Communication systems** These define whether ER is to be largely formal or informal, and what means are to be used. This includes definitions of briefing systems, newsletters, staff consultation, participation and negotiation activities. This again, is likely to help define the overall ER remit of senior management, management representatives, union and other staff representatives.

■ **Committee systems** These define what committees are to be constituted for ER purposes and how they are to operate. Some organizations are required by law to have works councils, or to bring them in by certain dates, and the EU is at present determined that this requirement is to be extended. Other organizations decide upon, and constitute, joint consultative committees, joint negotiating committees, safety committees and other staff consultative committees and fora for their own purposes (see Summary box 8.2).

Summary box 8.1   ER aura and climate

The aura or climate of ER remains a constant feature, and yet is equally as constantly difficult to define. Having in mind the desired aura is nevertheless fundamental to successful ER design and operation.

The ER aura is akin to organization culture. It is concerned directly with ER rather than organization culture overall. Some useful parallels may nevertheless be drawn.

The aura may be:

- designed – reflecting the particular standards required, expected and anticipated by all concerned
- emergent – in which the quality and value of ER activity is left to particular vested interests, and the ad hoc qualities, capability, expertise and interest of particular managers
- formal – in which everything is written down (clearly or otherwise) for the absolute guidance of all concerned, or where a clear set of guiding principles is written down, to which everyone is required to operate
- informal – often reflective of people or task cultures in that the prevailing culture is so positive that people know almost by instinct what is acceptable, and what standards are required; reflective also of power cultures where people come to understand the nature of the aura in relation to the centre of power
- strong – in which there are clearly understood ways of doing things, responding to crises, managing disputes and grievances
- weak – in which no clear organizational standards are set in these matters.

If this view is adopted, clearly it is highly desirable to have a strong and designed organization ER aura. It is true that others may be successful for a time and that, for example, a strong emergent aura may come to be recognized, by custom and practice, as the 'ways of doing things'. It may also be seen as:

- positive – where people know that they can act with the confidence that problems, disputes and grievances will not arise except where there are serious misunderstandings, and where they do arise, there is a commitment to resolve them as quickly as possible
- negative – where people are unwilling or even frightened to act for fear that, should they make a mistake, they will instantly be the subject of organization discipline.

Also when viewed in this way, it is apparent just how critical the ER aura is to the wider effective management of operations; and why therefore, it is necessary that organizations and their senior managers pay it so much attention.

Summary box 8.2   ER committee systems

Works councils

Works councils are bodies formally constituted by organizations. Representatives are drawn from all sectors of the workforce. The broad remit of works councils is to deal with employment issues on the same basis and status as shareholders and boards of directors (or governors of public bodies) deal with financial and operational issues.

The proposed European Company Statute takes this matter a stage further (see Chapter 2) in that companies constituted under this format will be required to address employee and employment concerns in exactly the same way as they address shareholder interests and financial and operational management issues.

It should also be noted that the concept of 'the social partnership' takes the standpoint that employee and shareholder interests are inextricably intertwined anyway – that long-term shareholder value can only be maximized and optimized if effective and productive workplace institutions, including a positive aspect to ER, are in place.

Joint consultative committee

Joint consultative committees are constituted, and exist, for the purpose of providing a formal means of information distribution. Staff – via their representatives – are kept informed of organizational strategies, plans and progress through this means, and matters are then discussed a) with a view to securing the cooperation of those involved in their implementation and b) with an exchange of ideas for their implementation, including seeking employee views as to the best way forward.

Joint negotiating committees

Joint negotiating committees (JNCs) exist for the stated purpose of negotiating those matters that are judged by the organization to be negotiable. Historically, JNCs were greatly concerned with pay bargaining, and especially the annual pay round. The subject of negotiations – and the concept and practices of collective bargaining that go with it – are dealt with later in this chapter. Formally constituted JNCs work to negotiate settlements on specified issues acceptable to all.

JNCs become cumbersome or unworkable when timetables for specified negotiations drift or when matters not specified for negotiation nevertheless somehow become negotiable. In these cases, it is very difficult to prevent trade unions and/or staff representatives from seeking to push back the boundaries of what is negotiable as far as they possibly can.

Staff consultative committees

Staff consultative committees exist a) alongside committees where unions are represented in organizations that recognize unions and b) as the main fora for consultation and negotiation where unions are not recognized. Again, the remit and purpose of the committee must be precisely specified. Where unions are recognized, many organizations and their managers perceive staff consultative committees as a useful additional forum; this is especially the case since the Employment Act 1988 when the 'closed shop' was outlawed. If a staff consultative committee is also constituted, it confirms to the staff that they are being treated equally, whether or not they are a member of a recognized trade union.

Safety committees

Safety committees are constituted for the express purpose of monitoring and evaluating the health and safety record of the organization and its particular activities, for pinpointing problems and for providing general advice and guidance to the organization concerning improvements in these areas. They work most effectively when they have a precise remit, a good deal of authority on which to conduct their affairs and the power to make recommendations that the organization undertakes to follow. They are less effective when they work purely in an advisory function.

Other committees

Organizations may also choose to constitute other committees according to their own particular needs. It is quite usual to provide, for example, joint shopstewards committees (where more than one union is recognized), joint management and supervisory boards (where large, diverse and complex employee relations are being conducted), technology implementation committees (for the express purpose of managing the ER and employment relations side of technological changes, work practice changes, changes in shift patterns and working hours), work improvement groups and quality circles (which have an express purpose of improving production and service quality, but which nevertheless enhance general staff and management relations).

■ **Written procedures and agreements** These define the stated terms of ER. They also imply certain terms and conditions and reinforce the ER aura. They cover:
  - substantive issues – the constitution of particular committees, regularity and frequency of meetings and prescribed agenda
  - operational issues – discipline, grievance, disputes, dismissal, training, safety, redundancy and redeployment

- procedural issues – which may be divided into two parts: a) procedures for electing representatives, officials and committee members and b) procedures for the conduct of disputes and other negotiations and activities (see Summary boxes 8.3 and 8.4).

Summary box 8.3   ER procedures 1: the importance of clarity

The ER agreement between Sanyo and EETPU (Appendix B) ran to 15 pages and covered all the activities and operations of a complex, dynamic and high quality industrial manufacturer when it was first constituted in 1982. In 1992, Kent County Council had a discipline procedure for the management of social workers that ran to 33 pages. In 1998, the East Kent Health Authority had a total ER procedure volume of 1200 pages. The more simple, clear and direct procedures are, the more capable they are of being understood and operated effectively.

Most important of all, simple procedures, fully understood and operated effectively, free up organization and managerial resources for primary organization purposes. Complex, convoluted, unclear – and inevitably contradictory – policies require the employment of expert staff to understand, advise on and operate them.

The best procedures are written in order to clarify standards and principles. The worst are written with the purpose of predicting and identifying every possible human situation, and the total range of possible responses. As a consequence, they always fail.

Summary box 8.4   ER procedures 2: the value of effective procedural agreements

The best procedural agreements define both deadlines for action or progress, and also the steps that are to take place at or within those deadlines.

At their best, they are an excellent discipline on both management and staff representatives of large complex organizations because they define and require progress to be made at a particular speed. They also regulate the conduct of disputes and conflicts so that if an issue is not resolved, everyone knows what the next step is and when it has to be taken.

Anything that is more complex than this tends to confuse. In the worst cases, this leads to discipline and grievance issues being needlessly dragged out. It also leads to pay bargaining rounds being delayed, and the consequent demoralization of the workforce.

■ **Role and function of union and staff representatives** The best designed ER policies state clearly the boundaries of these roles and functions, and the legitimate areas of interest and activity of all such representatives. Some organizations provide training for their representatives or insist that they undergo training (see above); trade unions also provide this, normally as a matter of course (see Summary box 8.5).

Summary box 8.5   The role and function of union and staff representatives

At its fullest, this role is highly complex and has its own very distinctive expertise. A staff representative is likely to be required to act as:

- advocate, for example, in discipline and grievance cases
- monitor, for example, in health and safety matters
- mediator, capable of understanding and representing all relevant points of view
- evaluator of company information and specific proposals
- proposer of issues and matters affecting those whom they represent.

In some organizations, the position of staff representative is effectively full time. In these cases, the individual involved is given the equivalent of a secondment away from their place of work for the period of their election. In others, organizations expect individuals to combine this role with their normal occupation.

There are no absolute guidelines for this. Ultimately, it is in the interests of everyone to have effective staff representation and representatives. It is a key part of organizational ER design to assess what is fair and reasonable in the circumstances, and this is necessary in each individual case.

■ **Trade unions** The question of trade union recognition has to be addressed at the ER design stage. The main issue concerns the overall remit – the extent of desired and legitimate union involvement. There is also the question of whether to recognize trade unions or not; different organizations and their managers will come to their own conclusions. There is the question of which unions to recognize (if any), and if more than one is to be recognized, whether the same overall remit is to be applied to each. Unions acceptable to the organization and its management may not be recognized, the remit and extent of staff consultative committees and other representative fora has to be addressed in the same way (see Summary box 8.6).

Summary box 8.6   Union recognition

Trade unions may be recognized for any or all of the following purposes:

- social partners, including a wide general consultative remit on all employment matters, as well as specific ER issues
- conduct of negotiations, in which specific items (especially pay) are negotiated and agreed between organizations and union representatives
- consultation, in which the trade union takes an active part in the exchange of information, and in the implementation of management policies and direction
- participation, in which the trade union representative acts as a general advocate, leader and director of employee wishes in particular matters
- training, in which training arrangements and training agreements are drawn up between organization and union representatives
- safety, in which union representatives have a key voice on safety committees and other institutions
- individual representation, in which union officials accompany employees on specific matters, especially when they are the subject of discipline or grievance issues
- group representation, in which the union representative acts as an advocate or proposer for the wishes of a particular work group
- representation of non-union members, which is increasingly being allowed by organizations, who take the view that it is better to have somebody with the individual who knows what they are doing, and understands the broader situation, than to risk subsequent difficulties (including tribunal cases) if the individual concerned is not properly or adequately represented or informed of their rights
- 'Fairness for All' (1998), which was published as a government White Paper. It sought to outline the boundaries within which trade unions were entitled to be recognized. The proposal was that an organization must recognize a trade union when 40 per cent of the workforce so desire. How this will eventually work in practice, however, is unclear. It is not clear, for example, whether the 40 per cent required must all want to belong to one union, or just to a union. It is also not clear whether the 40 per cent is to be a proportion of the total workforce or just of those voting.

- history and traditions: some organizations continue to recognize trade unions because there is a long history of trade unionism at their place of work and they understand, believe or perceive that to remove this trade union recognition would be both detrimental to their organization, and damaging to the general confidence of their workforce.
- single unions, which is the approach favoured by Japanese companies established in the UK (the Sanyo Agreement, Appendix B, is an example). The most serious problem with this is in finding a single trade union that enjoys the confidence of what is often a complex and diverse workforce.
- local officials: in unionised ER, a key relationship exists between the organization and its management representatives, and the local trade union full-time official. Both require mutual knowledge and understanding, and the inception and development of a professional and ultimately harmonious working relationship. However generally favourable relations between an organization and its trade union or unions are, the presence of an inappropriate full-time official can seriously damage this situation. Conversely, where institutional relationships are rocky, the presence of an expert and committed full-time official can ensure that the difficult passage is successfully traversed, and effective institutional relationships established in the future.

The outcome of the design is a framework for the conduct of workplace ER. As well as being strategically suitable for its stated purpose or purposes, it must be acceptable to, and understood by, everyone concerned and affected. It should be included as a key feature of staff induction programmes, management and supervisory training, and staff briefings.

It also must be designed on the basis that, as the organization changes, so must ER. All policies, frameworks and organizational designs must be capable of improvement, refining and streamlining, and in this respect ER is no different.

The design of ER has further key features as follows:

- the management of works councils
- the management of trade unions (where these are recognized)
- the management of consultation and participation
- the management of negotiations (including collective bargaining).

THE MANAGEMENT OF WORKS COUNCILS

As stated above, works councils are a legal requirement of organizations with more than 1000 employees and/or which operate in two or more EU countries; their purpose may be summarized as representing employee and employment interests, in the same way that boards of directors (and governing bodies for public institutions) represent financial and shareholder interests.

In genuinely unitary organizations, acceptance of organizational values, attitudes and standards is a key to effective employee relations and, so long as properly constituted and organized, the works council plays a key role. In genuinely radical organizations – where staff own and control the means of production – there is absolutely no conflict between financial and employment interests.

In pluralist organizations, constitution of an effective works council depends on the organization's capability to reconcile the divergent and conflicting interests into an effective representative body. In the UK, the most vociferous resistance to works councils – and therefore to the placing of employee interests on a par with financial concerns – comes from large, complex and diverse organizations where shareholder interests have always been paramount. There is also resistance from very small organizations, which tend to perceive the imposition of works councils as being an additional layer of bureaucracy and administration. Employer representatives, especially the Confederation of British Industry, the Institute of Directors and the Federation of Small Businesses, have lobbied hard against the introduction of works councils, and until 1997, it was UK government policy not to force their introduction under the 'opt-out' from the European Social Charter.

When the UK Labour government came to power in 1997, it signed the Social Charter; and also the Treaty of Amsterdam. The principle of establishing works councils is therefore enshrined.

Design and constitution of works councils

The first step in this part of effective ER management is to ensure that the works council is both representative of all employee interests, and also that its remit is both suitable and effective in a particular set of circumstances. Design of the works council may be carried out by:

■ the organization, normally in consultation with its employees and their representatives, in order to establish a format that is feasible and workable

- a special negotiating body, or project group, which is charged with this task and has been established especially to do it.

The constitution, remit and agenda of the works council are therefore established in either of these ways. The precise approach and the way in which items are covered, is unique to each organization. Overall, the issues for legitimate concern are:

- financial plans and company structures
- acquisitions, mergers, takeovers, investments, divestments and withdrawals
- closure and redundancy
- transfers
- changes in work practices
- the introduction of new technology, and the training schemes that go with this
- changes in working hours and work patterns
- redeployment and changes in location
- payment and incentive schemes, including profit-related, performance-related and company employee share schemes
- the relationship between sales, profits, prices and employee reward and remuneration
- the operation of HR and personnel policies
- health and safety at work
- recognition of trade unions, including recognition of specific trade unions
- the roles and functions of all employee representatives, including members on negotiating and consultative committees and health and safety committees
- long-term human resource strategies
- factors concerned with organization and performance development and improvement
- organization discipline
- the source, management and control of conflict and disputes, including the standards by which different disciplinary actions are determined.

The constitution and composition of the works council varies between organizations. It normally ensures adequate coverage of the following:

- direction and senior management, including adequate representation of the perspective of the board of directors
- human resource and employee relations specialists
- representation of recognized trade unions

- representation of work groups not represented by trade unions
- representation of all sites and locations in which the organization operates (for large organizations, a separate works council may be required for each site)
- specialist input from, for example, health and safety representatives or those with responsibility for consultation
- adequate representation of part-time, shift, and other members of staff who work irregular or non-standard patterns.

Advantages of works councils

As stated above, the institutions of the EU and its forerunners have always held the belief that the views of employees and their representatives were a major contributor to economic and financial performance. Other advantages claimed for the effective operation of works councils include the following:

- It requires management to seek consensus with employee representatives on strategic and operational issues.
- It is a means by which problems and issues can be raised early, and is therefore a major contributor to the avoidance of industrial action.
- It gives the employees a stake and responsibility for the continued well-being of the organization.
- It gives the employees a stake and responsibility in arriving at agreement on their major areas of concern – work methods and patterns, pay and reward, the constitution and operation of procedures.
- Changes in work practices, working methods and technology can be more easily introduced, since employees will be used to proposals in these areas from an early stage, and will have had their opportunity to have their input into how these are to be successfully achieved.
- It is an open and legitimate forum for the exchange of information and ideas – and therefore breaks down physical barriers, problems of alienation between ranks and hierarchies in the organization, and between different work groups, departments, divisions and locations.
- It encourages a human as well as professional and occupational relationship.

Disadvantages and criticisms of the works council system

In the UK, the practice of works councils is neither well known, nor well documented. Apart from anything else, therefore, organizations have tended to resist the introduction of works councils on the grounds that 'this is not the British way of doing things'.

Otherwise, the disadvantages cited are as follows:

■ They add an additional administrative and cost burden.
■ It is perceived that employees may not understand broader strategic perspectives and directions (though there is no empirical evidence to support this).
■ Employees may adopt short-term perspectives, especially if they see the long-term future as being uncertain.
■ Operational problems arise where the works council fails to arrive at consensus. If matters ever get put to a vote, then it is possible that 'block votes' can be lobbied.
■ Redundancy and lay-offs may be difficult to agree, due to resistance on the part of staff representatives.
■ It is possible to get bogged down in issues that should remain at departmental, divisional, functional, operational or location level.

The effective management of works councils requires that the potential disadvantages are addressed. The constitution, remit and agenda must be devised so that these issues can be overcome. It is also necessary to recognize that, as a general forum for the exchange of information, the works council must be constituted so that this can take place adequately and effectively, so that everyone involved may have their say, and carry out the representations that they are required to do by the particular interest that they represent. Individuals involved must be afforded the time and authority to report back to those whom they represent.

More generally, the works council is a fountain of information that will be disseminated ultimately to the whole organization. Where dishonest, dubious or expedient practices are being contemplated (especially by top management, but also by trade unions and other vested interests), this will immediately become apparent. As well as being a vehicle for openness therefore, the works council also ensures that the worst excesses of all special and vested interest groups is made public at an early stage, and their influence limited.

THE MANAGEMENT OF TRADE UNIONS

Where unions are recognized, they have legal rights of access to the workplace and obligations to their members. Provided they conduct themselves in accordance with trade union law (see Chapter 2), they may not be required to pay costs or charges incurred by the organization as a result.

Strategically, the key feature is mutual confidence between union and organization. Where many unions are recognized, effective ER can only take place if there is mutual confidence. This has to be seen in the context that different unions inevitably have different priorities and objectives (see Summary box 8.7).

Summary box 8.7   The changing role of trade unions

Trade unions were once perceived to be all-powerful, heavily represented as they were in primary and secondary industry in the UK. During the 1950s and 1960s, they also came to gain both membership and influence in the commercial service sector (eg banks) and public services sectors (eg nursing and teaching, as well as administrative, professional, technical and clerical staff and manual grades). By 1969, there were 14.7 million members of trade unions affiliated to the Trades Unions Congress.

Influence was thus derived from the sheer number of members. Trade unions also had a substantial voice in government, shaping industrial, commercial and public services policy, as well as representing the specific interests of their members. The trade unions have always been the main backers of the Labour Party (though there are many signs that this is likely to change) and, thus, always had a substantial voice in Parliament. Trade unions, and their leaders, gained substantial media coverage during the 1960s and 1970s. The large scale of many disputes was also widely covered on television and elsewhere in the media. Trade unions also enjoyed immunities from prosecution and being sued for damages by organizations affected by an industrial dispute, provided that it could be demonstrated to be in pursuit of a legitimate trade dispute. To a great extent these immunities remain, and they remain, in any case, provided that procedures are closely followed during the conduct of a dispute.

During the 1950s and 1960s, a perception of union strength and managerial weakness grew among organizations and their managers. This was partly due to the fact that trade unions trained their representatives. It was also partly due to prevailing demarcation and restrictive practices that meant that one part of a process or service could

---

be shut down in pursuit of a legitimate trade dispute. It should also be noted, however, that organizations and their managers invariably encouraged collective bargaining processes – and therefore strong trade unions – in the interests of managing groups of staff.

Much of this influence has since declined and trade unions have sought alternative roles. Some attribute the decline in union influence to political and legal changes that took place in the UK under the Conservative governments of the 1980s. More important when understanding the decline in trade union influence, are the job losses in primary and secondary industry where trade unions were traditionally strong and the replacement of these jobs through companies that adopt different ER strategies. In many of the 'new sectors' there is no history of trade union involvement and many organizations have chosen not to recognize trade unions. Union membership density (ie the proportion of people remaining in trade unions) in public services remains high at 56 per cent in 1998.

The following have also added to the decline in trade union influence:

- There have been great changes and improvements in management training. It has been recognized that both management in general, and ER in particular, are key qualities, requiring distinctive expertise to be carried out effectively.
- There have been changes in union objectives and priorities. Above all, this has meant moving away from macro, political and media influence, towards concentrating on individual benefits and, especially, individual representation for employees.
- There have been changes in management approaches to trade unions. This is exemplified, above all, by the single union and single table approaches identified in Chapter 1. Each of these has sought to streamline procedures, reduce the complexity of ER activities and remove or minimize the inherent causes of conflict. Alongside this has been the requirement for organizations and their managers to pay much greater attention to the importance of ER, and the contribution that it makes to the successful running of activities. This has, in turn, led to enhanced management training.

Operationally, the key feature is the relationship between the organization and the union(s). Especially, this concerns the professional and personal relationships between organization management and ER representatives, and designated union full-time officials.

Behaviourally, the key feature is the confidence with which the members feel that they are being represented. Ultimately, it is vital to all that this is maintained. Organizations do not want to be in the position of making agreements and consulting with unions if their staff have no confidence in their union representatives or officials. Staff also do not want representatives who make agreements that they know, believe or perceive are not in their best interests in the circumstances.

Once recognized, unions and their representatives have legitimate areas of concern and involvement in the following:

- **Individual representation** This is undertaken in disputes, grievances, disciplinary, dismissal, accident and injury cases. Union representatives may not be refused access or involvement when cases falling under these headings take place.
- **Group representation** Where the agreement allows for it, and in terms of the remit, framework and design indicated above, unions have specific rights to participate in works councils, joint consultative and negotiating committees. They may also legitimately undertake collective bargaining where this is a part of ER policy.
- **Information** Unions should be provided with as much general information as possible, simply so that they understand as fully as possible the nature of the organization with which they are dealing, and the other pressures under which it is operating (eg commercial or financial market). Unions are not entitled to receive commercially sensitive information or trade secrets except where they can prove that they do need to know these for a particular reason (eg where they are representing a member disciplined or dismissed for allegedly misusing sensitive information, it would be legitimate for a union to know what the information was, though they would be required not to publicize it further, and may be liable to civil prosecution if they then did so).
- **When representing groups or individuals, unions are entitled to the full facts of the case.** It is illegal to withhold material information. Unions may, in certain circumstances, be entitled to see the complete personnel file of their members. The general point of view is that the greater the information available, the greater the chance of mutual understanding, and the greater the chance of problems and issues being resolved quickly and effectively.
- **The right to conduct disputes** This includes recourse to industrial action, provided that this is in support of a 'legitimate trade dispute' (see Summary box 8.8).
- **The right to facilities suitable for the purposes for which they are recognized** This normally includes office space. It may also include equipment – desks, filing cabinets and computers, and secretarial and administrative support. At times when formal disputes are engaged, organizations must make available to unions the means and time to consult with their members on the facts of the case (it is

also legitimate for employers to present their own view to their employees through channels of communication other than those afforded through the union).

Summary box 8.8   Forms of industrial action

The forms of industrial action that unions may use in pursuit of a legitimate trade dispute are as follows:

- **Official strikes** These take place after ballots have been held and notice given, in accordance with the law. The main point for managers to understand is that, because of the legal constraints and shifts in attitudes to official strikes, this action now only takes place where there is a serious misunderstanding or breakdown of relationships, or a serious employee grievance (see also Chapter 5 for a discussion of the management of conflict).
- **Unofficial strikes** These are far less prevalent than in previous times. When they take place, employers have recourse to law in the prosecution of those involved and the ability to sue trade unions for losses incurred. They may also discipline and dismiss the strikers. In the pursuance of this, however, it is essential to remember that normal effective and profitable relationships have to be retrieved after the dispute is settled. Any legal or punitive action contemplated is therefore ideally to be thought of as an aid to restoring normal relationships and this is certain to be the case in some circumstances. In others, however, it needs to be treated with great caution and should only be considered following a full review of the broader situation, and especially of the real causes of the unofficial strike.
- **Working to rule** This used to be a favourite form of industrial action. It was extremely disruptive in those organizations and industries where rule books effectively instituted overtime and other fringe allowances. It was also extremely disruptive where rule books were inadequately or incompetently drafted. It is much less of an issue now because there exists a greater organizational and managerial understanding of – and expertise in – the purpose and aims of rules and operational procedures.
- **Overtime bans** This again used to be a favourite form of industrial action in the UK. Again, it is much less common than in previous times. It remains a problem where overtime is institutionalized, expected or accepted as the norm.
- **Implied duties** This is where staff refuse to carry out any activities not precisely specified on their contracts of employment or job descriptions. It is currently used extensively by, among others, teachers, doctors and nurses, refusing to fill in forms or complete paperwork returns.

- **Short strikes** These are where the staff involved in a particular dispute withdraw their labour or expertise – either on a group or individual basis– for very short periods of time. The usual forms are:
  - striking for periods of between half an hour and three hours, either on a group or rotating individual basis. This is a preferred form of action, for example, among those teaching in schools and colleges. It also means additional complex work for their employing authorities in making precise calculations of the amount of salary to be stopped;
  - striking for periods of one day, either on a group or rotating individual basis. This is a preferred form of action in the road, rail and air transport industries and in some public utilities. Again, it also means additional complexities for organizational management, because at the end of the dispute further disruption is invariably caused because the coaches, lorries, trains and planes are in the wrong place to recommence work to schedule.
- **Human contact** This is where relationships between the protagonists are purely formal, and no 'human warmth' is permitted. Insignificant in theory, it is extremely demoralizing in practice.

Each of these may be legitimately called by trade unions, provided that they follow the procedures required by law. Failure to follow procedures instituted in rule books normally leads to organizations contemplating legal action against their recognized trade unions.

It should also be noted that there is extreme potential in all these forms of industrial action for serious damage to be caused to both structural, and inter-group employee relations.

Advantages of recognizing trade unions

These are as follows:

- **History and tradition** People in many occupations are used to being represented by unions, and they expect this virtually as a basic condition of work, for example, at Ford, Vauxhall and also the new car companies Nissan, Toyota and Honda. In these latter cases, the companies have newly constituted workforces who are, however, drawn from those who used to work in traditional industries before they were closed down, and where there was a history of extensive trade union involvement.
- **Prestige** In some sectors and organizations it is considered a mark of prestige to have unions representing the workforce or particular parts of it, for example, the Royal College of Nursing in National Health Service and private hospitals, the British Airline Pilots

Association representing staff at airlines and the Professional Footballers' Association representing the wider interests of a perceived elite group of employees.

■ **Organizational confidence** Some companies, for example, Sanyo, Sony, Nissan, and other Asian companies inwardly investing in the UK, are so confident of the quality and integrity of their organizational ER that they are totally happy having the staff represented by an outside and independent body. They see this as being preferable to creating an in-house union, staff association, or other form, where independence might be questioned if there were hard decisions to be made.

■ **Simplicity and directness** Many organizations take the view that it makes sense to conduct ER on a collective rather than individual basis, because if they do it effectively, it is much less time and resource consuming and is perceived as fair to everyone affected.

■ **Employee benefits** Unions are able to offer a wide range of employee benefits including training, health schemes, pension schemes and financial benefits (eg visa cards at reduced rates) as well as individual representation (effectively a form of employment insurance akin to private health insurance). Each of these is attractive in some circumstances to different types of employees.

■ **Watchdog** Here, the union, because of its independence, is able to raise broader issues of legitimate concern, both with the organization and, where appropriate, elsewhere (eg the media).

Disadvantages of trade unions

Disadvantages and criticisms of trade unions include the following:

■ **Best practice** The best employers take the view that, as they have removed all the reasons why people historically needed or wanted to join a trade union, they have no need to have them along at all.

■ **History and tradition** Many employers (and also employees) point to the failure of trade unions to secure the long-term future of employment for their members. They cite heavily unionized former industries in support of this, for example, printing, docks and engineering.

■ **Bureaucracy** Many employers take the view that unions create proliferations of committees, paperwork and organizational support functions (eg specialist human resource and ER departments that would not otherwise be necessary).

■ **Inertia** Many employers take the view that unions act as a barrier to progress. They are concerned with defending the status quo and their own vested interests, rather than securing the long-term future of the organization.

■ **Politics and prejudice** This is reflected in views to the effect that unions (in the UK at least) are 'all communist', 'the Vanguard of the Red Army', 'the enemy within', or 'concerned with global revolution', and so on. To some extent, some of these views persist.

■ **Multi-unionism** Trying to harmonize the divergent agenda and priorities of different unions that were recognized was a managerial nightmare, and was too resource-consumptive in terms of managerial and organizational time, energy and finance.

■ **Watchdog** Many organizations remain of the view that instead of being a legitimate watchdog and monitor of broader interests, trade unions will engage media interest on spurious and self-seeking grounds, rather than in the interests of organizations and those members of staff that they represent.

It is clear from this that the effective management of trade unions in ER is concerned with designing and arranging the remit under which they are to operate, if they are to be recognized. In the UK, trade unions have lost much of their national influence, while at the same time, expertise in the organization and management of ER has greatly increased. There is also no particular history and tradition of trade unionism in 'the new industries' of the UK – especially retail, tourism, financial and other services. Some organizations – for example, Marks & Spencer, Virgin, Body Shop – have gone to great lengths, and have made substantial investment, in removing the reasons why people would normally have joined trade unions from their ambit or operations. It remains true, however, that inward investors – especially from the Far East – continue to recognize and value the role and contribution of trade unions, both to ER in particular, and to their organization at large.

The EU view of trade unions as social partners – as both a legitimate interest in the overall management of organizations and as a key representation of the employees as stakeholders – must, however, be recognized. This has to be seen in the context that the EU is certain to require all employers to take an increasingly broad view of their responsibilities to their employees and, at present, they see trade unions in all member states as having a major function in ensuring that this happens.

The key to effective management of trade unions, and to ensuring that they make a positive and enduring contribution to workplace ER in particular, and to the continued well-being of the organization in general, is communication. In the best organization–union relationships, a genuine professional relationship is generated, akin to that with any other legitimate priority stakeholder. Formal channels of communication are expressly designed for particular purposes and developed, streamlined and updated as necessary. The quality of communication is consistently high, two-way, and founded on mutual interest. A facility for instant or near instant telephone communication is also available at all times, so that if an emergency or crisis does occur, a mutual understanding of the situation can be arrived at quickly, as a precursor to speedy, fair and effective remedial action.

THE MANAGEMENT OF CONSULTATION AND PARTICIPATION

Consultation and participation takes place at a variety of levels, and through a range of means (see Summary box 8.9). The precise mix – and quality – varies between organizations. Some, or all, of the following are normally present:

- departmental, divisional, functional and locational briefing groups
- addresses by top and senior management, including question and answer sessions
- staff meetings, which may be short and frequent, or less frequent, long and substantial
- macro meetings – akin to works councils, even if not formally constituted as such
- work improvement groups, quality improvement groups, quality circles – while not necessarily constituted for ER purposes, they remain an effective forum for dealing with ER issues when they do arise
- feedback and focus groups – either generally constituted or else for particular purposes
- problem-solving groups – of a special value when changes in technology or work practice are being contemplated
- professional, technical, expert and managerial cluster groups
- project groups and organization development activities (see Summary box 8.10).

Summary box 8.9   Consultation and participation: employee involvement

I always think we complicate the affairs of industry in respect of employer–employee relationships by creating too much mystique. People are beings with emotions, fears, desires, hopes, in whatever situation – their homes, their leisure, the places where they work. Why, therefore, we have to complicate our relationships at work has always been beyond my understanding. If people feel involved and know that they matter, of course they will respond. Belonging is a basic need of every human being. I am sure very often it is the remoteness of relationships in industry which cause problems.

Experience has taught me that communications are vital and are generally good within well-organized companies. To my mind, the spoken word is the best method of communication because sooner or later, it leads to understanding. Communication in whatever form must be simple, understandable and truthful. It must be regular, on-going and personal. Unless this is so, joint decision taking is impossible because if we reach the stage where a joint decision is necessary, and we are still thinking of them and us in industry, we have failed to reach a basic understanding and a joint decision becomes a travesty.

We must beware of the trap of thinking that because we have been talking to one another we are necessarily in harmony. The main purpose of communication is to bring people closer together, but if we just talk with no intention of seeing the other person's point of view, we are deceiving ourselves. We must make sure we all understand one another and come to a point of trust.

The route of good employee relations is belonging, and involvement through good communications.

Ron Nethercott, member of Transport & General Workers Union (1981)

There are so many really urgent problems that are facing us. Problems of unemployment, inflation, lack of investment – these are only some of the areas where we sometimes feel overwhelmed and need to grasp all the sources of help that are available to us. In industry, we have come increasingly to recognize the immensity of the contribution which employees can make if only we will involve them. And in involving them we are only recognizing the obvious fact that it is the people who are engaged in an enterprise who determine its success or failure.

Now, it is a fact also that management must manage. Equally, employee representatives recognize areas where it is their duty to participate. But in between these two areas there is third area which is neither managing nor is it participation. Here there is a great list of subjects which can be explored jointly, management with employees. This is an area where the skills of employees, their special abilities, their special workplace knowledge, can be harnessed to management's ability to organize and to finance. The result can only be for the good of both sides.

Paul Blake, general manager, May & Baker Ltd (1981)

Source: Baddelay, J (1981) *Understanding Industry*, Buttersworths/Industrial Society, London

---

Summary box 8.10 Consultation and participation development: Sealink UK

In 1993, the Sealink cross-Channel ferry company undertook an organization development project on board one of its ships operating between Dover and Calais, the 'Invicta'.

The project was designed to research customer perceptions and attitudes to the quality of each aspect of the service that they received while on board the ship and, from this, to make recommendations as to how this could be improved, in order to compete with the Channel Tunnel, which had just come into full commercial operation.

However, the results were mostly concerned with employee and employee relations. For the first time, a project group had been constituted that consisted of staff from different occupations – catering, security, ship's crew and officers, and information and public relations.

Improvements to customer service were recommended. The key contribution, however, was in the breakdown of barriers that had hitherto existed between the groups. Each now understood the constraints of the others and recognized the degree of isolation in which they all worked, and the problems that this created. As a result, mutual personal and professional confidence was built up. Effective means of communication, based on personal as well as professional contact were commenced. The effect was to reduce the number of disputes and grievances caused as the result of misunderstanding the priorities of the different groups.

Source: 'Sid's Heroes': Sid Joyner (1993) BBC/Open University 'Management In Action'

The consultation approach is not new (as seen by the dates of the quotes above); indeed, the principle of macro consultation and participation was enshrined in the European Coal and Steel Community Treaty of 1951, in which the concept of social partnership between organizations and their employees and trade unions, was first recognized. The range of issues covered may be as broad as the organization wishes to make it, and spin-offs in the development of employee relations and ER may be apparent from other activities (see Summary box 8.10 and also references to the Hawthorne experiments in Chapter 3). In general, however, a strategic approach to consultation and participation requires organizations and their top management to be prepared to open up all the secrets of the organization to their employees, with the purpose of gaining a greater understanding and mutuality of interest and direction.

Specific ER issues that arise are normally concerned with long-term employment prospects, potential for change in technology and occupation, changes in work patterns and hours of work, training and development programmes, and the improvement and streamlining of specific ER rules and regulations, procedures and practices.

Inevitably, there are also effects on this from broader consultation, such as the promulgation of information concerning markets, products and product development, service improvements, changes in customer demands and requirements, and changes in expectations of financial performance.

In the UK, there is still resistance to the principle of full consultation and participation. This is partly a traditional factor again ('it is not the British way of doing things') and there is some resistance as the result of this becoming an ever-firmer plank of EU social – and therefore ER – policy. Again, the resistance is especially strong among pluralist organizations, which admit a diversity and conflict of objectives, and which often tend to distinguish especially between financial and employee performance.

Disadvantages of consultation and participation

The disadvantages most often quoted, both by those organizations and views indicated above, and also by those who do not use the approach are as follows:

■ It is expensive in terms of time, especially management time.
■ It wanders from the point, which is about improved workplace ER (though this is easily remedied by designing a precise remit into the consultation and participation process).
■ It raises expectations, not all of which can be satisfied (see Summary box 8.11).
■ It blurs the divides between departments, divisions, functions and ranks in hierarchies.
■ It may throw up facts, beliefs and perceptions of inequalities in different locations of multi-site organizations, which management may then have both to justify and, where necessary, address, and may consequently be required to engage in costly strategic ER repositioning.

Summary box 8.11   Opposition to consultation and participation: examples

Example 1

The Chairman of a major global telecommunications company retired in 1995. In his retirement speech, he first thanked the shareholders, and the directors whom they had elected, for their continued confidence during what had been a successful period of financial performance. However, in the future development of the company, he went on to exhort his successors 'not to let the employees get ideas above their station'. This would, he maintained, represent a dilution of organizational purpose and be detrimental to financial performance. At the time, nobody questioned his wisdom, nor the point of view from which it was delivered.

Example 2

The Chief Executive of a large national airline was removed from office in 1982, as the result of impending bankruptcy. His approach to employee consultation and participation was simple and direct: 'We are not letting the monkeys run the zoo'.

   The Chief Executive gained himself a job at another large airline. He adopted the same approach to his employees as previously and, again, the airline went bankrupt.

Both points of view show a fundamental lack of respect for the energy, commitment and expertise of the staff who carry out the work. While not all opponents of consultation and participation exhibit the same contempt for their staff by any means, it is an issue which those who resist the approach have to overcome. Employees – where they are not consulted – tend to feel excluded from true identity with the workplace, and this is inevitably detrimental to long-term and enduring high levels of motivation and morale.

Advantages of consultation and participation

Proponents of consultation and participation advocate the total approach, fully institutionalized and supported by the organization, and cite the following advantages:

- It breaks down barriers, helps to remove alienation and psychological distance.
- It creates mutuality of interest, understanding, confidence and direction.
- It creates understanding of total direction and the place of each department, division, function, individual and group in that total direction.
- It brings serious problems and issues out into the open early, requiring senior management to face and tackle issues that perhaps they would rather not undertake.
- It acts as a counter to real or potential inertia that can occur when everything is strictly formalized.
- It builds inter-group, departmental, divisional and functional respect, esteem, value and regard.
- It enables wider human and professional knowledge and understanding.
- Once everyone understands that there are problems and issues to be faced, they can be tackled openly and quickly.
- It develops morale and motivation overall.

It is true that when this approach is first introduced, there are problems of raised expectations and continuing – as well as initial – organization commitment, and this has to be resourced. So long as the policy, purpose, direction and remit are made clear, its proponents argue its case as a key to the development of the organization as a whole, enhanced staff commitment to all aspects of their work, and a major feature of the advancement of effective and harmonious ER.

THE MANAGEMENT OF NEGOTIATIONS AND COLLECTIVE BARGAINING

Collective bargaining is a uniquely UK employee relations arrangement. Its purpose is to make collective (as distinct from individual) bargains or agreements on behalf of those involved. Collective bargaining takes place at industrial, organizational, plant, divisional and unit levels.

The key to effective collective bargaining is negotiation. The strength of the approach is that each party comes to the bargaining table with a clear view of what they want – for example, what level of pay is required or on offer, hours of work required or on offer, other terms and conditions of employment required or on offer. Its great weakness is that it tends overwhelmingly to be adversarial and time consuming. It is compounded by facts, beliefs and perceptions that, on the one hand what employees and their representatives demand is unreasonable in the circumstances, and that what employers and their representatives have to offer is designed to ensure that they keep the lion's share of whatever is available for themselves and their shareholders.

Collective bargaining is overwhelmingly about pay, terms and conditions of employment. It is concerned with the following:

■ **Substance** This is what is on offer or demanded, the context in which it is on offer/demanded and any other limiting factors – for example, increased work commitments in return for increased pay rates.
■ **Behavioural** This requires special attention to the forms, processes, rights and rituals of the situation, to matters of media presentation, to gaining the known or perceived moral high ground and to the use of forms of language in reaching agreement, and in implementing those agreements.

In this context, agreements are made as follows:

■ **At national level** Here, minimum pay, terms, conditions and performance rates are established, which give a clear guideline to all those in the sector.
■ **At regional or local level** The national minima may be topped up according to special local needs – the need to compete for scarce labour resources, the inability to recruit at minimum levels and so on.
■ **At organizational, divisional or plant level** The national minima are accepted and will again be topped up through specific attention to productivity, payments and targets, overtime requirements, specific issues concerning other work patterns – for example, shift work, part-time work or short time work.

Consideration of local factors gives rise to the phenomenon known as 'wages drift'. Wages drift upwards when specific local factors are applied. This is always taken into account by employers' associations at national level when they are establishing their agreed minima.

Negotiating

Whenever anyone concerned with effective ER enters into any form of negotiation, they must have their own aims and objectives and understand above all what their preferred outcomes are. In such cases, they will have in mind:

- their own 'dream' scenario, in which everything is settled on precisely their terms
- a baseline, below which they will not drop
- a field of negotiation in between the two, in which there is scope for agreement.

Those concerned should always prepare their own case, establishing what they are seeking, when, where, how and why. They need to know any constraints within which they have to act. They also need to be aware of any opportunities afforded by a wider consideration of the matter in hand. They must have an understanding (if not sympathy) with the position of the others involved, and of what they want, when, where, how and why, and of the substance, merits and demerits of their case.

Anyone who promises anything in a negotiation must be able to deliver it if it is agreed. If they do not, they simply cause much deeper conflict, and long and damaging mistrust (see Summary box 8.12).

Summary box 8.12   Labour negotiations: the education sector in the 1980s

In 1982, teachers in secondary schools and further and higher education colleges were told by the Department of Education that they would have to accept annual performance appraisal as part of their terms and conditions of employment. In return for this, the then Education Secretary, Sir Keith Joseph, promised all concerned a 15 per cent pay rise.

The proposal was accepted lock, stock and barrel by the trade unions representing the school and college teachers.

The offer was promptly withdrawn. To this date, no effective performance appraisal scheme exists in secondary schools and colleges. There was a widely held view – never denied – that the offer was made simply on the grounds that the Department of Education and Secretary of State were absolutely certain that it would be rejected, and that consequently school and college teachers could be portrayed as seeing themselves as above the constraints imposed on other people in other working situations.

Conducting effective negotiations also requires a complete understanding of the behavioural norms of the situation. If it is necessary to let someone have their say and if by doing so the process is advanced, then this must be allowed.

If there is a potentially explosive or extreme situation, all those involved must be able to deal with this; they must recognize where the crisis or outburst is likely to come from, and take steps to manage it if it does arise.

By understanding these factors, the creation of an effective environment for negotiations is possible. Those concerned must also have regard to any precedent set in the past, and to the implications of making agreements that may set further precedent for the future.

It is also necessary to be aware of the continuing need to work effectively and harmoniously at the same time as collective bargaining is being carried out. Even where the matter in hand may result in a serious dispute, this should not hide or obscure the basic requirement for the eventual promotion of a harmonious working environment.

Those concerned in ER negotiations therefore require strategic, tactical and situational awareness, empathy, judgment, situational understanding and the ability to communicate in the correct ways according to the nature of the situation.

Collective bargaining

Collective bargaining is the traditional process in the UK by which agreements between employers and employees, or their respective representatives, are made. Agreements may be at national, regional, local, sectoral, or plant and unit level. This may involve very senior and highly trained personnel at sectoral or national levels, and elected lay representatives at local levels.

Two separate strands can be identified – the substantive, or what is to be negotiated, and the procedural, or how it is to be done, and how procedures and other regulatory instruments are to be used.

Collective bargaining is based on mistrust and conflict – that is, that there is a fundamental divergence of interest between employers and employees. At stake, initially therefore, is a basis on which the two can agree to cooperate together at all. This is made more difficult or extreme where there exists a long history and tradition of workplace conflict.

Collective bargaining is a strategy and structure for the management of this conflict. Summary box 8.13 shows the ritualized nature of labour relations and bargaining. Much of the process is therefore stylized and ritualized, and anyone who wishes to operate it effectively must understand the importance of this. The purpose must be to use the instruments and the language involved to gain workplace agreements that at least contain conflicts that are inherent.

Summary box 8.13   Behavioural theories of labour relations

Walton and McKersie (1965) distinguish four interrelated processes. These are as follows:

- **Distributive bargaining** This is the classical collective bargaining process, involving the resolution of conflicts of interest. It includes a consideration of the costs, benefits and opportunities afforded by each side of an industrial dispute, the ability and strength of each party concerned, and the bargaining position, tactics and postures to be adopted. The process consists of assessing the opponent's standpoints and likely responses to particular moves, the use of tactics that influence the opponent's perceptions, the manipulation of the opponent's perceptions of his own position of strength, either by changing his views of the value of his own demands or by changing his view of the unpleasantness or unacceptability of the other side's proposals, affecting the costs of the disputes to one's own advantage, setting deadlines, 'final deadlines', 'final, final deadlines' and so on, and manifesting all of this in a degree of commitment that is necessary to ensure victory in the dispute. Finally, in such a situation it may or may not be necessary to demonstrate that one side or the other has won at the expense of the other; in such cases forms of words and other face-saving formulae may need to be devised.
- **Integrative bargaining** This is the process by which common or complementary interests are found and is the means by which problems are resolved in the interests of all parties concerned. In this way, both sides gain. The purpose is not to conduct a dispute but to find a means of resolving it in the interests of all concerned. The confrontational postures and stance indicated above do not form part of integrative bargaining. The process adopted rather uses a problem-solving model – that is, the identifying of the issue or matter of concern, searching for alternative solutions and extrapolating their consequences, and from this choosing a preferred course of action.
- **Attitudinal structuring** This is the process by which each side influences the attitudes of the participants towards the other. In this situation attitudes are formed and modified by the nature of the orientation that each party has towards each other and towards the matter in hand. This may either be competitive, whereby the parties are motivated to defeat or win the other over to their own point of view or individualistic, in which the parties concerned pursue their own self-interests without any regard for the position of the other, or it may be cooperative, whereby each party is concerned about the other as well as its own position. An extreme form of this may be a form of collusion, whereby the parties concerned form a coalition in which they pursue a common purpose possibly to the detriment of other groups within the organization.

- **Staff relations** The final matter to be considered here is the form of intra-organizational style of staff relations that is concerned to maintain a balance and equilibrium about the organization and to prevent issues from arising that affect this balance. The main part of this process is to ensure that people understand the true nature and strength of their own position, to ensure that people's expectations are met in such situations and to ensure that the two are compatible.

The bargaining framework

There is a broad bargaining framework to understand (see Figure 8.1):

- The first offer or claim is always made on the basis that it will be rejected (if for any reason it is accepted straight away, it generally causes resentment rather than instant satisfaction).
- There then follows a process of counter-offer and counter-claim, with each party working its way gradually towards the other.
- The content of the final agreement is usually clearly signalled before it is made, and the basis of what is genuinely acceptable to each party is signalled also.
- Serious disputes occur either when one side is determined not to settle or when there is a genuine misreading of the signals.
- Settlements reached are normally couched in positive terms in relation to all concerned, to avoid the use of words such as 'loss', 'loser', 'climb-down' and 'defeat', which have negative connotations for anyone associated with them, and tend to store up resentment for the future, and polarize attitudes for the next round of negotiations.

The following standpoints in the bargaining process may be usefully identified:

- It may be necessary to settle with one group or part of the workforce, at the expense of others.
- It may be possible to resolve problems to the satisfaction of all concerned.
- It may not be possible to satisfy everyone.
- It may be necessary to take a hard initial stance to try and persuade the other party to revise its expectations.

Part of the function of the process is also to structure the attitudes of each party towards the other, and to try and build impressions of honesty, trust, openness, firmness, reasonableness and fairness, as necessary. A fundamental credibility must also be established.

Substance and process	Other factors
Initial offer and response claim	Strategic nature of offer
Adoption of postures	Strength and validity of cases
Ritual: movements and processes	Strength of each party Morale of each party Attitudes of each party
Negotiations	Public sympathy and support
Further offers/responsibilities	Government sympathy and support
Basis of agreement	
Final offer/response	Media coverage

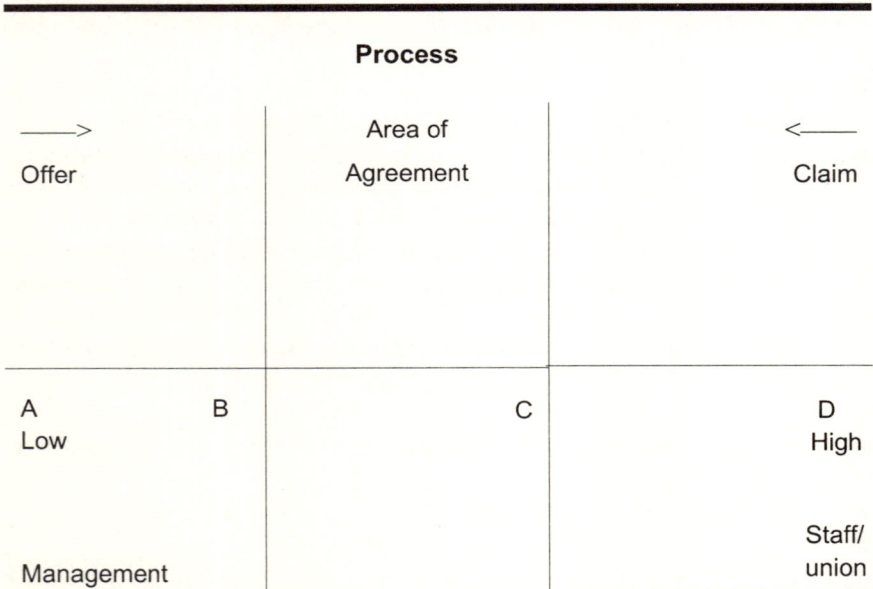

Process

——>		Area of		<——
Offer		Agreement		Claim
A	B		C	D
Low				High
				Staff/
Management				union

Figure 8.1 *The collective bargaining process: offers between A and B rejected by staff; between C and D instantly accepted by staff; claims between A and B instantly accepted by management; between C and D rejected by management; B–C is basis for negotiated settlement; normal first offer is around A, which leads to instant rejection; normal first claim is around D, but engages the process*

Objectives of bargaining systems

Within this context, collective bargaining systems have three specific objectives:

- to provide a means for agreeing the price of labour
- to provide a means of industrial governance and workplace rules and regulations
- to provide a means for controlling the stresses and strains inherent in any work situation
- to provide the means for resolving serious problems.

Formal and informal bargaining systems

There are both formal and informal systems to be considered. The former is constituted with agenda, objectives, purposes, outcomes, deadlines and timescales; the latter is the means by which the former is oiled, and consists of corridor meetings, contacts and networks that enable the formal system to function. Public services, municipal and local authorities and multinational companies tend to have both sophisticated formal procedures and highly developed networks also.

Work organization traditions

There are histories and traditions of work organization to be addressed also, either through the reformation of bargaining activities, or through the effective management of a wide range of employees' representatives and multi-unionism. All this has its origin in the differentiation of occupations, demarcation, restrictive practices and barriers to occupational entry, devised by groups of workers to protect their trades and give them a measure of exclusivity and allowed to grow by employers, partly because their need for staff was overwhelming, and partly also because they had no alternative to offer.

Employee expectations

Finally, there are employee expectations that have either to be met, or understood and dealt with. In the immediate past, employees have expected an annual percentage pay rise and improvement in conditions, devised partly to offset the effects of inflation – the 'annual pay round' is a feature of the industrial West. There have also arisen concepts of 'pay leagues', whereby a given occupation would offer terms and conditions of employment in relation to other occupations – to alter these 'leagues' generated resentment on the part of those occupations that perceived themselves to be moving down the 'table'. Closely related to this is the general concept of the 'going rate' for a job – the anticipation that, by joining a particular occupation, a known range of benefits will be forthcoming.

ER AND REALPOLITIK

In ER terms, this is the art of being effective in the total organization in which activities are being carried out. It requires full situational knowledge and understanding. From this, those concerned will devise their own means and methods of becoming effective.

They must be able to survive long enough to do this. It follows from this that they must understand and be able to work within the formal and informal systems of the organization and to establish their place in them (see Chapter 3). Especially in the informal system, they will need to find their own niches and from there go on and develop networks and support within the organization and its ER mechanisms. Large, complex and sophisticated organizations have many layers of informal organization, determined by profession, location, status, department and division, and people in such situations must discover those that are suitable, those that are unsuitable, those that are supportive and those that are antagonistic.

They will therefore develop a keen environmental sense. This comprises the ability to spot straws in the wind, to gain access to the grapevine, to become aware of particular and possible changes, developments, innovations and crises. It requires recognition of the departments, divisions, functions and individuals where actual power and influence truly lie. It also requires access to, and generation of, sources of information from within the complexities of the organization, and away from its formal channels.

Those concerned need to assess their own genuine position in the organizational pecking order and the extent to which they carry true influence in the process of creating effective ER. They will assess their own strengths and weaknesses in it, the sources of support, the sources and reasons of antagonism and jealousy, and the capabilities and capacities that are required in order to be effective.

They will identify where inter-group frictions (and sometimes hostility) lie and assess the reasons for these, and in the same way, identify where inter-group alliances are formed. It is necessary to assess where people's loyalties truly lie and whether they have their own secondary or hidden agenda. Especially in collective bargaining, and other traditional ER situations in the UK, it may be necessary to form alliances on the basis of 'if you support me in matter X, I will support you in matter Y', and so on.

It should be clear from this that the potential for organizational damage, and damage of relationships between individuals and groups within organizations, is extremely high. Much of the operation of collective bargaining, and the organization realpolitik that goes with it, is extremely negative (see Summary box 8.14). If it is not conducted as effectively as possible, given the extreme constraints indicated above, it is extremely demoralizing and debilitating, both on the staff and on the organizations, customers and clients. Ideally, when organizations recognize the problems and pitfalls inherent in these situations, it is necessary for them to take remedial steps, both in the short term to alleviate immediate problems and also in the medium to long term, to devise more effective and positive ER strategies.

Summary box 8.14   Collective bargaining and the EU

Many opponents of the collective bargaining approach to employee relations also tend to view the EU concept of 'social partners' with deep suspicion. There is a widely held view that the social partner approach is simply collective bargaining under another name.

There is no need for this to be the case. The EU standpoint, and language used, are both different. The EU cites a 'partnership', rather than a series of conflicting, divergent and entrenched self-interest groups. It also cites ER as being a key feature of overall organization direction and strategy, integral to commercial success and well-being, rather than as a separate – and costly – organizational activity.

Moreover, as the EU develops its social policy, the place of organizations within it, and the interests of employees, it is clear that these objectives are not to be achieved by recourse to traditional UK collective bargaining processes. The adversarial perspective is contrary to the view advanced by the EU and its institutions for the development of economic prosperity and social harmony. The partnership of the approach requires openness and mutuality of interest whereas the collective bargaining approach reinforces the divergence and divisions between the interests of particular groups.

CONCLUSIONS

The key to this part of the effective creation and management of ER is communication. It should also be recognized that, from whichever point of view these matters are addressed – consultation and participation, the involvement or not of trade unions, the use or not of collective bargaining – there is a large measure of agreement of the core issues that require attention. These are as follows:

■ Effective ER is based on agreements that everybody understands and accepts and on high quality, continuing and full information.
■ There must be adequate channels of communication.
■ There must be a recognition of the effect that broader organizational activities have on the development and advancement of ER.
■ There must be a recognition of the fact that, whatever the overall design of ER, its effective implementation can only be achieved if there is clear direction and precise principles of design on the part of the organization, and if effective institutions, procedures and practices are then generated so that it can be managed, maintained and improved on an operational basis.

9

EMPLOYEE RELATIONS MANAGEMENT: MOTIVATION, GROUPS AND INDIVIDUALS

INTRODUCTION

Whatever the soundness and reasoning behind the design of ER strategies and frameworks, they may only be successfully implemented if as full an understanding as possible of the motivation of people at the place of work is understood. It is necessary to consider this from the point of view of an understanding of the principles of motivation and the organizational factors and features that tend to contribute to, or detract from, individual and group motivation.

It is then necessary to develop this into a broader consideration of how groups and individuals function in places of work, the roles and priorities that they bring with them, and how these are best understood in the generation of effective employment relations. This is based on:

- a general appreciation of how human beings behave in particular situations and in response to their needs to satisfy and fulfil basic drives, instincts, needs and wants. Some of these are instinctive, others are the product of the civilization in which we live, and the organizations in which we work
- the effects of the organization and occupation held by the individual in terms of education, training, ethics, standards, aspirations, expectations and rewards

■ the nature of the work that is to be carried out: the total mix of work, the components of individual jobs, and the effects that these have, or are likely to have, on those who carry out the work. This includes attention to questions such as personal, group and organizational health and well-being, as well as the application of expertise

■ the wider standards and expectations of the relations between humans at the workplace. This includes relations within groups, relations between groups, and relations between individuals

■ the organizational culture, structure, style and ways of working: organizations cannot be all things to all people. They can only accommodate a range of divergent interests and aspirations among their people in so far as these can be made to accord with their overall purposes and values. Dysfunctions arising from these divergences, and the inherent conflicts of interest, exist to a greater or lesser extent in all organizations; they are most common in multinational hierarchies and in public institutions and services.

MOTIVATION

A full understanding of the principles of motivation is essential. The major theories of motivation are as follows.

Rensis Likert: System 4

Likert's contribution to the theories of workplace motivation arose from his work with high performing managers; managers and supervisors who achieved high levels of productivity, low levels of cost and high levels of employee motivation, participation and involvement at their places of work. The work demonstrated a correlation between this success and the style and structure of the work groups that they created. The groups achieved not only high levels of economic output and therefore wage and salary targets, but were also heavily involved both in group maintenance activities and the design and definition of work patterns. This was underpinned by a supportive style of supervision and the generation of a sense of personal worth, importance and esteem in belonging to the group itself.

The System 4 model arose from this work. Likert (1961) identified four styles or systems of management (see Figure 9.1):

■ System 1: Exploitative authoritative, where power and direction come from the top downwards and where there is no participation, consultation or involvement on the part of the workforce. Workforce compliance is thus based on fear. Unfavourable attitudes are generated, there is little confidence and trust, and low levels of motivation to cooperate or generate output above the absolute minimum.

■ System 2: Benevolent authoritative, which is similar to System 1 but which allows some 'upward' opportunity for consultation and participation in some areas. Again attitudes tend to be generally unfavourable; confidence, trust and communication are also at low levels. In both Systems 1 and 2, productivity may be high over the short run when targets can be achieved by a combination of coercion and bonus and overtime payments. However, both productivity and earnings are demonstrably low over the long run; there is also high absenteeism and labour turnover.

■ System 3: Consultative, where aims and objectives are set after discussion and consultation with subordinates, communication is two-way and teamwork is encouraged at least in some areas. Attitudes towards both superiors and the organization tend to be favourable, especially when the organization is working steadily.

Productivity tends to be higher, absenteeism and turnover lower. There is also demonstrable reduction in scrap, improvement in product quality, reduction in overall operational costs and higher levels of earning on the part of the workforce.

■ System 4: Participative, in which three basic concepts have a very important effect on performance – the use by the manager of the principle of supportive relationships throughout the work group, the use of group decision-making and group methods of supervision and the setting of high performance and very ambitious goals for the department and also for the organization overall. This was Likert's preferred System.

Likert saw the various management systems as having causal, intervening and end result variables.

The causal variables are independent variables that determine the course of developments within an organization and the results achieved, as well as management policies, decisions, business and leadership strategies, skills and behaviour.

The intervening variables are those that reflect the internal state and health of the organization. These include loyalties, attitudes, motivations, performance goals and their achievement, the perceptions of all members and their collective capacity for interaction, communication and decision-making.

The end result variables are the dependent variables reflecting the achievements of the organization in terms of its productivity, costs, efficiency, product quality and earnings.

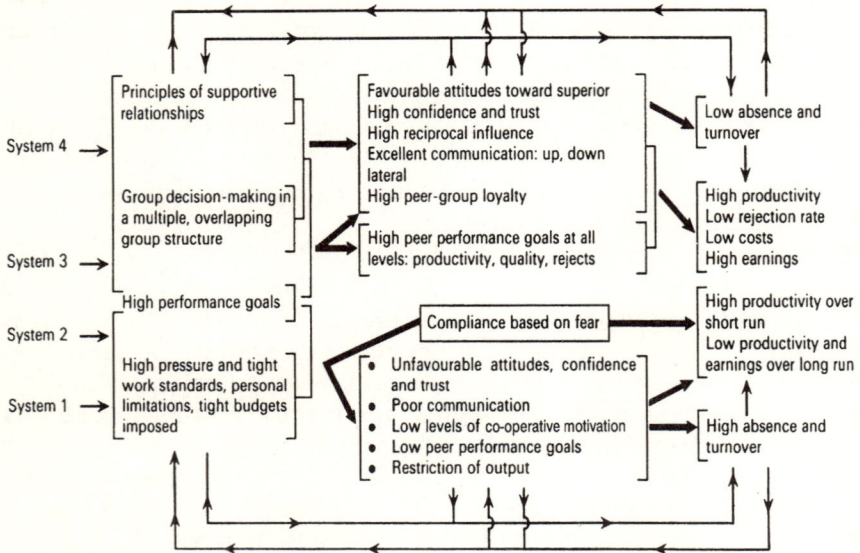

Figure 9.1 *System 4* (source: Likert, 1961)

Abraham Maslow: a hierarchy of needs

Abraham Maslow was a behavioural scientist whose researches led him to depict a hierarchy of needs, which explained different types and levels of motivation that were important to people at different times. This hierarchy of needs is normally depicted as a pyramid (see Figure 9.2). The hierarchy of needs works from the bottom of the pyramid upwards. It shows the most basic needs and motivations at the lowest levels while those at the top are created by, or fostered by, civilization and society. Maslow identified five key needs:

1. physiological: the need for food, drink, air, warmth, sleep and shelter; basic survival needs related to the instinct for self-preservation
2. safety and security: protection from danger, threats or deprivation and the need for stability (or relative stability) of environment
3. social: a sense of belonging to a society and its groups, for example, the family, the organization or the work group, the giving and receiving of friendship; basic status needs within these groups, and the need to participate in social activities
4. esteem needs: self-respect, self-esteem, appreciation, value, recognition and status both on the part of the individuals concerned and the society, circle or group in which they interrelate; part of the esteem need is therefore the drive to gain the respect, esteem and appreciation accorded by others
5. self-actualization: the need for self-fulfilment, self-realization, personal development, accomplishment, mental, material and social growth and the development and fulfilment of the creative faculties.

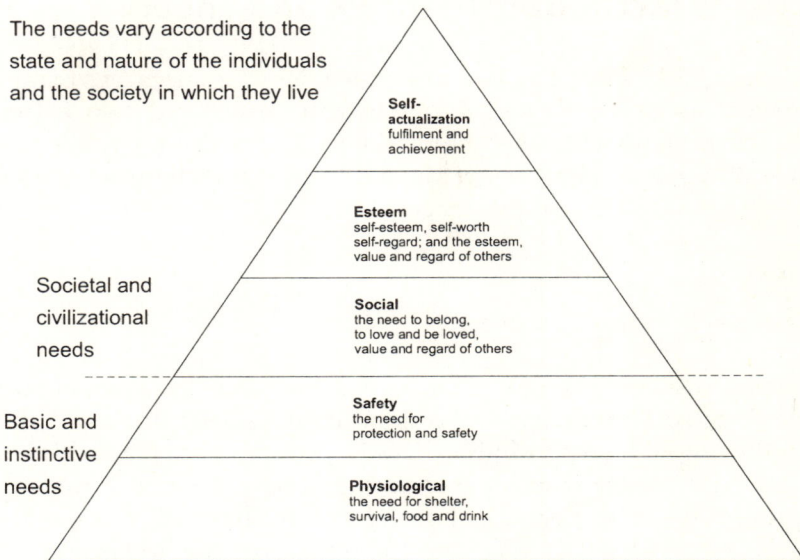

The needs vary according to the state and nature of the individuals and the society in which they live

Self-actualization
fulfilment and achievement

Esteem
self-esteem, self-worth self-regard; and the esteem, value and regard of others

Societal and civilizational needs

Social
the need to belong, to love and be loved, value and regard of others

Basic and instinctive needs

Safety
the need for protection and safety

Physiological
the need for shelter, survival, food and drink

Figure 9.2 *Maslow's hierarchy of needs* (source: Maslow, 1960)

This was the hierarchy of needs outlined. Maslow reinforced his model by stating that people tended to satisfy their needs systematically. They started with the basic, instinctive needs and then moved up the hierarchy. Until one particular group of needs was satisfied, a person's behaviour would be dominated by them. Thus the hungry or homeless person will look to their needs for self-esteem and society only after their hunger has been satisfied and they have found a place to stay. The other point that Maslow made was that people's motives were constantly being modified as their situation changed and in relation to their levels of adaptation and other perceptual factors. This was especially true of the self-actualization needs in which, having achieved measures of fulfilment and recognition, people nevertheless tended to remain unsatisfied and to wish to progress further.

Maslow's work was based on general studies of human motivation and as such was not directly related to matters endemic at the workplace. However, matters concerning the last two items on the pyramid, those of self-esteem and self-actualization, have clear implications for the motivation (and self-motivation) of professional, technical and managerial staff in organizations. There are also implications for the management of all staff in all forms of work.

Douglas McGregor: Theory X and Theory Y

McGregor (1980) identified two distinctive sets of assumptions made by managers about employees. From this he articulated two extreme attitudes or views and called them Theory X and Theory Y. His thesis was that in practice most people would come somewhere between the two, except in certain circumstances.

Theory X

This is based on three premises:

■ People dislike work and will avoid it if they can. They would rather be directed than accept any responsibility; indeed, they will avoid authority and responsibility if they possibly can. They have no creativity except when it comes to getting around the rules and procedures of the organization. Above all they will not use their creativity in the pursuit either of the job or the interests of the organization.
■ People must be forced or bribed to put out the right effort. They are motivated mainly by money, which remains the overriding reason

why they go to work. Their main anxiety concerns their own personal security, which they alleviate by earning money.

■ People are inherently lazy, they require high degrees of supervision, coercion and control in order to produce adequate output.

Theory Y

This is based on the premise that work is necessary to one's psychological growth:

■ People wish only to be interested in their work, and under the right conditions they will enjoy it. They gain intrinsic fulfilment from it and they are motivated by the desire to realize their own potential, to work to the best of their capabilities and to employ the creativity and ingenuity with which they are endowed in the pursuit of this.

■ People will direct themselves towards given accepted and understood targets, they will seek and accept responsibility and authority and they will accept the discipline of the organization in the pursuit of this. They also impose their own self-discipline on themselves and their activities.

Whatever the conditions, management was to be responsible for organizing the elements of productive enterprise and its resources in the interests of economic ends. This would be done in ways suitable to the nature of the organization and its workforce in question; either providing a coercive style of management and supervision or arranging a productive and harmonious environment in which the workforce can and will take responsibility for erecting their own efforts and those of their unit towards organizational aims and objectives.

Frederick Herzberg: Two-factor Theory

Herzberg's research was directed at people in places of work (see Figure 9.3).

It was based on questioning people in organizations in different jobs, at different levels, to establish:

■ those factors that led to extreme dissatisfaction with the job, the environment and the workplace

■ those factors that led to extreme satisfaction with the job, the environment and the workplace.

The factors giving rise to satisfaction Herzberg called motivators. Those giving rise to dissatisfaction he called hygiene factors.

The motivators that emerged were achievement, recognition, the nature of the work itself, level of responsibility, advancement and opportunities for personal growth and development. These factors are all related to the actual content of the work and job responsibilities. Where present in a working situation, these factors led to high levels and degrees of satisfaction on the part of the workforce.

The hygiene factors or dissatisfiers identified were company policy and administration, supervision and management style, levels of pay and salary, relationships with peers, relationships with subordinates, status and security. Where they were good or adequate, these factors would not in themselves make people satisfied. If it were ensured that they were indeed adequate, then dissatisfaction was removed, but satisfaction was not in itself generated. On the other hand, where these aspects were bad extreme dissatisfaction was experienced by all respondents.

Organizations that failed to provide adequate hygiene factors tended to have high levels of conflict, absenteeism and labour turnover and low general morale.

The work of Herzberg has tended to encourage attention to such factors as good and adequate supervision, which encourages and extends the workforce rather than restricts it, job satisfaction, which can often be increased through work restructuring, job enrichment and job enlargement programmes and the setting and achieving of targets and objectives based on a full understanding of what they are and why they have been set. Some organizations have also concentrated on removing the dissatisfiers or hygiene factors to ensure that causes of intrinsic dissatisfaction with the workplace and its environment are minimized.

| Factors on the job that led to extreme dissatisfaction but not satisfaction | Factors on the satisfaction but |

Percentage frequency   Percentage fre

| 50% | 40 | 30 | 20 | 10 | 0 | 10 | 20 |

Achievement

Recognition

Work itself

Responsibility

Advancement

Growth

Company policy and administration

Supervision

Relationship with supervisor

Work conditions

Salary

Relationship with peers

Personal life

Relationship with subordinates

Status

Security

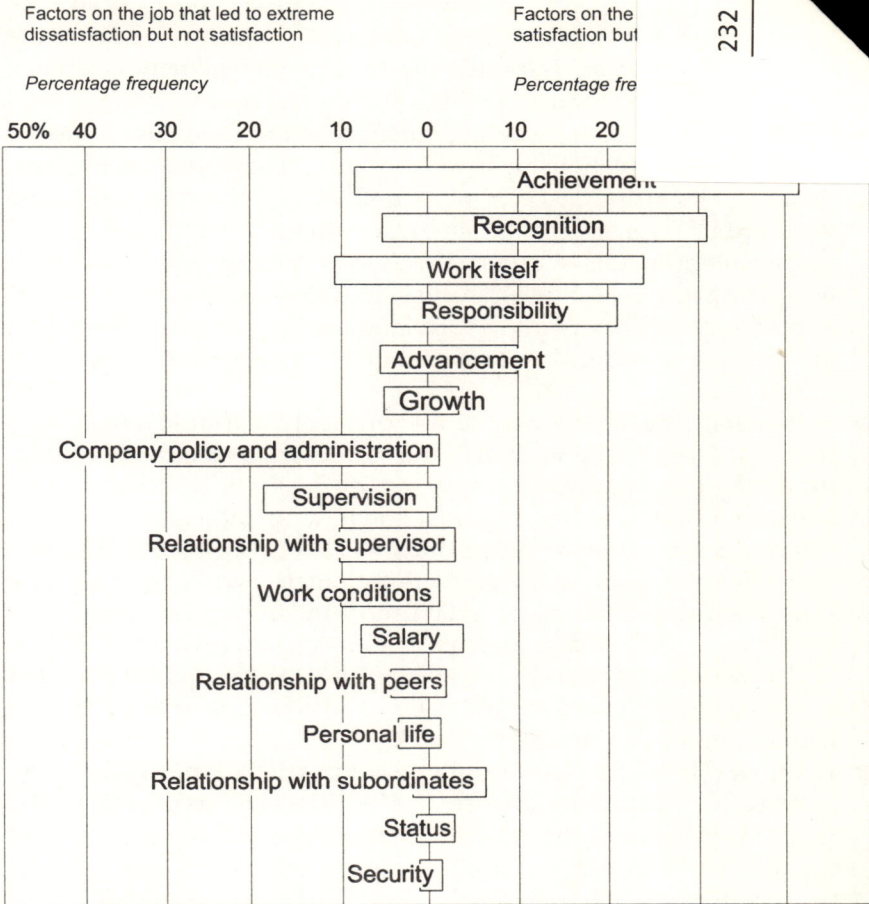

Figure 9.3 *Two factor or hygiene theory* (source: Herzberg, 1962)

Edgar Schein: a classification of people

Schein (1990) classified people in four ways:

■ **Rational economic** These people are primarily motivated by economic needs. They pursue their own self-interest in the expectation of high economic returns. If they work in an organization they need both motivation and control. As they intensify their pursuit of money they become untrustworthy and calculating.

Within this group, however, there are those who are self-motivated and have a high degree of self-control. This is the group that must take responsibility for the management of others. They also set the moral and ethical standards required.

■ **Social** These people are social animals, gaining their basic sense of identity from relationships with others. They will seek social relationships at the place of work and part of the function of the work group will be the fulfilment of this necessity. The role of management in this situation is therefore greatly concerned with mobilizing the social relationships in the pursuit of operational effectiveness and drawing a correlation between productivity and morale, and taking an active interest in the development of the work group.

■ **Self-actualizing** These people are primarily self-motivated. They seek challenge, responsibility and pride from their job and to maximize the opportunities offered by it. They are likely to be affected negatively by organizational and management style, external controls, scarcity of resources and other pressure. They will develop their own ways of working, their own objectives and integrate these with those established by the organization. The inference is that this is strongest among professional, technical, skilled and managerial staff, however, all work groups have tended towards higher levels of motivation and morale when given a greater degree of autonomy at work.

■ **Complex** These people are complex and variable; they have many motives, differing and diverse and which vary according to the matter in hand and the different work groups in which they find themselves. They will not fulfil all their needs in any one situation but rather require a variety of activities in order to do this. They respond to a variety of stimuli according to their needs and wants at a particular moment. Schein's view of 'complex people' in organizations is that of a psychological contract, based on mutual expectations and commonality of aspirations. It is therefore a partnership.

Expectancy

In essence, this approach to motivation draws the relationship between the efforts put into particular activities by individuals, and the nature of the expectations of the rewards that they perceive they will get from these efforts.

The expectancy approach to motivation draws a relationship between:

■ the expectations that people have in work situations
■ the efforts that they put in to meet these expectations
■ the rewards offered for successful efforts.

Understanding individual aspirations and the extent to which work can satisfy these is essential. It is also necessary to recognize the need to balance expectation, effort and reward. If expectations are raised and then not fulfilled, effort declines. If high levels of effort turn out to be unproductive, expectations are repositioned downwards. If the anticipated rewards are not forthcoming, effort declines. The effect of each is always to demotivate and demoralize. This is clearly centred on the individual and relates to the ways in which the individual sees or perceives the environment. In particular, it relates to his/her view of work, expectations, aspirations, ambitions and desired outcomes from it, and the extent to which these can be satisfied at the workplace or carrying out the occupation in question. For example, the individual may have no particular regard for the job that they are currently doing but will nevertheless work productively and effectively at it and be committed to it because it is a stepping stone, in their view, to greater things. These expectations constitute the basis of the individual's efforts and the quality of these efforts. This is compounded, however, by other factors, such as the actual capacities and aptitudes of the individual concerned on the one hand and the nature of the work environment on the other. It is also limited by the perceptions and expectations that the commissioner of the work has on the part of the person who is actually carrying it out. There is a distinction to be drawn between the effort put into performance and the effectiveness of that effort – hard work, conscientiously carried out does not always produce effective activity; the effort has to be directed and targeted. There has also to be a match between the rewards expected and those that are offered – a reward is merely a value judgment placed on something offered in return for effort, and if this is not valued by the receiver it has no effect on his motivation.

Consequently, there has to be an understanding of the nature of the motives and expectations of the individual, related to an ability to satisfy these on the part of the organization if it is to address effectively the issue of motivation. The approach required is, therefore, to take both an enlightened and specific view of what constitutes job satisfaction (rather than assuming that it exists or exists in certain occupations at least) and an understanding of the processes of perception and the nature of reward in relation to the aspirations of those conducting the work.

The works referred to here constitute the major investigations into the subject of human motivation, both in general and at the place of work. The overall purpose has been to indicate both the importance of the subject itself and the relationship between effective human motivation and effective work performance, and the level of understanding and application required of the subject of those who aspire to manage others.

Motivation and achievement

The general correlation between motivation and achievement is a common theme that runs through all of the work to which reference has been made. There are lessons to be learned.

Organizations can and should develop characteristics within their staff to generate in them improved and higher levels of commitment and performance that relate to higher levels of achievement. These characteristics are activity (rather than passivity), degrees of workplace autonomy, long-termism (as opposed to short-termism), self-discipline, self-motivation and self-awareness. Work conducted by Chris Argyris in the USA (1990) concluded that traditional style organizations tended to encourage the opposite of these characteristics (ie passivity, dependence and expediency), leading to both individual and corporate frustration and ineffectiveness.

All people, whatever their work, need to have achievements. In recent years the organizational concept of 'the high achiever' has become prevalent. The term implies an individual who regularly completes work to high degrees of quality, output and effectiveness. Such staff require tasks and targets against which their achievements may be measured, and regular feedback on the extent to which these have been fulfilled. It is prevalent in task cultures and high pressure and output-oriented occupations.

Motivation and money

It is stated elsewhere (Herzberg, 1962) that money does not enhance the intrinsic nature of the work. Indeed, in the most extreme cases it will not affect the employee's motivation at all (as with voluntary work, where the driving force is to do with commitment or vocation) while at the other extreme it may simply make working life bearable for a very short period of time (no matter how much one is paid for sweeping roads, the job to be done is still the sweeping of the roads). However, there are additional points to be borne in mind:

■ Wage and salary levels reinforce such matters as self-image and t.. esteem that others hold of the job or occupation. A high salary reinforces the status and responsibility that the job holder is felt to have. A low salary may diminish this. A low salary for a professional person may give the aura of professional commitment at personal expense.

■ Wage and salary levels form the basis of inter-occupational comparisons and expectations. Wage and salary rises, also, have to be seen in behavioural terms, both against what is 'the going rate', and also against what others in both related and wholly different occupations are getting (or perceived to be getting). If one is at the top of this measure, there will be a tendency towards greater satisfaction than if one is at the lower end.

■ Wage and salary levels reflect the value placed upon an employee by the organization. They also reflect the value and relative value of the occupation range that is carried out in the organization. They also impart information that relates to the true nature of the work being carried out (eg a high sounding job title that carries with it a low salary is likely to mean that the level of work carried out is actually less than the job title implies).

■ Reinforcement elements such as bonuses and incentives may also be used by organizations to generate additional output (in whatever terms that is measured) or to reward loyalty. The approach to the management of such payments must be positive and dynamic; such payments should never be allowed to become institutionalized, or their effect is lost.

Motivation and employee relations

It is clear from the preceding pages that motivation is a key feature of effective ER. It indicates the key attention required to the human side of all managerial activities and the positive and negative effects.

Specific lessons may be learned from each approach.

System 4

This approach stresses the importance and value of consultation and participation, bearing in mind that the research was carried out in high achievement and highly successful organizations. In these situations, a direct relationship was drawn between high levels of motivation and enduring high levels of performance and output.

An understanding of the drawbacks of the non-participative approaches is defined, which is not to say that adequate levels of output cannot be maintained in such situations. However, it does indicate and support the organizational, as well as ER, problems inherent in such approaches. System 4 also outlines the key features of trust, openness and honesty, that are implicit in all such situations.

Hierarchies of needs

The approach based on hierarchies of needs is adaptive, as people's priorities and levels of motivation in particular matters alter as their circumstances change. In ER situations, and where either adverse news or great change is envisaged by the organization, this underlines the value of early information and consultation. People adapt when they understand why they have to adapt, and people fail to adapt when they do not see the need. Early warning or notification of crises and upheavals is therefore a key to effective employee relations.

The hierarchies of needs studies were carried out on the subject of human, rather than specific workplace, motivation. The need for self-actualization – self-fulfilment – was found to be a common factor. At workplaces, therefore, whatever the occupation, people tend to seek the need to progress as far as they possibly can. Lack of capability, or scope or space, to do this, is widely demotivating. This was a fundamental error of the original 'scientific management' approach of Taylor (1947), in which it was felt that 'the workers' would carry out any job, however boring, mundane or repetitive, as long as wages were maintained at high levels. This approach has subsequently been found to be detrimental to both physical and mental health.

The hierarchies of needs also indicates fundamental needs of safety and security. Again, the implication is clear – when people know and understand, for example, that their job security is being threatened, they will respond in positive ways to preserve it and, again, the key is knowledge rather than ignorance. It is important, however, to recognize that this response may take two forms. According to the way in which information is presented, either of these two positions indicated may be adopted:

- entrenchment, in which a defensive position is established, akin to that of the print workers at the Wapping dispute of 1982 in which industrial strife was seen as the best form of self-preservation (which subsequently turned out to be wrong)
- commitment, in which the efforts of the staff are engaged in more productive and prioritized directions so that extraneous or subversive activities are excluded. The motivation of staff even in such situations is therefore not simple.

Theory X and Y

Those treated from the standpoint of Theory X tend to respond in kind. This approach reinforces perceptions of lack of value, lack of worth and lack of esteem. In the long term, anyone who is threatened, bribed or bullied comes to regard their protagonist with contempt. This remains true however high the bribe or financial consideration may be and eventually none of these approaches is ever enough to sustain high levels of output in the long term (see Summary box 9.1).

Proponents of the Theory Y approach point in particular to the enduring high levels of motivation of volunteer staff to work in remote and deprived parts of the world, and the continued ability of organizations to attract recruits to do this work.

In times of employment stability, there is a tendency in some organizations towards a median point on the spectrum between the two extremes. This may be summarized as 'the nice little job' in which a modicum of reward was issued for a modicum of output in medium quality working environments, and all of this was a trade-off for long-term enduring, job, salary – and subsequently pension – certainty. In times of industrial turmoil and occupational uncertainty and upheaval, the median approach does not work. In ER terms, people seek increased levels of reward, alongside increased levels of satisfaction, achievement and the potential for advancement.

Summary box 9.1   High levels of remuneration

Here is a simple example. If the entire content of the job is sweeping roads, repetitive actions, or washing up dishes, the intrinsic worth of the job does not alter however much is paid. Again, the Taylor approach to deskilling – in which production line operatives carried out a very small task repetitively for very high levels of wages – did not prevent bad employee relations and industrial strife.

Two further current examples may be considered:

- **Real Madrid** In 1998, the minimum level of wage paid to the top footballers who play for this club was £42,000 per week. This does not prevent a substantial level of demotivation on the part of some of the players, leading ultimately to contempt for the club.
- **The Spice Girls** In 1998 also, Geri Halliwell left the group, in spite of the fact that by remaining she would have retained commercial endorsements to the value of £15 million.

Two-factor theory

The two-factor studies were carried out at places of work. The evidence was overwhelming: sources of disputes and grievances were attributable to the 'hygiene factors' – those things that, if present, did not tend to motivate particularly, but if negative or absent, tended towards greater demotivation. The sources of disputes and grievances were nearly always to be found in bad or inappropriate management style, inability to follow procedures, inability to get problems and issues resolved quickly, inter-group strife, short-term demands for overtime and adversarial, negative and dividing cultures. Again, throwing money at ER problems – in the form of enhanced bonuses or pay rates – mollified individuals for a short period of time, rather than resolving long-term institutionalized problems. The genuine resolution of problems caused through prevailing 'hygiene factors' is remedied by strategic approaches to the training and development of managers; and to the development of the organization as a whole.

Classifications of people

This approach identifies a totality of those factors that need to be present in effective working and ER situations, rather than identifying issues that it is possible to trade-off or balance against each other. All people, when they come to work, want all of the factors to the extent that these are possible in their particular occupations. Above all, it is the responsibility of organizations to make overtly mundane jobs – such as in industrial production, catering or clerical work – as interesting and rewarding as possible in intrinsic terms, rather than merely paying wages for them (and again, the word merely tends to be either stated or implicit in such situations) (see Summary box 9.2).

Expectancy theories

ER problems are caused when the expectancy-effort–reward relationship is distorted. People become demoralized, and there is an increase in disputes and grievances, especially when rewards anticipated in return for efforts exerted are not forthcoming. This is a key issue in pay rates and pay rises. People anticipate that by taking the effort to gain extra skills, they will gain extra rewards. People anticipate 'a going rate', usually expressed in percentage terms, for the annual pay rise; when the pay rise is less than 'the going rate' demoralization ensues. While the output of strikes and other more extreme forms of industrial action is much rarer than previously, the fundamental problems of motivation and morale remain. It is the manifestation of these that has changed – not the reality.

Summary box 9.2   Semco

Semco is a Brazilian industrial company, which manufactures, distributes and services pumping equipment across the world.

The company chairman and chief executive is Ricardo Semler. He has the following distinctive views on the performance of mundane activities:

- All filing, photocopying, and administration should be carried out by those who generate the paperwork. Semco does not employ secretaries or clerks. Semler himself does not have a secretary. There is a small core of those charged with producing company documentation, but this is carried out by staff who also have extensive information and data processing responsibilities. Otherwise, if staff wish to produce memoranda, letters and invoices, they must do so themselves.
- Staff are employed for the key contribution that they make to the organization, not for the hours that they fill in. Semler himself takes at least two months' holiday a year and the rest of his staff are expected and required to take at least six weeks. He quotes examples of having highly expert staff sitting around in the company offices, doing nothing in particular, because he knows that when their expertise is required, they will go into action, whatever the time of day or night, and wherever in the world they are required.

Semler also quotes an occasion on which he was visited by the wife of one of his staff. The wife 'complained' that her husband was no longer as grumpy or irascible as he used to be – and she was wondering what the company was doing to produce this wonderful effect!

Source: Semler (1992)

Factors common to all

All the studies of motivation discussed highlight the following areas as a matter of general staff management concern, and as key features in the development of effective ER:

- There is a need for working relationships to be based on long-term, mutual and enduring respect and value, esteem and regard. It is a mutual obligation. However, it is the organizational responsibility and prerogative to create the conditions in which this can exist.

- Variety, interest and development in work occupation must be open and available to everybody. Again, ultimately it is a mutual partnership, however, the conditions necessary in which progress and development are sought by everyone must be created by the organization and its managers.
- There must be equality, equity and fairness in all activities. Apart from anything else, this is a legal requirement. The penalties for prejudice, discrimination, victimization and harassment are unlimited and imposed on organizations that treat their staff apart from these principles with ever-increasing severity.
- The need for 'self-actualization' – advancement, achievement and fulfilment of potential – is present in everyone. It is a most complex aspect of organizational, industrial and human motivation. It is of particular concern to organizations and their managers in deciding how much achievement, advancement and fulfilment can be offered in the particular places of work and where the limitations on this lie. It may, for example, be necessary to ensure that people do understand that they only have limited career potential and that there will come a point where the organization cannot offer them any further advancement. This is, however, not to be seen as a catch-all, nor an abdication of responsibility. The problem lies rather in ensuring that people do have a highly fulfilling period of employment while they are with the particular organization, and that opportunities – both internally and in other organizations – are made available as and when they become known.
- There is a need for security, including the removal of uncertainty, based on the fundamental human drive for security. Again, this is not possible in all organizations (and some would say that this is not possible in the current turbulent state of business, commercial and public activities). However, there are lessons to be drawn from those organizations in terms of the high levels of commitment and motivation, and low levels of ER problems ensuing, that seek to provide 'lifetime employment' – through organization, management and staff development programmes – in order to address this basic need.
- The constraints of the situation, which need to be a continued matter of organizational and senior management concern, are important. The tendency towards the strategic policy and directional requirements of engendering high levels of motivation, tend towards the openness necessary for a real understanding of specific, organizational and situational constraints. On the one hand, it is very easy and comfortable to remain remote, isolated and alienated, whatever the occupation. However, as there is no prognosis for the return to steady-state, enduring and certain organizational activities,

either in commercial and industrial sectors or public services, the clear implication is that this form of organization management, and ER style, is no longer appropriate. This is to be seen alongside the prevailing view that effective ER is a key business, as well as expert support function, activity.

Motivation, ER and groups

Groups and teams are formed, constituted, disbanded and re-formed over periods of time for all work purposes, from short-term projects, production lines, administrative functions, support teams and professional services departments, to top management teams and boards of directors.

Two key features may be distinguished:

■ synergy, which is the principle that the whole is greater than the sum of its parts
■ cohesion, which is the ability of the group to stick together in pursuit of the stated purpose.

Groups may also be:

■ formal – constituted and directed for a purpose, to solve problems, develop products and conduct projects; these will have formal and organized key results, agenda, constitutions and composition
■ informal – in which the staff organize themselves in ways important or necessary to themselves, for example professional development, information generation, improved inter-departmental working, self-regulation, professional and occupational clusters. More insidiously, they may form canteen cultures, pressure groups, special interest groups, lobbies and vested interests
■ purpose – drawn together for a stated purpose, usually with a formalized remit and lifespan.

In the creation of effective ER, special attention must be paid to the following group functions.

Groups have their own core values, reasons for belonging and commonality and universality of purpose. In order to function effectively, mutual trust, honesty, openness and understanding must be present.

ER problems within groups are kept to a minimum if attention is paid to the group formation process and the group management process.

The group formation process

A useful summary of this formation process is as follows:

- **Forming** This is the initial bringing together of individuals for the designated purpose, the initial meeting, initial establishment of mutual interests and confidence and the initial results.
- **Storming** Here there is a rush of creativity and purpose, the first burst of creative and positive group activity with continuing output and results.
- **Norming** This is the establishment of operational rules and norms, the development of respect and confidence and continued attention to results.
- **Performing** Finally, there is the harnessing of individual talents and energy for the good of the group, the obtaining of key results, successes and failures and the activities devised to ensure a productive and positive purpose to the group.

Potential for ER problems exist at each stage. It is therefore essential that sufficient attention is paid to each part of the process to ensure that potential for conflict is recognized, principles of equality and fairness are established, the basis of each contribution is recognized and acknowledged, and that rewards and responsibilities are evenly shared. This removes the causes of both underlying loss and damage to morale and also the potential for individual grievances, disputes and personal and professional clashes.

This remains true also when group rejuvenation, re-forming and re-energizing take place. This happens either when the remit is changed, or when new persons are brought in. They have to be inducted into the ways of working, as well as the specific remit and objectives. They too will share in the successes and responsibilities.

ER problems may also arise at the ending of the group. If this is not properly managed, feelings of alienation, loss and demoralization are experienced. This also has implications for future group work in that, if no proper ending is made, or results noted, people asked to join such bodies in the future will do so reluctantly. Again, this may dilute organizational purpose as well as cause ER problems.

The group management process

Specific attention is therefore required to the following, if ER problems in group work are to be kept to a minimum, and if high levels of motivation are to be maintained:

■ **Management of the task** This involves attention to work methods, timescales, resource gathering, problem-solving and maintenance functions.

■ **Management of the process** This involves the use of interpersonal skills and interaction with the environment to gain the maximum contribution from each person.

■ **Managing communications** This is important between individuals within the group and also with other groups with whom they must work.

■ **Managing the individual** It must be ensured that individual talents, attributes and expertise is maximized.

■ **Leadership and management style** There must be acceptance and adoption of a style that is both positive and dynamic, and also suitable to the management needs of the situation.

■ **Maintenance management** This ensures that administration and support services are suitable, and that they do not conflict with the aims of the group.

■ **Shared values, aims and objectives** It must be possible to harmonize people's individual aims and objectives, while paying attention especially to standards of behaviour and attitudes with which all members of the group can agree.

■ **Group and team spirit** This requires a combination of shared values, together with ethics, mutual harmony, trust, respect, loyalty and integrity, so that rewards and responsibilities are shared.

Problems may also be caused in formal groups through:

■ their size (large groups tend to the formation of cliques and subgroups)
■ the nature and mix of personal, professional and occupational backgrounds from which members come
■ questions of representation, especially proportional representation where, for example, one department, division, function or expertise is given too great or too little a weighting in relation to the others
■ group remit and agenda, which may not enjoy the support or understanding of everyone concerned.

Problems may also arise where members of one group participate in different ER fora and agreements, according to the nature of their professional, technical or other occupational factors. They may get differences of information, both in quantity and quality, from their colleagues.

Where informal groups are concerned, people will always gather socially or professionally, whatever their actual occupation. Problems arise where these groups give rise to canteen cultures and other 'over-mightiness', enabling them to have a direct effect on the behaviour or orientation of the organization, in spite of any genuine authority commanded by the group. This is prevalent where there is no clear direction, ER policy, or broader organizational culture. Such groups flourish at their best – or worst – where an organizational vacuum exists. In extreme cases, they are very damaging to the organization as a whole, causing loss of public reputation and confidence (see Summary box 9.3).

Summary box 9.3   Informal groups and serious problems

The North Yorkshire police

In November 1997, two female members of the North Yorkshire Police. Force received compensatory awards from employment tribunal to the value of over £150,000 each.

The reason for this was that they were subject to systematic sexual victimization, harassment and bullying at their places of work. Male colleagues consistently made disparaging remarks about their capability to do the job, as well as about their gender. They were treated as objects rather than work colleagues.

The case against them was defended by the North Yorkshire Police Authority. They cited 'a traditional male culture founded on machismo' as their explanation as to why this situation had been allowed to arise.

Dismissing this as the defence, the employment tribunal ordered the North Yorkshire Police Authority to put its house in order. It stated unequivocally that this form of behaviour was unacceptable in the UK in the late 1990s.

The broad general lesson for all those concerned with the effective management of ER is that however things were carried out in the past, this is no excuse for allowing them to prevail in the present and into the future. Above all, it indicates the organizational and top management responsibilities for ensuring that canteen cultures are nipped in the bud when they do become apparent, and the requirement to create an organization culture, and overall standard of behaviour, that precludes this from existing in the first place is implicit.

Motivation, ER and the position of the individual

Individuals come into organizations to take up positions and roles within them, to carry them out, develop them and move them on, and to change roles, especially as the result of advancement. Individuals also have their own needs and wants, not all of which are easily harmonized or reconciled with the organization and its demands.

The rest of the organization will ascribe certain preconceptions and expectations to an individual occupying a particular job or role. This consists of a number of factors drawn from a combination of preconceptions and expectations, the aspirations of the person concerned and the ways in which he/she is perceived to carry out the job.

Roles are reinforced in various ways. A common form of this is the wearing of a uniform; work colleagues, as well as society at large, ascribe particular characteristics, expertise and features to uniforms. Other symbols include job titles, an office, the location, having personal staff and other personal trappings and features acquired as the result of holding a particular job.

ER conflicts arise where the following exist:

■ role ambiguity and uncertainty, which exists where a definition (perceptual or actual) of the role of the individual is not comfortably or satisfactorily achieved
■ role conflict, which is where the uncertainty and ambiguity develops into the need to adopt more than one role in the same situation
■ role confidence, which denotes the relationship between the role holder and the role itself and the wider confidence that work colleagues, and others in the organization, have in the individual to carry out the role
■ conformity, where the individual adopts the role constructs and symbols, and carries it out in ways that may or may not be satisfactory to the organization, but which are perceived as unsatisfactory by those on whom they have immediate impact.

Individuals may also be required to adopt several different roles (sub-roles) during the course of their work. They may also have different roles in different groups. A role carried out in one group may, therefore, cause conflict in others to which the individual belongs. From a behavioural point of view, people have great difficulties in handling ambiguities and uncertainties and it is important to recognize this as a potential source of ER conflict (see Summary box 9.4).

Summary box 9.4   Role acceptance and rejection

Role acceptance and rejection is usefully summarized as follows:

- **rejection:** a refusal to accept the role
- **indifference:** where the role is occupied without any form of personal or professional commitment
- **compliance:** where the role is occupied because the individual perceives it to be in their current interests
- **conformity:** where the occupation of the role is based on accepting rules and direction but not necessarily on interest or commitment
- **internalization:** where the role is occupied based on interest, commitment, and acceptance of organizational procedures, rules and regulations, and where there is personal and professional commitment to use the skills, knowledge and expertise in the organization's best interests.

In the pursuit of effective ER, all staff are expected to move to the position of conformity, if not internalization, rather than simply complying. Organizations expect it and it is a key feature of induction and orientation programmes. It is a major contributor to the reduction in potential for conflict and to the removal of causes of organizational conflict. It is also a key feature in the building of shared values, attitudes and organizational beliefs that lie at the centre of unitary and conformist organizations.

CONCLUSIONS

The main conclusion lies in the understanding of the place of human motivation as a key to the effective construction of successful workplace ER. Managers in particular, need to be able to assimilate all of this, and understand the complexities of behaviour involved, if they are to be able to adapt and develop particular situations and to use the processes, skills and qualities inherent in them in the promotion of effective and successful ER activities.

It is therefore necessary to learn the basic approaches to motivation, and the ways in which the motivation process is affected and influenced. Managers need to be able to recognize that which is inherent in particular situations. It is much better to take this approach, and use it as part of the basis on which effective ER is to be built, than simply moving from one dispute, grievance or conflict to the next. It is also essential to understand this as a key contributor to effective work and to the design of successful and productive work patterns.

10

EMPLOYEE RELATIONS MANAGEMENT: WORK PATTERNS

INTRODUCTION

In the creation of an environment of effective and harmonious ER, specific attention must be paid to the prevailing patterns of work. ER design and structure has to be capable of being integrated with these, as well as contributing to their design and being sufficiently flexible to accommodate changes as and when they become necessary. Become necessary they certainly must, and will continue to be so, as organizations strive to maximize and optimize customer services and returns on investment and as people hitherto excluded from the workforce now find themselves able to take advantage of developments in shift patterns and opportunities afforded by homeworking, teleworking and other patterns based on technology.

Patterns of work arise from the following:

Social and cultural aspects

This is the prevailing, perceived, national, regional or local standard and pattern of work. Nationally in the UK, and much of the EU, this is still perceived as being based around Monday to Friday, 9am to 5pm.

This represents a basis of regular hours of work on the same days each week, leaving the weekend clear for non-work activities.

The view is tempered as follows:

■ People have always expected certain products and services to be available, 24 hours per day, seven days per week, and are inconvenienced and upset when, for any reason, they may not be accessed.
■ Health, social, emergency and security services, and the energy and transport sectors, have always had to be available around the clock.
■ Advances in the development of customer and consumer services – for example, in banking and financial services, information services, retail and distribution – have led on the one hand, to people being required to work at hours convenient to customers and, on the other, to requirements for the ever-greater extension of these services because of the non-standard and therefore 'non-social' patterns of work being created. This has, in turn, led to a great proliferation in non-regular hours and patterns of work.

Industrial, commercial and public sector standards

In some sectors, standards continue to accord with these social standards. In others, distinctive patterns of work were, and remain, the norm, and these are well understood and accepted (to a greater or lesser extent) with retail and leisure services being offered at times suitable to the core activity in question (see Summary box 10.1).

Summary box 10.1   Sectoral work patterns: examples

Some useful points may be illustrated by consideration of the following:

- **Coal mining** When it was a major UK industrial activity, coal mining was both the dominant employer in the area, and also the key from which other institutions took their lead and developed their work patterns. As a consequence, there were early experiences in these locations of extended openings of shops, bars, sports and leisure facilities, transport and distribution activities.

- **Power generation** Because of the need to generate power at all times, those communities in which large numbers of people work at the power station have also experienced a long history and tradition of having other services open to them. This also had – and continues to have – effects on local facilities such as public transport, which are required at times suitable to shift changes at the power station. This is because people are drawn from further and wider to work in such institutions, and is thus distinct from the mining industry in that communities grew up in close proximity to the mines themselves.
- **London markets** Fish, meat, vegetable and other produce markets of London, and other big towns also, open for work at approximately 2.30am. The working day runs from this time until approximately 11.30am. Business communities in micro grew up around these markets, and they continue to flourish at these times. It is therefore possible to find cafes and public houses open during these times, restaurants serving lunches from 5.30am onwards and a wide range of retail activities, including 'metro' supermarkets.

It is a useful indication of the interrelationship between organizations and other activities in their area, and the consequent effects on work patterns. It also underlines the importance of managers taking the broader situation into account when considering the vagaries of ER in their own organizations.

Occupations

Specific occupations and professions carry clear implications for patterns of work. Those going to work in health, emergency and security services have always known that they would be required to work non-standard hours. This has now been greatly extended, and covers both the areas indicated above, and also a substantial range of other industrial activities, commercial services and support functions, as the result of drives for managerial efficiency (see below) and the need to try and fit people with skills in short supply into places of work and, where necessary, to fit these around their other commitments.

Management standards

Organizations and their managers have sought to change and extend hours of work and to adopt more flexible and creative work patterns in order to try and secure greater efficiency in terms of returns on investment, as well as broadening customer bases and market and sectoral coverage. This is also driven by the needs and demands for ever-increasing quality and totality of customer service, whatever the sector (see Summary box 10.2).

Summary box 10.2   ER and return on investment: examples

The major reason for the proliferation of patterns of work and staffing arrangements is the defined strategic aim of organizations to maximize their return on investment. Examples are:

- supermarkets, which are extending their opening hours, and therefore their customer base potential in terms of their competition, in order to maintain and extend market share
- information management and information services, which have made a strategic move away from the provision of these services at hitherto traditionally accepted retail and physical access outlets, as the senior management of these organizations has come to realize that this may not always be the most appropriate form of activity
- banking, insurance and financial services, which are increasingly being made available around the clock and which now (in many cases) offer the full range of banking services, parallel to those offered at traditional outlets, and during traditional hours. At present, the traditional remains the major contribution to the banking and financial services industries; should the telebanking approach become the norm, this will radically alter all patterns of work hitherto accepted as standard in that sector – and it will inevitably have knock-on effects on other aspects of the service, including personal contact with customers; personal contact with other members of staff and personal access to managers.

Alienation

The main ER problem to be faced is alienation. This is especially an issue when those carrying out the work do so at times different from those who have authority in solving problems, resolving conflicts and disputes. It may be compounded by a request to attend training and briefing sessions and staff meetings during more 'socially normal' hours.

There are also perceptual problems to be overcome. In terms of organization attitudes and values, it is essential that those working outside 'normal' hours receive the same fundamental equity and equality of treatment afforded to everyone else.

There may also be ER managerial problems caused by having different managers at different times, who overlap with each other in terms of staff hours. These occur, for example, in the management of disputes and grievances and disciplinary issues, when staff know, believe or perceive that they receive different levels of treatment over the same matter, depending on which manager happens to deal with the matter when it first blows up.

Each of these instances requires close attention if ER problems are to be minimized.

Expatriates

Expatriates and those working away from home for long periods require special attention. Especially those working overseas, who sometimes experience significant domestic problems that reduce their value to their employer. Social and family upheaval has to be managed as an ER issue, including consideration of schooling and other family arrangements, and the wider need for social settlement.

Other specific issues that have to be addressed include:

■ salary levels, including any perceived perks or benefits, or additional payments, that are to accrue as the result of living and working overseas, which is likely to put the individual's reward package out of kilter with those elsewhere in the organization

■ creating effective and harmonious reporting relationships and reconciling the problems of fundamental equality of treatment, with the fact that such staff work in very different environments, cultures and circumstances

■ problems of physical distance, compounded by international factors – of quality of telecommunications, ease of access, visibility and also the problem of generating effective staff identity and loyalty with an organization with which they may have no particular affinity, especially if they are locals who see the employer purely as a means of economic support

■ problems of perceived social disadvantage, including the inability to integrate into local society and avail themselves of the use of leisure facilities, sports facilities, public and commercial services.

These issues need careful management. There remains also the question of what happens to the individual when he/she returns to the domestic situation after a period of expatriate employment. In these cases, as well as reintegration into the organization's structures, there are problems of potential cultural dysfunction, new forms of authority, and domestic ways of working to be addressed.

While these need not necessarily cause strikes, disputes and other traditional ER outpourings, they do represent issues that, if not properly managed, are likely to affect motivation and morale.

Professions and expert occupations

The 'classical' professions are medicine, law, the priesthood, and the army. The following properties were held to distinguish these from the rest of society:

■ distinctive expertise not available elsewhere in the society
■ distinctive body of knowledge required by all those who aspire to practise in the profession
■ entry barriers in the form of examinations, time serving or learning from experts
■ formal qualifications given as the result of acquiring the body of knowledge and clearing the entry barriers
■ high status: these professions are at or near the top of the occupational tree
■ distinctive morality: for medicine, the commitment to keep people alive as long as possible; for law, a commitment to represent the client's best interests; for the Church, a commitment to Godliness and to serve the congregation's best interests; for the army, to fight within stated rules of war
■ high value: these professions make a distinctive and positive contribution to both the organizations and individual members of the society, and their expertise is held in high respect and demand
■ self-regulating professions set their own rules, codes of conduct, standards of performance and qualifications
■ self-discipline: these professions establish their own bodies for dealing with problems, complaints and allegations of malpractice, and there is commitment to personal standards of behaviour in the pursuit of professional excellence
■ unlimited reward levels: according to preferred levels of charges and the demands of society

- life membership: dismissal is at the behest of the profession, and ceasing to work for one employer does not constitute loss of profession
- personal commitment to high standards of practice and morality; commitment to deliver the best in all circumstances
- continuous development of knowledge and skills and a commitment to keep abreast of all developments and initiatives in the field
- governance by institutions established by the profession itself.

In addition to these occupations, others aspire to the position of near-professionalism – for example, nursing, teaching, accountancy, aircraft piloting and sea navigation. Moreover, many occupations point especially to their high levels of expertise and distinctive standards of qualification, together with necessary commitments to continuous development, as being worthy of distinctive recognition. These areas include engineering, construction, other transport occupations and capability in information technologies.

The main ER issues here are the management of professional standards and the management of interprofessional and occupational relationships.

The management of professional standards

Problems arise when someone is asked by their organization to do something that they know, believe or perceive is at variance with the requirements of the professional occupation. This is compounded when:

- professionals operate for long periods in their working lives away from direct contact with managers (eg surgeons, airline pilots, sea captains)
- the professional group has a distinctive or specialized organization remit (eg the maintenance of production lines) into which there is no specific managerial input
- the profession or occupational group knows, believes or perceives that their expertise, quality of work, or distinctive work pressures are not fully understood, or are misunderstood by management (see Summary box 10.3).
- when the profession or occupational group knows, believes or perceives that their expertise, quality of work or distinctive work pressures give them a form of elite position in the organization, leading them to be able to set their own norms and standards of work practice

■ when the managers of professional or occupational groups fight shy of confronting organizational and managerial issues because they know, believe or perceive that the particular group is likely to be hostile or resistant to what they need to be told.

Summary box 10.3   The management of professions: junior hospital doctors

In 1990, a junior hospital doctor working in the West Country went to carry out an emergency visit to one of the patients on his ward. He had been roused from sleep during a long period of duty. He went and examined the patient, then returned to his room.

A complaint was made to management that, when he carried out this examination, he was wearing no clothes. He was therefore disciplined by the hospital authorities for being 'improperly dressed' during periods of work.

In his defence, the junior doctor stated the following:

- that he had been on continuous duty for five days prior to the incident
- that the particular day on which the incident occurred had been especially busy, and that he had worked for a period of approximately 16 hours without a break
- that he had finally returned to his room about an hour prior to the incident occurring
- that he could not remember the incident in question – he had no recollection of either being roused from his sleep, or going to treat the particular patient, or of returning to his room. Indeed, the only evidence that he had been to the ward was his signature on the patient's notes in a clipboard at the end of the bed on the ward.

The doctor was disciplined, but not dismissed.

It is essential to recognize the potential for ER strife and conflict inherent in these situations. Professionals and experts, and their groups, take refuge in allegations of bullying, victimization and harassment against their managers and while many of these issues are clearly valid, some inevitably are not (see Summary box 10.4).

Summary box 10.4   ER and professional staff: heart surgeons at Bristol

Over the period 1989–95, 56 heart operations were carried out on child patients at a major hospital in Bristol.

Of these patients, 33 died. This was known by all concerned to be a mortality rate totally unacceptable to everyone. Concerns were raised at an informal level. The matter was widely discussed in professional surgical circles, and questions about absolute standards of practice were asked by the profession at an early stage.

All such problems are at least minimized when regular organization channels of communication are kept open, regular meetings held, and the basis of a mutually interested relationship established. Where this does not occur, professionals and experts take refuge in their professional and occupational groups. They build behavioural defensive walls and these are very difficult to break down once attitudes harden and positions become entrenched.

Restrictive practices

A restrictive practice is where only designated or defined persons may carry out a particular occupation. Restrictive practices occur where:

■ the job or occupation requires by law that those who carry it out have first completed a period of professional, technical, expert or occupational period of study, training or work experience. This applies to certain professions, for example, law, medicine and accountancy, and certain other occupations, for example, engineering, London black cab taxi driving, airline pilots, railway and road haulage driving and emergency services

■ the job or occupation requires that people will normally be expected to demonstrate proficiency prior to the commencement of employment, even if there are no legal requirements, for example, estate agency, certain financial occupations and managerial positions

■ the job or occupation requires membership of a professional body prior to commencement of employment, and where this membership may be gained via one or more recognized route, whether legally constrained or not, for example, marketing, journalism, purchasing and supply

■ the job or occupation requires that people are either a member of a recognized trade union prior to commencement of work or that they undertake to join a recognized trade union as a condition of work and at the point of commencement. Formally known as the 'closed shop' or 'union membership agreement', this is now illegal in the UK and across the EU
■ the job or occupation requires that people have their capacity to work countersigned by statutory bodies, training lead bodies, trade unions and professional bodies, for example, health, social service and other medical professions, teaching, professional social work, engineering professions and crafts, catering and hairdressing.

In the past, much of this has been reinforced by requirements to join specific trade unions or professional or occupational bodies and this was a peculiarly UK requirement. It was further enhanced by the very specific descriptions of some trade unions, for example, wheel tappers and shunters, the boiler makers union or the navigation union. While all of these specific examples have been subsumed, and the occupations long since lost, specific industrial descriptions still persist, for example, the Police Federation, Rail, Maritime and Transport Union, Manufacturing, Science and Finance Union and so on. The same also applies to professional bodies, such as the Institute of Marketing, Institute of Personnel and Development, Institute of Administrative Management and so on.

The perceived advantage of restricting the ability to practise in these ways is that by limiting the numbers involved in the occupation, wage and salary levels will be driven up. In the past, this led to the formation of general trade unions, such as those now known as the Transport & General Workers Union, General, Municipal and Boiler Makers Union and the National Association of Local Government Officers. The approach also puts value on specific industries, reflected in union names such as the National Union of Mineworkers and the National Union of Railwaymen.

Alongside this, other activities tried to generate for themselves a distinctive identity. For example, clerical occupations created their own form of language for communication with each other, so that only they could understand what was being said or written. In this way, they would enhance their own value and, therefore, salary and reward. However, the people for whom they worked got round the problem, simply by writing to each other, rather than employing clerks to do it on their behalf.

Restraint of trade

The reverse of restrictive practice is restraint of trade. This occurs where an employer prevents or seeks to prevent an employee from applying their expertise elsewhere. Restraint of trade falls into two categories: legitimate and illegitimate.

Legitimate restraint

This is where:

■ an employer makes a condition of employment that their employees will not work for a customer, client or competitor of their organization on a part-time, self-employed, consultancy or advisory basis during the period of their current employment
■ an employer for sound organizational and operational reasons, makes as a condition of employment that their employees will have no other paid occupation during their period of employment. It is generally necessary for the employer to be able to demonstrate that this is a sound organizational and operational reason.

Illegitimate restraint

This is where an employer seeks to prevent an employee or ex-employee from pursuing their chosen occupation. This may involve failing to allow someone to move on to other work at the end of a fixed term contract or placing a notice period sufficiently extensive as to make them unattractive to the next prospective employer (see Summary box 10.5).

Summary box 10.5   Restraint of trade: the Bosman ruling

The judgment that has come to be known as 'The Bosman ruling' was delivered by the European Court of Justice in March 1995. It concerned a professional footballer, Jean-Marc Bosman, whose contract with one football club finished. However, the club failed to allow him to move on; it also failed to pay him wages, so that not only was he unable to carry out his particular trade, he was also prevented from earning a living.

He pursued the matter through the courts to the European Court of Justice. The outcome set the following precedent:

- no one may be prevented from seeking other work at a time when they are out of contract with the previous employer; nor may they be prevented from seeking other work at a time when it becomes apparent that their contract is ending and may not be renewed; it is illegal to place any restraint on employees in their quest for work.

The second point brought into question what, in the UK, had always been regarded as a grey area. This is where an employer places a condition on the contract of employment, preventing an employee seeking work or accepting a job with a competitor, customer or client for a period of time at the end of the current period of employment. The reason most often stated for this is commercial confidentiality – the ability to offer trade secrets, product specifications, customer and client lists to the new organization. In practice, it is always better to avoid falling into disputes over this, except where it can be proven that the employee in question has stolen products or client lists. If an organization ever pursues or prosecutes an ex-employee for such a reason, it carries the burden of having to prove that a form of theft or industrial espionage of this sort has indeed taken place.

FLEXIBLE WORKING

Flexible working has first to be seen in its broadest context, as follows:

- careers and occupations that last 40 years, based on a 40-hour working week, for 48 weeks of the year are no longer viable; everyone (whatever their expertise or preference) must expect to experience great changes in occupation, changes in the ways in which things are done, the obsolescence of some occupations and the creation of new ones
- earnings levels no longer rise steadily, nor are they the product of a combination of loyalty, promotion and enhanced expertise; people tend to expect enhanced rewards today, rather than the promise of enhanced rewards tomorrow
- core and peripheral activities, in which organizations increasingly structure their workforce according to the peaks and troughs of activities, drives towards contracting out specialist activities to specialist organizations rather than retaining expensive expertise in-house, especially when it is only occasionally required, the creation of networks that can be called upon at short notice to handle problems or cater for sudden upturns in activities

- the extension of part-time and intermittent patterns of employment to cope with the peaks and troughs of business demand
- the extension of activities covered by alternative patterns of employment, especially homeworking and subcontracting
- the nature of the organization's activities and the particular pressures and constraints that are present, production and operational pressures, any constraints placed by technology, the demands of customers and the nature of their relationship with the organization
- the blurring of the distinction between full-time and part-time patterns of employment; in the UK there is now very little difference in basic employment rights between full-time and part-time staff, and it is normally best practice to treat them exactly the same.

This is the context in which consideration of different patterns of employment and hours of work takes place. The overall drive is to synchronize employee working hours with operational demands. This has the purpose of having people present when they are needed, and not present when they are not needed. It reduces costs, improves the effectiveness of the human resource and ultimately improves organizational performance.

In terms of work content and design, whatever the hours worked, or nature of the job to be done, the following characteristics need to be satisfied:

- people should have some degree of autonomy over the way tasks are to be achieved
- people should have a certain amount of responsibility for their own work, for the resources that they use and for the way in which they structure and organize their working day
- variety and autonomy should be present
- repetitive tasks should be kept to a minimum
- people should receive regular feedback on their performance, and this should be carried out face to face in the course of normal supervision
- the place of the job in the wider scheme of things should be clearly understood
- social contact should be available wherever practicable
- learning, training and development opportunities should be in-built into work patterns
- people need to know what is expected of them in terms of performance, attitude, behaviour and demeanour
- people should be treated fairly and evenly at all times

■ work should have distinctive measures of success and failure; people should know and understand the means by which success and failure is evaluated.

From the employee's point of view, therefore, the hours should be long enough and regular enough to enable a sufficient amount of work to be carried out to give feelings of satisfaction and achievement. The longer and more regular the hours, the quicker a real identity and commitment is generated. Where hours are short and intermittent, there is a pressure on managers and supervisors to take additional steps to build this identity and commitment quickly.

From the employer's point of view, the issue is the ability to integrate this with the frequency, regularity, length of work period that the employee is present and the output that is required, feasible or achievable. People on different hours and patterns of work have to be integrated with one another so that an effective working environment and relationship is created. The greater the ability to do this, the greater the reduction in the use and administration of procedures and problem-solving, thus freeing up time and resources for productive and profitable activities.

Whatever the nature or patterns of work, everyone works better in a clean, comfortable and wholesome environment. This does not mean luxury. Moreover, there are work pressures and constraints to be considered, especially where work is to be carried out in extremes of heat or cold, wet or dry, or in dangerous conditions. Within this context, it should normally be possible to provide everyone with basic standards of comfort and cleanliness, rest, refreshment and meal time arrangements, car parking or transport to and from the workplace and adequate standards of warmth and comfort. Making this available to everyone reinforces the value, respect and esteem in which everyone is held regardless of their pattern of work or length of working hours.

Alternative patterns and hours of work

The main patterns are:

■ annual hours: where the number of hours of work required each year of the employee is established and patterns of work agreed between the individual and the organization; in the UK the normal upper figure on this is 2,000 hours (which represents an equivalent of 40 hours per week for 50 weeks of the year)
■ compressed working: where 'full-time' hours are worked, but compressed into fewer working days – for example, instead of

working 8 hours a day for five days, people work 10 hours per day for four days or even 12–15 hours per day for three days

■ term time working: in which those with responsibilities for school age children are either given extensive unpaid leave, or else required to take their annual leave during the school holidays

■ continental shifts: whereby people follow patterns of work such as four days on and two days off, or three days on and two days off so that the whole week is covered in a fair manner

■ hours to suit: where the demands of the work are reconciled with the work time preferences of the employees

■ twilight shifts: where work is offered between 5.30pm and 10.30pm to people (often married women, students and those of school age) enabling them to fit work around their other commitments.

■ flexitime, based on:
  ▪ core periods, when attendance is compulsory, either for a given period every day, or for a given period on certain days
  ▪ optional time, which is attendance at other than core times, enabling employees to choose the time suitable to themselves when they are most productive and again to reconcile this with their other demands and commitments

■ job sharing: where a single position is shared out between two or more persons. Job sharing works best when the post is shared between two persons. For reasons of administration and control, it is both unusual and impractical to share the post between more than three persons (see Summary box 10.6).

Summary box 10.6   Job sharing

The form of work known as job sharing became widely used in the late 1970s and early 1980s in the UK. The main reasons and attractions for this form of work were as follows:

• it enabled women to balance work and other commitments (especially family) on a fully standardized employment basis
• it gave full employment protection to those under job sharing arrangements, as the shared job was designated as full time
• it enabled employers to retain expertise, albeit on a reduced hours basis
• it was heavily promoted as one way forward in the granting of equal opportunities.

It remains true that it has worked, and continues to work, in many situations. However, with the removal of distinction between full-time and part-time patterns of employment, and employment rights, employers are now looking very much harder at the benefits. In particular, the following problems have become apparent:

- When one of the sharers moves on, it may not be possible to replace them adequately.
- Work loadings that were acceptable when the sharing started may become unacceptable as both employer and customer demands change.
- If the employer offers additional benefits, it may be necessary to duplicate those benefits, rather than share them out.
- Pension schemes and other statutory bodies are ambivalent towards the role and function of job shares, both when a full-time job is shared, and at the end of a sharing period, when the position reverts to a full-time arrangement for one of the sharers.
- Employers also perceive problems in age discrepancies (eg if one of the sharers has only a little while to go to retirement age, while the other has many years to go); this is seen as a barrier to effective job sharing.

Moreover, as part-time and flexible patterns of work become ever more developed and sophisticated, the formalized boundaries around job sharing become an increasing administrative burden that can be coped with much more effectively by adopting other patterns of employment.

Summary box 10.7   Consideration in the design of work patterns

- On the face of it, having one member of staff working long hours of, say, up to 60 hours per week and possibly taking work home in the evenings or on their days off (or failing to take all their leave entitlement) is attractive, because a large return is being made on one salary. If there really is 60 hours worth of high quality work to be done each week, this can only be sustained by one person in the very short term. Over longer periods, the quality of work, personal health and personal life all suffer.
- There is a culture among managerial, professional and white collar staff in the UK of the 'work based lifestyle'. This consists of putting in long hours to demonstrate commitment, loyalty and dedication. In many cases a proportion of social life becomes centred around work. Long hours are invariably necessary once in a while. If they are continually necessary, it is either because the job is too big for one person, or because the job holder is not capable of doing it.

- This applies to other occupations. Employees, often quite willingly, carry out overtime or work additional periods during their time off. The end result again is stress and burn out. Moreover, the employee becomes disappointed, frustrated and angry when the overtime and extra shifts come to an end as their standard of living then suffers.
- If hours are too short and intermittent, the employee has no opportunity to build up any true working relationship with colleagues, managers and supervisors or the organization. The result is frustration and disappointment. This occurs even if for some reason employees have chosen their hours of work. Where short periods of work are required and where part time is the normal employment pattern, hours should still be long and regular enough to build up a mutual identity and positive beneficial relationship.
- Hours to suit should only be offered on the employee's terms alone, where the work permits this, or where there is otherwise no possibility of filling the vacancy.
- Flexitime is attractive and popular with people, because it normally allows them to build up additional leave entitlement through the amount of hours that they work during the optional period. It is most commonly found in white collar and service sectors, and is increasingly being extended to production and sales functions.
- Problems with job sharing arise when, for some reason, it becomes impossible for the job sharers to continue to work together.
- It may also be necessary to consider variations in work pressures, for example, where the job share splits the working week into mornings and afternoons, and where it is more stressful in the mornings, or where the working week is divided at Wednesday lunchtime and the work is more pressurized on Thursday and Friday than Monday and Tuesday.
- If additional hours are required, these should first be offered to existing staff. This is especially important where people are on patterns of low or infrequent attendance, as it gives the opportunity to develop the total working relationship. This also reduces the need for unnecessary recruitment, selection, induction and job training, and the administrative burden that these create.
- Those on distinctive patterns of employment, for example, Saturday and Sunday crews in retail and permanent night shifts, need the same positive identity and commitment to be generated as everyone else. Otherwise, these groups may become isolated and this tends to lead to unofficial work regulation and canteen cultures.

Whatever the hours agreed, the main issues are:

- to get the best possible work out of the member of staff
- to gain a proper professional and committed working relationship
- to give the member of staff the opportunity to earn a fair living
- to build a positive and mutually productive continuing relationship.

Other patterns of work

Enrichment

Job and work enrichment has the purpose of making all work as satisfying and fulfilling as possible. It applies to any form of work that becomes mundane, repetitive or routine, all of which tend to lead to disaffection and boredom – and, therefore, to loss of performance. It takes the following forms:

■ **Rotation** Here the employee is changed or rotated through a variety of tasks, activities and work stations. This should occur regularly enough to generate interest, but not so regularly as to fragment the work being carried out.
■ **Enlargement** Here the employee is given additional tasks and (increasingly) responsibilities attached to the main duties. Additional tasks often include quality control, customer liaison and dealing with problems and queries.
■ **Consultation** This obtains the employee's view of the best way of carrying out the work, on new work and work station design, on the choice of new equipment and on problems with existing equipment.
■ **Training and development** This may be offered for current activities, for the future, to identify potential and aptitudes and to enable individuals to pursue personal choices and preferences.
■ **Project work** This is based on a combination of organizational requirements and personal drives. Much of this often stems from suggestion schemes and membership of work improvement groups and quality circles. Some of this may also arise from secondments and from the continuous need for fresh approaches to problems.

Enrichment builds on and reinforces positive attitudes and commitment. It strengthens the mutual identity and interest of employee and employer. It identifies personal potential and aptitudes, and enlarges the fund of talent and expertise available.

Empowerment

Empowerment is a form of job enrichment that involves employees in any or all of the following:

■ taking on additional responsibility for administration, customer satisfaction, record keeping or cashing up (eg in restaurants and checkout work)

■ taking on extra duties such as bank and retail, cash desk and checkout staff, taking on sales and customer service functions
■ being allowed to use initiative in acting in the organization's best interests in its dealings with its customers
■ work improvement groups, quality improvement groups and quality circles that are given broad remits in which to work and allowed initiative and responsibility to carry out their tasks
■ suggestion schemes, especially those which give employees scope, and sometimes a budget, to put their proposals into practice and which reward them for extra profits made or reductions in costs.

Apart from tackling specific problems and issues, these activities contribute to employee and organizational development and reinforce commitment to product quality and customer service.

Homeworking

Homeworking is attractive all round. For the employer, there is no need to provide expensive production, operational or office space as that is the employee's home. For the employee, there is no need to travel to work. Homeworking is well established in various sectors – for example, computer software, fashion and clothing sales, journalism, financial services and cosmetics. Its potential is limited only by the approach and attitude of organizations and the strong demands of large sectors of the population that they physically separate their working and non-working lives. There is great potential for administration, financial management, purchasing and supply to be carried out by people working at work stations established in their own homes – and potential therefore for organizations to curtail their premises' requirements.

Notes

■ Homeworking employees need to be provided with all the facilities and equipment that they would have if they were working on the employer's premises. For white collar staff this includes phone, computer, fax, stationery and access to copying, mail and postage facilities. For those engaged in production activities, this includes any tools of the trade, access to supplies and means of delivery. For those engaged in sales, this is likely to include a car as well as other office equipment.
■ Payment for homeworking normally covers the use of any domestic equipment for work purposes (eg telephone, computer, fax). It also normally includes paying an allowance in return for the member of staff using a part of their home as a workplace.

■ Homeworkers feel isolated; this is often because they are cut off from the mainstream of their organization. Homeworking requires the establishment of effective channels of communication. Regular face-to-face meetings, reviews of performance and the ability to discuss progress are essential and must form part of the way of working.

■ People must be prepared to cope with the lack of regular contact and the loss of social interaction and regular attendance at a designated place of work.

■ Homeworking must be fair to everyone concerned. Those who are not offered the chance of homeworking feel let down. Those who are offered the chance of homeworking often feel that they are being marginalized and that their opportunities for promotion and variation are limited.

Fixed term contracts

This is where people are taken on for a specific period of time to do a particular job, where there is a requirement for absence cover (eg maternity) and where people are taken on for the duration of a project however long that lasts.

The boundaries are clearly stated in advance so that it is known to both employee and employer when the work is to finish.

A form of fixed term contract is also often used for research jobs and to pursue ideas to see if they have potential. Employers normally place a deadline by which likely results should at least become apparent.

Piecework and 'job and finish'

This is where the employee is paid per item. Most commonly used in industrial and production work, it is less popular now than in the past because the volume of work possible is governed by production technology and because it tended to concentrate on volume rather than quality.

Fee paying work

This is for employees who carry out work above and beyond the call of duty (one-off payments or honoraria).

Autonomous work groups

This is where the group has a set amount of work to carry out and how this is to be done is agreed by group members and its manager.

Autonomous work unit

This is where the unit is a distinctive feature of a larger organization. It works in line with organizational policies and aims, and its performance is affected by its location.

Unit managers are responsible for getting the best out of the unit in the prevailing local conditions. They are given resources and support from the centre, and autonomy and authority to act independently within these constraints.

Seasonal work

This is used in order to cope with seasonal pressures (eg Christmas, summer).

On-call

This is where individuals and groups do not work regularly for the organization, but where they may be called in at short notice to cover for sudden upturns in demand or to handle crises. Some on-call schemes pay a regular retainer; others include this in the form of increased payments when the work is actually carried out.

Other ER factors in the management of patterns of work

Alienation

Alienation occurs overwhelmingly where there is no positive identity between organization and staff, or between or among groups of staff. The result is that staff seek refuge in professional and personal allegiances, causing divisions between and among staff and work groups. It is caused by bad or inappropriate management style and practice, the quality of work and the working environment. Symptoms of alienation are as follows:

■ Proliferation of discipline, disputes and grievances on minor issues. This is often compounded by a known, believed or perceived truculence when staff approach supervisors and managers on these issues and when staff invoke procedures for the management of disputes and grievances before the organization has had sufficient time to respond to the initial request. This is also symptomatic of a fundamental lack of trust and belief in the organization as well as (or even instead of) in the manager or supervisor in question.

■ Recourse to trade union or staff representatives to get problems solved. This may be done rather than putting the problems directly to managers and supervisors, or using organization processes which are after all, open to everyone.

■ Joining trade unions, whether they are recognized or not. Where they are not recognized, employees are taking out union membership as a form of employment protection insurance. Where unions are recognized, substantial increases in union membership and activity have to be viewed as reflecting feelings of alienation. This may also be true of increased activities of professional and occupational bodies.

This has to be seen in the broadest context, however. Unions and professional bodies may be offering a range of perks and benefits that more than repays the subscription, or they may recently have appointed lay or full-time officials who are much more committed to membership increases than previously. There may be a local social history of union identity and membership. However, it does indicate the need for organizations and their managers to take an active interest based on analysis and evaluation as a key feature of maintaining effective ER.

Pay and rewards

Effective pay and reward systems must meet a variety of purposes and considerations. They must reward productive effort, expertise and output. They must provide an adequate level of income on a regular basis for those receiving it. They must attract people to the work in the first place and be of a sufficient standard to maintain continued interest and satisfaction, and to encourage commitment, and they must motivate and generate energy and activity.

They must meet the expectations of those carrying out the work, and the reward systems in place must meet the expectations of the organizations that design them.

The systems must be fair and honest to all concerned, transparent and open, and with rules and regulations published and available to all (see Summary box 10.8).

Summary box 10.8   Pay and reward systems

Pay and reward systems are normally broken down into two components: pay and benefits.

Pay

The following elements of payment can be identified:

- **Payments** These may be annual, quarterly, monthly, four-weekly, weekly, daily, hourly, by commission, by bonus, in increments, as fees or as profit, performance and merit-related payments.
- **Allowances** These may be for attendance, disturbance, shift working, weekend working, unsocial hours, training and development, location and relocation, absence from home, or for special conditions, such as dangerous and hazardous locations and occupations.

Payment mixes adopted by organizations in devising and implementing reward strategies for different staff categories cover a variety of aims and purposes in response to particular situations. The general purpose is to address the following:

- **Expectations** This is to meet the expectations of the job holder.
- **Attractiveness** This is for the purposes of attracting and retaining staff.
- **Motivation** This is based on value, effort, expertise and future commitment.
- **Mixes of payment with other aspects** People in the UK expect to receive a 'reward package' – a combination of pay with other benefits and rewards. This varies according to the particular situation.
- **Occupational aspects** Here, part of the reward package is likely to include the provision of specialist, expert and continuous training.
- **Performance and profit-related elements** These are related either to the achievement of particular objectives, or to overall company performance.

Where it is based on targets, the scheme must be believed in, valued and understood by all concerned. Targets must be achievable. They must be neither too easy nor too difficult. Targets must be set in advance; if they are achieved, payment must always be made. The purpose is to reward effort and achievement on the part of the staff.

Where pay is related to company profitability and performance, the best and fairest approach is to pay everyone the same percentage of their salary. For example, a 10 per cent performance-related element would result in someone on £3,000 receiving a bonus of £300, while someone on £30,000 would receive a bonus of £3,000 and so on.

Where performance is to be rewarded in the issuing of share options, this again should be on an equal basis. The availability of share options should be there for anyone who wants to take advantage of them; where restrictions are placed, again this should be done as a percentage of individual salary.

Where pay is related to team performance, all members should receive the same percentage bonus.

Where pay is related to individual performance, there must be absolute trust and confidence between assessor and assessee.

Notes

- If the hourly rate is too low, no effective wage–work relationship is possible. Pay is a mark of value, and low pay in the eyes of the employees means low value. People take low paid jobs only because they have to and until something better comes along.
- Turnover, absenteeism and low productivity all rise where the employees are, or perceive themselves to be, unvalued or undervalued.
- Overpayment does not make mundane or boring work more interesting. It makes it more bearable (see Chapter 9). When pay rates rise, there is a short-term benefit. This is followed by employees reverting to previous levels of activity and approach.
- Those who work from a variety of locations are normally provided with transport, travelling time, expenses and additional allowances. These are either paid separately or else worked into the total salary package.
- Those who work on a variety of jobs, which change frequently or regularly, or whose hours and shift patterns change frequently and regularly, are provided with additional payments to compensate. This is done either by:
  - making a point of itemizing each of the elements included in the wage or salary. This satisfies the perceptions and expectations of employees. It requires additional administration and in large organizations, with highly complex work hours and shift patterns, this is a heavy additional cost
  - paying a relatively high single wage or salary in return for which the employee works as necessary and directed. This takes a greater level of introduction and understanding; the payback is to remove the administrative burden indicated above.
- Integrity and equality – any system of payment must be understood and valued. It should treat people equally and with respect.

There is never a sound or honest reason for rewarding one group of the workforce at the expense of others. The effect is always to demoralize those who lose out. The longer-term effect is to enhance any divisions that already exist between the different elements of the workforce as they jockey for position to ensure that they are not the ones to lose out in the future.

By law, an itemized pay statement is required for all employees. This shows each element that makes up the gross pay and each deduction made before payment, and the amount of net pay.

Pay rises, bonuses and other rewards should always be paid on the date on which they are due. Again, this is a mark of respect and value.

Economic rent is the payment of very high rates for particular forms of expertise. While this is clearly essential in some circumstances, care is to be taken that the appearance of overpayment of some individuals does not have a detrimental and damaging effect on the rest of the workforce. Payment of high salaries that distort the general pattern should only be contemplated when all other approaches have failed.

Payment of low rates is certainly possible for unskilled staff in periods of high unemployment (eg the UK in the mid 1990s). Again, this should only really be contemplated if there is no alternative, for example, if the organization is going through a lean time. Under-payment is a mark of contempt for the staff.

Pay freezes and reductions are also demoralizing and damaging to the staff. Again, they should only be contemplated when there is no other alternative.

Benefits

Benefits are items and services offered by employers to employees as part of the reward package. They consist of the following:

- **General benefits** These include loans (eg for season tickets), pension (contributory and non-contributory), subsidies (on company products, canteen, travel), car, telephone/car phone, private health care, training and development and luncheon vouchers.
- **Flexible benefits** These are packages that all staff members can have access to if they wish to do so and which are offered to all staff members on the same basis.
- **Chains of gold or super-benefits** Examples of these are schools holidays (teachers), cheap loans (banks, building societies), free/cheap travel (railways, shipping, airlines) and special pension arrangements (for older and longer serving staff).

The main reasons for using benefits are as follows:

- to encourage certain types of behaviour, for example, paying for training courses, paying subscriptions to professional associations and expert bodies or paying for accommodation while employees are working away from home
- to encourage potential employees to join the organization, for example, relocation expenses, travel packages or use of company cars
- as a way of retaining employees, for example, the opportunity to buy shares, increases in holiday entitlements in line with length of service and enhanced pension rights
- the recognition of long service, for example, with presentations after specific time periods
- as a demonstration of being a caring employer, for example, sick pay, occupational health schemes, life assurance, health insurance and private health care plans and school fee plans.
- a commitment to equal opportunities, for example, nurseries, career break schemes and sabbaticals and flexible hours and locations.

Flexible benefits may also be used as a means of recognizing and indicating enhanced status, for example, allowing certain grades of employee to travel first class, stay in 4 and 5-star accommodation and providing high quality cars. However, this invariably detracts from the fundamental basis of equality that is essential to all flexible working arrangements.

In general, therefore, benefit packages will be made available to staff on an even footing. The only exceptions are where the benefit is work related to certain categories of employee; even in these circumstances, the offering of benefits to certain groups of employees but not others must be on operational grounds alone.

Notes

The mix of benefits available depends on the patterns of work of the employees and the nature of the organization's business. Some organizations do have hook-ups with others, for example, working for a travel agent entitles the opportunity of free travel on certain airlines, shipping and railway companies, and some organizations provide discount cards for their staff to be used at department stores, supermarkets, travel agencies and finance companies.

Benefit choice is most effective when things that are offered benefit all employees, where the ability to choose is based on personal and occupational circumstances and where the benefits are not seen as privileges only available to a chosen few.

Some organizations allow their staff either to choose the benefit or to take a cash equivalent. For example, if it is not possible for an employee to use up their total annual leave allowance during the course of a year for operational reasons, then a cash alternative should always be made available. If it is not possible for a parent to bring their child into the company nursery, a cash payment should be made instead.

Giving individuals the choice of determining which benefits they require from a total package enables them to weigh up their own current needs and how their organization can best serve them. This reinforces the positive message that the organization cares about them as individuals as well as employees.

Chains of gold are extremely attractive to employees when they first come to work and for as long as the relationship between employee and employer remains productive and positive. They become a burden on the individual when the relationship is lost. This is especially true where a financial commitment has been entered into as an integral part of the employment package, such as a free or cheap loan from a bank or building society, or a subscription to a pension or life assurance arrangement as part of a flexible benefits plan. There is at least a moral duty on employers to make arrangements as painless as possible to be entered into when the employee seeks to leave the organization. In this way, the employee concerned is looked after to the best of the organization's ability for the whole term of their employment. It also gives positive messages to those remaining, in that they are reassured that if they do suddenly need to leave, they will be taken care of properly.

The main ER issues here are:

■ wage and salary levels, and the extent to which they continue to attract, retain and motivate, and the extent to which they are known, believed or perceived to place adequate value on both the people concerned and the work that they carry out
■ differentials between occupational groups, within occupational groups and between ranks in the hierarchies
■ salary scales, whether a single scale is chosen for the whole organization and people placed on it or whether different scales are chosen for different groups, ranks, occupations, divisions and functions and, if so, the extent to which they are nevertheless fair and equitable across the whole organization; fairness and evenness in the issuing of increments and other pay rises
■ criteria for the establishment of profit-related pay, performance-related pay and other 'merit pay' schemes, application of these criteria in a fair and equitable manner
■ organizational attitudes to perks and benefits and any differentials concerned, regarding the rights of individuals and groups to access to these benefits
■ different rates of increase, levels of pay, advantageous scales and incremental approaches for so-called 'key' members of staff (see Summary box 10.9)

■ attainable and unattainable performance targets for which bonuses are paid or not paid
■ attendance allowances, which used to be extremely popular, but which have now fallen into discredit (see Summary box 10.10).

Summary box 10.9   Payment and key members of staff: examples

The aspect of pay at which organizations have to work the hardest to support and justify, concerns reward packages for top staff. Examples are as follows:

- **British Gas** In 1994, the Chief Executive of British Gas received a 60 per cent pay rise, taking his salary up from £190,000 per annum to £400,000 per annum. It also emerged that he was to be paid this salary in US$, because this was his preference. At the same time, he was asking showroom, technical and maintenance staff to take a pay freeze for two years.
- **Camelot** This is the company that runs the UK national lottery. In 1998, it announced a percentage profits increase of 15 per cent comparative to the previous year. As the result of this, some directors' salaries went up by 19 per cent. This was far in excess of staff salaries, the overall average increase of which was 3.5 per cent. Because of the nature of the activities, there was also a widespread belief that directors were benefiting to the detriment of the charities and good causes for which money was supposed to be being raised.

This is directly at variance with current approaches based on 'best practice', in which percentage increases are supposed to be applied across the board, so that absolute positions in the pay order are not disrupted. It is also the approach of Japanese organizations in the UK, and one factor cited as a key to their organizational, behavioural and ER success (as well as commercial).

The universal point is that this form of pay differential presents the individuals, or groups of staff, that are paid detrimentally, as having lesser value to their organization. There is also a very strong perception that those responsible for the pay and reward policies, and the broader structure of ER in general, are using the system to benefit themselves.

Summary box 10.10   Attendance allowances: Allied Irish Bank

In 1992, the Allied Irish Bank introduced a form of incentive that was designed to ensure that staff attended when they were supposed to attend and, in particular, that they did not take days of 'self-certificated sickness' when requiring the odd day off. They accordingly proposed that anybody completing a full year's work without a day of 'self-certificated sickness' absence would receive an extra week's holiday the following year.

In practice, what happened was that anybody who genuinely took a day's 'self-certificated sickness' absence, simply made sure that they took the other four days in any case, so that they did not lose the additional perceived week's holiday that was on offer.

The key to effective ER in the management of pay and reward is empathy – the ability of those responsible for the design and delivery of pay and reward policies to understand the range of responses on the part of those at the receiving end. Contentious and demeaning issues can thus be recognized at the outset. Where possible, they can then be designed out of the system; where this is not possible, the potential for conflict, dispute and loss of morale can at least be assessed in advance, so that the organization and its managers know and understand the nature and scale of the problems they are storing up for themselves (see Summary box 10.11).

Summary box 10.11   Payment and the manufacture of lemonade

A large soft drinks company operating in the south-east of the UK decided at an early stage of its development that it would be unable to pay sufficiently high levels to retain operative staff (those directly involved in the manufacture and packaging of the lemonade) for long periods of time.

The company therefore paid the minimum possible in the circumstances. Rather than facing regular disputes and grievances, it concentrated on ensuring a steady supply of staff, all of whom it knew would only stay for periods of up to six months.

Turnover

Staff turnover comes about for a variety of reasons and when considering these the broadest view is necessary. They are not all symptomatic of ER problems. They are as follows:

■ **Size, scale, scope and nature of work** All these may be limiting factors in those seeking substantial advancement or variety and in these cases the best organizations actively encourage their staff to move on rather than risking demotivation and conflict borne of frustration.

■ **Location of work** This may again mean that wider opportunities are limited. Or it may mean requiring staff to work in extremes of heat, cold or isolation, in which case the limitations of the location need to be in-built into work patterns. Or it may require people to commute to work, which has implications for working hours (start and finish times), attendance (eg where public transport is unreliable) and perks and benefits (eg the provision of free or subsidized season tickets and travel).

These may or may not give rise to ER concerns. Of more precise concern as a barometer of organization ER is the relationship between labour turnover and the following:

■ **Management style** This may be appropriate to some groups of staff but not to others.

■ **Expectations** These may suit some groups of staff but not others.

■ **Levels and nature of prevailing conflict** This is personally as well as occupationally demoralizing, and causes people to look elsewhere.

■ **Wage and salary levels** These are of concern when they are plainly uncompetitive, unevenly applied, or where there is no other overriding reason for employees to stay.

■ **Knowledge, belief or perception of inequality of treatment** This could be within and between groups, departments, divisions, occupations and locations.

■ **Inequality of opportunity** This could be felt within and between groups, departments, divisions, occupations and locations, especially where those working in one location are known, believed or perceived to receive preferential treatment for promotion opportunities and advancement.

The whole question of labour turnover can be addressed through structured exit interviews. Provided that matters covering confidentiality and impartiality are adequately addressed, they indicate the extent and prevalence of general questions of human resource management and managerial style, as well as the specific ER issues.

CONCLUSIONS

Work patterns are individually constructed in each case. The contribution to the management of ER therefore lies in understanding the nature of work patterns, their composition, the expectations and aspirations of those involved in them and the potential for conflict arising out of each of the areas indicated.

The fundamental principle for the management of that part of ER concerned with work patterns lies in equality. Whatever the length of service, occupational profession, hours of work or pattern of attendance, all staff must be treated fairly and equally. This is a fundamental management lesson; it should also concern all those – including staff representatives, trade unions and employers' associations – who are concerned with the promotion of effective and positive ER. The acceptance of the principle of equality and fairness in the treatment of all members of staff, whatever their circumstances, is also a fundamental management quality.

11

MANAGEMENT QUALITIES

INTRODUCTION

However adequate the strategy, design and approach of organizational ER, it is only implemented effectively and successfully if the required management qualities are available. These are underpinned by the reality of the conduct of organizational ER, and the extent to which this coincides with its policy and direction, by the attention and priority it gives to the expertise of its managers and supervisors in these activities and, in particular, by the consistency of operation of disciplinary grievance, disputes and other procedures. These factors are then in turn reinforced by the extent to which top managers support and reinforce the position of their more junior colleagues in day-to-day ER operations and activities and their attitude to the conduct and outcome of particular cases (see Summary box 11.1).

Summary box 11.1   ER in practice: examples

Different approaches may be illustrated as follows:

Sanyo

This company seeks to create conditions in which problems do not occur. This is not a hands-off approach; rather, managers and supervisors are expected to conduct their ER activities and general staff management to keep the occurrence of disputes, grievances and disciplinary activities to an absolute minimum. This means that the company insists that its junior managers and supervisors remain visible to the staff at all times and take a fundamentally positive attitude to staff issues as and when they arise.

Post Office

In early 1998, the Post Office published a radically revised staff management and ER handbook. In this, the required attitude, together with the very distinctive procedures to be used, were detailed. To date, the majority of issues that have fallen under this particular procedure and publication have arisen as the result of a lack of fundamental shift in attitudes on all parts, together with insufficient staff training.

Police

Most police forces publish distinctive sets of standards by which ER is to be conducted. Recent problems – including those highlighted elsewhere in this book – have arisen because of the tolerance of different approaches and standards and the fact that different groups of staff are known, believed or perceived to have had their cases conducted from different standpoints.

Whichever the approach used (and there is no single right answer) the following must be present in daily ER practice:

- a lack of tolerance of varying standards, and a determination to ensure that everybody is treated under the same set of principles
- the publication of codes of practice (including the Sanyo example shown in Appendix B)
- total institutional support for all activities, which must be supported by a fundamental integrity of approach.

With reference to the second point, it is the operation of the approach that is at issue, rather than its design. Life is very much easier if the design is clear and straightforward, and is supported by staff briefings and training. However, training is not an end in itself.

STRATEGIC AND DIRECTIONAL MANAGEMENT

A manager needs the fundamental capability to devise and implement suitable ER policies, perspectives, standards and approaches to organization ER in general, and discipline in particular, based on a complete understanding of the nature of activities and the nature of those carrying them out. This must be supported by the capability to devise and implement operational procedures, means of staff representation, and corporate attitudes to ER problems and issues.

Ideally, this means recognizing the position of staff as stakeholders, with a legitimate interest equivalent to that of shareholders. Where this is neither acceptable nor possible, it is still essential that these attitudes and approaches are present when ER principles and policies are devised, even though this will be a part of the pursuit of shareholder (or for public services, political) interests.

Whichever the approach, universal attitudes are required as follows:

■ Openness, transparency and honesty are essential in the policies created and in their operation. This should be supported by a clearly understood rationale for any material differences in the treatment and standards for staff with different levels of expertise or rank, or for those who work in different places or varying patterns of work.
■ In the constitution of representative bodies, there must be clearly defined terms of reference and objectives that make the required contribution to total organizational performance.
■ There must be capability and willingness to develop ER institutions, policies and practices when required. This is significant in all aspects of ER. It must be in-built into ER capacity when takeovers, mergers, withdrawals and divestments are being considered, or when a change of status is being contemplated for the whole or a part of the particular organization (see Summary box 11.2). Remember that all policies and practices may be streamlined, improved and developed.

Summary box 11.2   Takeovers, mergers and withdrawals

When takeovers, mergers, withdrawals, sell-offs and divestments occur, there are legal obligations on all organizations involved to accept the main terms and conditions of employment of the staff, together with specific ER practices, as a condition:

- **Takeovers and mergers** Both the organization being taken over, and the organization effecting the takeover, must understand that staff terms and conditions of employment, and specific ER policies and practices, are acquired 'lock, stock and barrel'. Changes of status may not take place for the purpose of reducing wages, or trade union derecognition. Nor may they take place for material variations in terms and conditions of employment. Specific rights – especially pension rights – are also preserved as a part of the takeover.
- **Sell-offs and divestments** An organization selling or divesting a part of itself (or the whole of itself) must be sure in advance that the receiving organization can meet the obligations indicated above.
- **Change of status** This applies especially to government privatizations and the translation of activities and industries that were hitherto in the public sector into limited company or trust status. These activities may not be carried out for the purposes of materially reducing terms and conditions of employment. They may also not be carried out with the express or implied purpose of reducing the quality or integrity of ER.
- **Common factors** These may be summarized as follows:
  - legal obligations – whenever any of these activities are contemplated, there is a statutory duty on the part of all organizations involved to consult with representatives of all staff groups, to provide total and complete information in ways that are easily understandable, and to accommodate, so far as is reasonably practicable, the individual as well as collective interest
  - moral obligations – the EU Social Charter (Appendix A) requires that employers take a broader and more enlightened view of their continuing and residual obligations, as well as adhering specifically to the letter of the law. This means that organizations and their managers can be asked to account for their actions during mergers and takeovers, even though what was done may have precisely fitted the particular regulations in force at the time.

■ A distinctive approach is required to the institutions with which ER is to be conducted, especially trade unions and other employee representatives, employers' associations and their approaches, influences, values and priorities, and statutory bodies such as ACAS and the HSE. Ideally, this is founded in the positive and open, and is responsive especially to the views of expert bodies. Where it is not, for example, where the organization is sufficiently confident that its own standards will meet every legal, moral and directional issue anyway, the approach remains effective overall as long as this remains a priority.

In pluralist situations and more complex organizations greater attention is needed. This is because, both historically and traditionally, it is easy for this aspect of organizational policy to become clouded, or to lose its priority, in other operational activities. There must be understanding of the effects of business policy changes on ER, and of the potential for conflict if the two are not managed together. For example, where the organization takes a policy decision to shift from purchasing stockpiling to 'just in time' methods, there are implications for the work of the purchasing and supply function, and activities concerned with goods inward, storage and distribution. This is the sort of change that may lead to redundancies, redeployment and retraining; it is almost certain to require reconstitution of work groups and key tasks and may also require fundamental job and work evaluation (see Summary box 11.3).

Summary box 11.3   ER and job evaluation

Job, work and occupation evaluations go on all the time. Their purpose is to assess the nature, volume and priorities of work to be done, together with its value, to parcel it up into jobs and occupations, and to rank it or grade it in ways that are both fair, and also seen to be so. ER problems in job evaluation arise when:

- the job evaluation process is not transparent, understood or acceptable for some reason
- some groups of staff are known, understood, believed or perceived to have gained advantages through the system at the expense of others
- the process is long, complex and convoluted
- the appeals process is either cumbersome or constrained
- the process assumes greater importance than the work itself
- the process takes up a substantial proportion of organizational time and resources.

There are also derived problems that occur when:

- important or influential groups appear to have their position confirmed by the process
- non-influential groups appear to have their lack of influence confirmed by the process
- non-influential groups are found to require much greater importance than previously ascribed to them, and yet the organization does nothing about it

- important or influential groups are found not to warrant their previous importance or influence, and yet the organization does nothing about it
- the outcome of the process is radically to alter the salary or occupational structure. If this is done, it will be disruptive. If it is not, then those whose positions should have been enhanced will feel aggrieved (this is especially the case when staff groups have long felt that they were undervalued, because now the job evaluation exercise has given their dissatisfaction a form of legitimization)
- the outcome of the process is that certain departments, divisions, functions and categories of staff are no longer needed; this is always perceived by those affected that the job evaluation process has simply been used by senior management as a vehicle to cut costs.

Rigid job evaluation systems came to prominence in the UK in the 1970s. Their perceived advantage was to provide a line of reasoning for existing and developing hierarchical and occupational structures. They were eagerly seized on by organizations and their senior managers as a way out of constant dilemmas and conflicts, and having to cave in to the next point of pressure from the staff.

In many cases, all that happened was to change the pressure points and causes of conflict. Over the past 30 years, problems with job evaluation have reduced as managers have advanced their understanding of the process, and as the systems and processes themselves have become more simplified and flexible, and more appropriate to particular organizations. Residual problems – above all, ER and staff management problems – tend to remain where 'off-the-shelf' systems are brought in from consultants and are implemented by consultants who have no real understanding of the organization for whom they are working.

- There must be recognition of the need for harmony at board level between functional directors and top managers. Inter-departmental divisions and strife are major potential and actual causes of grievances and disputes, and this is only reduced where there is a measure of cohesion and universality of direction at the top. Even where this is the case, disputes are likely to arise, but at least their effects can be minimized and resolved early.
- The fundamental importance of ER as a business activity must be recognized. In the past, ER in many cases was an adversarial proceduralized activity, a device by which representatives of management and the workforce could engage in periodical ritualized battles. This is uncompetitive from a business point of view and therefore extremely unprofitable. It consumes financial

resources that could be better spent elsewhere. It is destructive to the morale of the organization as a whole and to its reputation among those with whom it does business (see Summary box 11.4).

Summary box 11.4   Negative effects of ER on the stakeholders

A summary of these is as follows:

- Shareholders form their own view of the presence of ER strife, in terms of affecting the potential for return on investment. Behaviourally, they may not wish to be associated with an organization that is permanently in strife with its employees.
- Backers of public services may seek to move public resources from where they are being consumed in industrial strife to areas where a better return is being made.
- Suppliers want to be reassured that, whatever the state of their customers, they will continue to receive regular orders and regular bills. Where strikes occur, this always affects the volume of business, and therefore profitability, carried out with suppliers.
- Distributors, customers and clients want at all times to know that the quality, value and regularity of what they receive will not be affected. In the past, it is true that some suppliers, customers and clients took sympathetic views of industrial strife; now this is not the case, and they may be persuaded to shift to organizations where their satisfaction can be guaranteed.
- Media coverage is always attracted by employee relations problems. The coverage may be localized for small activities (eg employment tribunal cases are always written up in the local press), while conflict affecting major public and private organizations always attracts widespread national media coverage.
- Community spirit and harmony is always adversely affected by strikes, disputes and continuing ER unrest. Also when staff are on strike or in dispute, their disposable income is reduced (because they do not get paid) and this has a knock-on commercial effect on other activities in the community.

Nobody ever wished to see the decline of coal, dock work, engineering or car manufacture in the UK. It is also true to say that their decline was not wholly attributable to the ER situation, although this clearly did not help. Incursions from containerization (docks), and foreign competitors (the other sectors indicated), occurred at the time when levels of strife in these sectors were at their greatest.

■ A clear distinction is required between the approach to the direction of ER and a commitment only to 'managing the mess'. Managing the mess occurs where there is directional vacuum or void. Where there is no clear direction, and especially where there is no clear responsibility, managing the mess becomes the alternative because the organization can at least be seen to be doing something (even if it is neither effective in problem-solving, nor a cause of real progress.

It is also very attractive to particular job holders. Organization ER officers gain reputations as 'trouble-shooters', or 'hard men/women', or a reputation for directness, toughness or some other perceived required quality. In the management of public service institutions, politicians use ER factors in support of their own interests, and to make a name for themselves. For the individuals concerned, therefore, managing the mess is very profitable and many have made, and advanced, careers on this basis. This is in spite of the fact that their activities have been extremely destructive to the organizations with which they have been involved and that they have purported to serve.

■ There must be recognition of the potential for the existence of special interest groups, vested interest and over-mighty subjects and departments. Again, these flourish best in a vacuum or void. Where no clear responsibility or direction exists, it is institutionally very easy to leave ER (and indeed other business and operational matters) in the hands of those who shout the loudest, or who push themselves forward. This is often in spite of any real authority or expertise in the area. Any genuine concern for the future direction and success of the organization on the part of the vested interest, is always tempered by the fact that it has its own priorities.

■ There must be understanding of the behavioural aspects that are created with the institution of ER. If trade unions are recognized then they will always try to raise their own image and value in the eyes of those whom they represent. They will publish and distribute their own version of what occurs in organizational ER and the committees and institutions that support it. As well as behavioural norms, they create their own rites and rituals and these also have to be managed (see Table 11.1). They also create themselves and their officials in their own desired image, and the signals and the cues that arise from this have to be managed (see Summary box 11.5).

Misreading or lack of understanding of all this diverts everyone from ER priorities and may cause extensive and expensive strife. It also remains true that nobody is required to put up with obnoxious behaviour; again, this underlines the need for precise and effective organization ER design if this is to be avoided.

Types of rite	Social consequences	Role in promoting/ Consolidating culture change	Examples
Rites of passage	Facilitate transition of people into social roles and statuses that are new for them	• Consolidate ways people carry out social roles • Promote new ways of social interaction	• Induction of new recruits • Create union/ work group/ vested interest identity
Rites of degradation	Dissolve social identities and their attendant power	• Provide public acknowledgements that problems exist • Defend group boundaries by redefining who belongs and who does not • Reaffirm social importance and value of role involved	• Firing and replacing top executives • Firing and replacing those who are known or seen to lose disputes
Rites of enhancement	Enhance social identities and their attendant power	• Spread good news about the organization • Provide public recognition of individuals for their accomplishments and motivate others to similar efforts • Emphasize social value of performance of work roles	• Triumphs for those who win disputes • Media coverage • Personal reputations
Rites of renewal	Refurbish social structures and improve the ways they function	• Reassure members that something is being done about problems • Focus attention on some problems and away from others • Legitimate systems of power and authority	• ER project management • Joint consultation • Visibility to trade unions/staff representatives
Rites of integration	Encourage and revive shared feelings that bind people together and keep them committed to a social system	• Permit venting of emotion and temporary loosening of various norms • Reassert and reaffirm, by contrast, moral rightness of usual norms	• Joint consultation • Joint negotiations
Rites of conflict reduction	Reduce conflict and aggression	• Re-establish equilibrium in disturbed social relations • Compartmentalize conflict and its disruptive effects	• Internal appeal systems • Union–management committees

Table 11.1 *Types of rite (ritual) and their roles in ER* (source: adapted from Trice and Beyer (1985))

Summary box 11.5   ER rituals

One trade union senior official, when conducting negotiations, always used to screw up the first offer presented to him ostentatiously, and throw it into the corner of the room.

This worked extremely well with those managers who knew him, and it also gained him a reputation among his members as an extremely tough negotiator.

It worked less well with those who did not know him, or who would not play the game. On one occasion, a dispute at an engineering firm was prolonged for a week when the company's ER director treated the union leader's opening gambit in exactly the same way. On another, the company in question moved to derecognize his union because they perceived his action as contempt rather than ritual. When he produced the same action with the ER committee of an employers' federation, they in turn, ordered that the union replace him with someone with better manners.

When he retired, he was widely venerated in the media as an icon of the trade union movement. Without doubt, he won many ER battles as well as losing a good few. In retrospect, however, no one could really pin down very many hard achievements, even though respect for his career endures to this day.

■ There must be a commitment to monitor, review and evaluate at a strategic level and as a board priority the contribution that the ER direction, style and institutions make to the effectiveness of the organization overall. This review is carried out through:

- consideration of desired and prevailing levels of motivation, morale and commitment
- attention to production and output activities, and consideration of the positive and negative contributions that are made by organization approaches to ER
- attention to ER statistics – health and safety, absenteeism, sickness, turnover, strikes, disputes and grievances, and consideration of these from a total organizational point of view.

A key policy contribution of ER specialists is an accurate interpretation of these statistics, and of where any resultant dysfunction can be attributed. A broader picture can then be taken in some detail so that problems can be seen as:

- structural – based on the nature of work, technology, lay-out of premises or location

- institutional – based on the totality of relations between organization and staff, and the extent to which ER policies surface positively and negatively
- operational – where the variations occur according to department, division or function, and whether, therefore, there is any necessity to consider the attitude and expertise of functional or operations management
- managerial and supervisory – paying special attention to the overall style, approach and expertise of those in managerial and supervisory positions and identifying whether their key targets and priorities cause ER problems and what, if anything, can be done about this
- behavioural – the nature of workforce attitudes and the reasons for these, both positive and negative. The key factor here is that where there are extensive positive attitudes, these are not regarded as an end in themselves, but rather as something to be nurtured and reinforced through continued attention to those facts that cause high levels of commitment, involvement or output.

OPERATIONS MANAGEMENT

The critical element of effective ER operations management is unity of purpose – with top management; with the committees, institutions and procedures created; and with the nature and composition of the workforce.

It is also to be seen in terms of a broader understanding. Department, divisional and functional staff require information in a format that they can understand and with which they can identify. Where this information is not adequate, complete or presented in such a format, staff create their own networks and grapevine, and this can be extremely destructive, especially where the standard is high overall but where there are some lapses. The total integrity is invariably called into question.

The principle of equality must be enshrined and reinforced through the operation of procedures. Lapses in decency and equality of human treatment are always punished. Where this does not happen, morale is destroyed (see Summary box 11.6).

Summary box 11.6   ER and inequality

An education authority in north-west England was ordered to pay £300,000 damages for sex discrimination to one of its members of staff, a deputy head teacher of a comprehensive school.

The woman in question had been a deputy for nine years. She was known to be capable, and always received excellent reports. Both the person for whom she worked, and also her school's board of governors, persistently recommended that she seek promotion, and gain her own headship.

She applied for several jobs, each without success.

Eventually, she approached the education authority to find out why she was not being successful. The chief officer concerned told her 'between you and me, this is sex discrimination. The authority does not wish to promote women to this level of position'.

As a result, the woman lost her career, her health, and her motivation and morale. She was eventually awarded the substantial damages indicated; the education authority were able to insist on 'a confidentiality clause' preventing her from telling her story more widely, or from naming the official who had victimized her in this way.

The particular official was promoted shortly afterwards, and subsequently picked up a deputy chief executiveship at a County Council elsewhere.

The mix of staff and potential for conflict inherent in this must be recognized. Within the main principles of access to information and equality of treatment, operations managers need to divide their attention to the creation of effective ER as follows:

■ understanding the hopes, fears, aspirations and expectations of everyone and the extent to which these can and cannot be satisfied
■ attention to both the human and the operational side of the enterprise, akin to the Adair model of leadership, organization and work group management (see Figure 11.1).

In the Adair model, the leader must address the key issues of achieving the task, building the team and developing individuals. The leader who concentrates only on the task by, for example, going all out for production schedules while neglecting the training, encouragement and motivation of the group will always have problems of dissonance and dysfunction.

The leader who concentrates only on creating team spirit while neglecting the job or individuals will not get maximum involvement and commitment, which only comes from an environment that is both harmonious and genuinely productive. Staff members would therefore lack any true achievement or feeling of success.

Achieving the task

Building and
developing
the team

Concern
for the
individual

Figure 11.1 *The Adair model of leadership, organization and work group management. The key leadership functions required are direction, communication, coordination, assessment, planning, appraisal, control and development* (source: Adair, 1975)

■ In ER terms, task vagaries and variations cause problems if some people are known, believed or perceived to be lumbered with the majority of the unattractive parts, if they get pigeonholed and stereotyped as a result of carrying out one set of activities, or if opportunities accrue to individuals as the result of 'being in the right place at the right time' – at the expense of others.

■ Team vagaries and variations are based on total workforce composition, the nature and mix of expertise present, the size of work groups and the influence, actual or potential, that is wielded by those with different expertise (see Summary box 11.7).

Summary box 11.7   ER and influence

The following occurred in early 1998 at a hospital in south-east England.

A consultant was doing his ward rounds. He was with his junior, and they had a heavy workload. During the round, the consultant became more and more stressed. He came to a patient who was suffering from breathing difficulties, and who was on an oxygen machine. The patient was very distressed and tried to ask the consultant questions. Eventually, the consultant became angry, and picked up a spare oxygen cylinder which he heaved across the ward. This caused agitation both to the particular patient, and to many others present.

At the same hospital, a nurse was called in to cover for a colleague who had gone sick. The nurse drove in and when he arrived at the hospital could not find anywhere to park. Accordingly, he parked in a surgeon's specified car parking space. He then went on to the ward, where he was the only qualified person in charge.

Some time later, the surgeon came to find him and told him to move his car. This, the nurse refused to do, because he could not leave the ward unattended. The surgeon hit him, and then told him again to go and move his car.

The nurse made a formal complaint about the surgeon. The hospital authorities told the nurse that, if he wished to continue with his career at the hospital, he should drop the complaint. The nurse was persuaded to drop the complaint. Both the nurse and the surgeon still work at the hospital.

■ Attention to the individual means addressing every problem and issue from a point of view of equity and fairness. Problems arise when it is known, believed or perceived that there are pecking orders in the issuing of benefits and opportunities, and even with such matters as holiday allocations – the ability to take annual leave when desired, rather than when the organization says so, or a restricted ability because others have got in first and booked theirs.

■ Problems arise when issues are resolved on a distributive rather than integrated basis – where one person gets what they want at the expense of others.

■ Problems arise when staff receive different levels of individual reward as the result of team efforts. This is both discussed and illustrated in Chapter 3. When it does occur, the outcome and individual problems arising invariably fall on the shoulders of the particular operations manager or supervisor. They have accordingly to deal with an institutional or structural issue over which they may have little or no control. This, in turn, reinforces the need for totality as well as unity of ER direction, because in such cases, the actual conflict is between individual and immediate manager or supervisor, whereas the cause and source of the real issue lies elsewhere.

ER operations management and different patterns of work

In present day ER, there are major issues to be faced through the creation and proliferation of non-standard patterns of work. As we have seen elsewhere, the main drive for these issues is the need to satisfy ever-increasing customer and client demands and expectations, together with drives for the maximization and optimization of return on investment (see Summary box 11.8).

Summary box 11.8   Management and organizational attitudes to flexible working

The first duty of all organizations in managing flexible working is to get the right attitudes and approaches from its managers and supervisors. Where flexibility is based on part-time, fixed term contracts and job sharing type work, the approach that demeans – 'They are only part timers' and 'They are only job sharers' – is unacceptable. It is absolutely certain that if people are treated as 'only' something, this is how they will turn out. Work, profitability, productivity, effectiveness and customer service are all certain to suffer. Moreover, this attitude is certain to spread to other full-time staff who will regard themselves as superior. It will then spread to part timers who are likely to develop some form of siege mentality. They are certain to develop defensive and negative attitudes. The result is to affect effectiveness and profitability.

All employees, whatever their hours of work or length of service, are to be treated fairly and equally. Any departure from this line is punished.

Any failure to do this is certain to result in grievances, court and employment tribunal cases, which are all costly and debilitating.

The management task is therefore to produce excellent and top quality staff who make excellent products and give high levels of service. This is the source of customer satisfaction, repeat business, enhanced reputation – and profits.

MANAGEMENT STYLE

ER is best supported by an open, honest and visible style of management and supervision. This is especially important where large numbers of part-time staff are present, and where people move around regularly between different tasks during the work periods. Visibility builds the trust and empathy essential in any effective working relationship. For part timers and those who do move around, this has to be built quickly.

Honesty and openness are also critical. Very often, there is an organizational issue at stake. The organization itself must first learn the difference between being open and not – and the benefits of the former and the drawbacks of the latter. In many cases, organizations lose sight of the reasons why certain things are kept confidential. While confidentiality clearly extends to customer bases and profiles, new products, services and initiatives and other operational brainwaves, there is very little else that needs this approach. The more that is kept from the staff, the more they conclude that the organization is hiding something.

A substantial part of the management job consists therefore of 'walking the job'. Where this is not possible – for example, where employees work from home or in regional centres – regular and positive telephone contacts are to be maintained. This should be supported by regular meetings.

Regular meetings are also essential where there is a large measure of contact through e-mail and fax. This breaks down physical and psychological barriers and enhances identity.

The priority is attention to operational requirements and the patterns of staffing necessary to make these effective.

Administration and procedures are to be kept as simple as possible. There is an administrative workload generated by the variety of work patterns indicated and used. This is accommodated by standardizing and simplifying as much as possible, especially forms of contract of employment and work procedures. Use and adherence to procedures is kept to a minimum, reserved for serious issues only. Smaller problems and issues are resolved by the work group, managers and supervisors on the spot. This frees up both time and resources for the primary purpose of pursuing customer satisfaction and product and service excellence. It also removes the need for employee relations, staff management and other administrative superstructures and subfunctions; this frees up resources for more positive and productive purposes.

Procedures for the handling of disciplinary and grievance matters should be kept as simple as possible. They should be used as infrequently as possible – because managers and supervisors have the capability of resolving issues before recourse to procedures is necessary. Where it is necessary to invoke procedures, strict time constraints should be imposed. This prevents issues from festering, people taking sides, and battle lines being drawn. The purpose is to get operations back on a successful and effective footing as quickly as possible. The vast majority of grievances will be resolved on the spot. Where procedures are invoked, this should take no longer than two weeks.

Disciplinary matters should follow the same pattern. The only constraint is to allow the employee time to prepare his/her response to an issue and to seek representation and support for his/her point of view. This is also the approach for reporting relationships between departments and senior management. Information required and provided should be suitable and effective. Continuous attention should be paid to the volumes and quality of information available, and the purposes to which it is put. Regular requirements – for example, for year end – are clearly signalled and structured into departmental workloads. Information systems should be designed and commissioned with the demands and requirements in mind in order to eliminate crisis requests, overloads and underloads.

Inter-departmental relations and relationships between operational and senior management are based on organizational effectiveness rather than adherence to procedures. Problems that do arise are to be resolved quickly and effectively, again with the emphasis on product and service quality and customer satisfaction. Where the issues concern staff, procedures must be followed and these are to be kept simple and effective.

This means reference to the totality of organization management style, including questions of the basic approach, supported by the desired standards of integrity. It is also necessary to consider the extent to which this totality is coordinated or fragmented in terms of departmental, divisional, functional and operations management. The nature of the style – adversarial, cooperative, participative, consultative, autocratic (whether benevolent or malevolent) also needs to be considered, because whichever is adopted, it is necessary that those with individual departmental responsibilities adopt their own format that is compatible. It is also necessary to consider management style in terms of organizational priorities, especially in relation to output, procedures, reporting relationships and relationships within and between groups. Again, it is necessary to recognize that there is no single right answer, but it is also essential to understand that whatever is created, must be sufficiently cohesive to give those that work in the organization a measure of stability, certainty and understanding (see Summary box 11.9).

Summary box 11.9 ER and management style

Another way of looking at this is to assess the factors that are rewarded by the organization and its top management. These factors include:

- adherence to procedures
- loyalty and length of service
- support for particular initiatives
- productive output and excellence
- measures of customer satisfaction and complaints

- speed and nature of the decision-making process
- agenda of ER committee structures and procedures.

Assessment of these factors gives a sound initial insight into the nature of organizational ER and therefore an idea of its strengths and weaknesses. This can then be used as part of the process of assessing the likely ER problems and issues that may arise, and the best ways of handling these. It may also be used to assess those parts of the totality of organization ER that need specific attention.

MANAGEMENT TRAINING

Training in the skills and qualities needed to manage the effective ER consists of:

- ensuring that managers and supervisors have positive attitudes and dispositions towards their staff and that managers and supervisors understand what constitutes customer satisfaction and expectations, and the nature and quality of activities necessary to achieve this
- developing interpersonal skills, as much of the supervision and management routines are concerned with promoting understanding, harmonizing persons on a variety of working arrangements, consultation and briefings, solving questions and problems without recourse to procedures
- developing high standards of communication, written and spoken
- developing managerial and supervisory habits of 'walking the job' (also known as managing by walking about)
- training in practical problem-solving in all activities – product and service quality, customer issues, staff and personal matters and questions – with an emphasis on quick and effective solutions with which those directly affected are satisfied and that can be accommodated within the wider organization
- appraisal, knowledge and skills, based on continuous assessment of performance with regular formal or semi-formal punctuation marks. Regular staff appraisals need not and should not take long; most of the work is best done as part of the continuous working relationship. Again, problems become apparent early and are easily nipped in the bud. This is essential when managing part timers and outworkers with whom regular face-to-face contact is limited. It is damaging to both production, quality and morale if issues are allowed to drag on without being resolved

- discipline and grievance procedures based on establishing and maintaining standards of working relationship that keep both to a minimum. Management and supervisory training in these areas is concerned with equipping those involved with the capabilities and autonomy to resolve issues before they become problems. Providing training in the operation of simple, direct and speedy procedures indicated elsewhere is in the context of maintaining staff morale and effectiveness
- continuous regular briefings concerning organizational, department, divisional, group and individual performance with the emphasis on the positive and the early identification and resolution of problems
- knowledge and understanding of all aspects of organizational operations and activities, where the individual manager or supervisor fits in, the nature of their required contribution, familiarity with the work of related departments, understanding required performance targets and understanding the constraints within which they have to work.

ER management training and development is a continued requirement. Some is clearly best pursued in-house. The pursuit of external courses and formal qualifications is also highly desirable because it broadens the general perspective and understanding of managers, enabling them to come into contact with people from other organizations, bringing fresh ideas to bear on existing issues and problems. Training also develops the fund, knowledge and talent available in the organization.

MOTIVATION

Understanding of the totality of human motivation is critical to the creation of effective ER. From the standpoint of qualities of management, work motivation is based on:

- demanding, interesting, varied and valuable work that people are capable of carrying out, recognizing and rewarding their achievements and taking early remedial action when standards fall
- treating everyone equally and with respect, creating workplace relationships based on trust, honesty, openness and integrity, creating a unity of purpose and mutual interest between organization and staff, developing positive work, professional and personal relationships within and between groups

- attending to individual needs, wants, drives, hopes, fears and aspirations, ensuring that everyone progresses, develops and improves operationally, professionally and personally
- high, regular and increasing levels of pay.

If all of this is in place, organizations are entitled to expect high quality, high value work. Creating these conditions is the organization's responsibility. The potential for this is much greater under some arrangements because so many more of the conditions are easier to satisfy. Moreover, people are coming into different patterns of working with raised expectations of security, employability, variety and opportunity. The basis of the whole relationship is clear – and positive.

Motivation is adversely affected by:

- management style and the invisibility of managers and supervisors, inability to solve problems quickly and adversarial approaches to staff
- physical and psychological distance, based again on visibility and also on forms of preferential treatment, inaccessibility and uncertainty
- bad interpersonal and inter-occupational relationships
- boring and valueless work
- bad and unclear communications, infrequently delivered and frequently changed, and where the message given does not relate to the reality of the situation
- inherent dishonesty, lack of integrity and unfairness in the treatment of people.

It should also be noted that individual motivation changes as the relationship between people and their organization progresses. The motivation:

- to apply for a job
- to turn up for an interview
- to accept a job
- to turn up on the first day
- to turn up on the second day
- to keep turning up

are all different. The individual is affected by the ways in which they have been treated on each of these occasions and their motivation is either enhanced or diminished accordingly.

Motivation is most likely to be adversely affected by pay levels, the quality or the value of the work, and this is enhanced where more general expectations are not met.

Where pay is low, it is a mark of low esteem and value. It reflects the level of worth placed on the staff. The only exception to this is voluntary or vocational work, and vocation should never be confused with professionalism or expertise. It is both unfair and unethical to take advantage of people's commitment to their customers and clients.

Where work value is low, jobs and, therefore, staff are dispensable and those involved will know this better than anyone. Work of low value is extravagant and wasteful and is either to be abolished or improved.

Where product and service quality is low, there is no personal, professional or occupational feeling of satisfaction from being involved. Indeed, there is often a desire not to be associated. Real achievement is based on completing things that are good and positive and give satisfaction, not just on completing something.

People's motivation is directly affected by the following:

- expectations: the outcomes that they anticipate as the result of being in a situation and carrying out work
- efforts: the amount of energy that they are prepared to put into the situation
- rewards: the benefits to be accrued by being in the particular situation.

Recognizing the balance between these three is vital. If rewards do not match expectations, efforts decline. If other expectations are not met, efforts decline. If rewards exceed expectations, efforts increase in the short term, though in the long term this becomes the new level of expectation.

Individuals – whatever their pattern of work or frequency of attendance – therefore act best when they have a reasonable expectation that their effort will lead to the desired rewards and outcomes. This emphasizes the importance of the individual in any form of working relationship. It also indicates that raising expectations leads to the anticipation of enhanced rewards and that lowering rewards reduces both expectations and effort.

Communication and understanding

Communication and understanding is the other main key to staff motivation. The nature, media, language, volume and quality of communications reinforces the working relationship. Again, where one or more of these elements is lacking or wrong, motivation suffers.

Communication is best and most effective face to face, supported in writing in clear, simple, direct language. Communication always suffers when this is not present. It is also damaged when it is not supported by managerial or organizational actions or integrity. When this occurs, people always look for hidden meanings and messages. This is counter-productive to effective work, damaging and ultimately destroying working relationships.

Where face-to-face communication is not possible (eg for homeworkers, sales staff and others working away from the organization for long periods), regular meetings are convened to get over the problems caused by working in isolation. These meetings should devote at least part of their time to general discussions about the overall state of affairs and filling in the outworkers on any and all matters of importance, general knowledge and concern. It is also the opportunity to ensure that achievements and successes are noted and recognized. Attendance at these meetings is compulsory. It is the only clear opportunity that organizations and their managers have of building on existing levels of confidence and identity, as well as resolving problems and points of contention. Serious problems should always be tackled face to face. To attempt to tackle them by e-mail or over the phone, or by fax, normally results in the situation getting worse.

These conditions are present in all effective working arrangements. Attention to motivating the staff can then be completed by:

- good and positive supervision that encourages and enhances rather than restricts
- work satisfaction, based on flexible structuring, enrichment and variety
- high levels of team, group and organizational identity
- positive and professional relationships between group members and different groups and teams
- recognition for work well done
- recognizing communication problems that are likely to arise in specific situations and devising patterns of supervision and the means of communication that address these to best effect
- an attitude that learns from failure rather than seeks to apportion blame
- attention to the general working environment, adequate standards of accommodation and cleanliness, a standard of facilities with which people can be comfortable

- relating status to work performance and organization membership rather than to job titles, group or department membership.

If all of this is in place, organizations are entitled to accept a reciprocal commitment from their employees, high levels of commitment and high standards and quality of work.

MANAGEMENT QUALITIES AND MANAGERIAL PERFORMANCE

Effective management of ER requires high quality and distinctive forms of expertise, based on the compatibility of the organization style with the managerial expertise and capabilities of those with departmental, functional or divisional responsibility. The manager or supervisor is the point of reference for all staff – whatever their length of service, level of expertise or hours of work. Universally, their people look to them for quick and effective decisions, solutions to problems, and the creation of an effective, positive and productive place of work.

The managerial qualities required are:

- setting and maintaining the required attitudes and values, and reinforcing these through personal conduct and performance, and remedying these where they fall short
- setting goals, aims and objectives for the department or division as a whole, and for teams, groups and individuals within it
- delegating, giving autonomy, authority and responsibility to subordinates to complete work as they see fit, and providing the space for personal, professional and organizational development
- improving and developing the expertise of all staff
- controlling the work and performance of persons on a variety of different expertise, experience, hours and patterns of work
- acting as advocate and spokesperson for the department and its members
- acting as supporter and confidante for the department and its members
- being receptive, evaluative and judgmental of ideas received from members of staff
- continuously seeking improvements to products and service quality; and for improvements to work methods and practices
- engaging in general communication, consultation, and information exchanges

- involving the staff in key operational, departmental and divisional developments – including choices of new technology, developments in work methods and practices, and involvement in both operational and specific ER activities
- creating and reinforcing the desired attitudes
- creating the basis on which mutual trust, integrity and harmony can be maintained
- knowledge and understanding of the pressures, opportunities, constraints and drives present in the workplace, and of those that can and cannot be controlled
- knowing and understanding what constitutes successful and effective performance, and the ability to take remedial action quickly when performance falls short (see Summary box 11.10)
- handling daily operational management in such a way that staff relations are not impaired, or conflict generated
- developing absolute standards in terms of equality, fairness and honesty, and also in the operation of health and safety matters, and in the attention to individual disputes and grievances.

Summary box 11.10   ER and time

As a general rule in ER, the longer a dispute is allowed to persist, the harder it is to resolve, and the greater the adverse change to working relationships and general motivation and morale.

When an issue arises there needs to exist a means of dealing with it swiftly and effectively. This means an organizational acceptance that this is the case, and that staff must be encouraged to raise issues early. This is so that issues can be resolved before they become serious problems, and so that managers can do this in the knowledge that they have full institutional support. Managers, in turn, must be both capable and willing to respond to matters raised.

The only exception to this is where it is easy for all parties to see clearly how an issue is to be resolved, and to agree to resolve it as such – but where a quick resolution would give the impression to others that the matter could not have possibly been thought through fully. In such cases, an early agreement is reached and it is published by common consent as soon as is behaviourally practicable in the circumstances.

CONCLUSIONS

The purpose of this chapter is to indicate the key organization and managerial qualities required for effective ER to take place, and also to indicate the context in which ER takes place. It should especially be noted that there is a fundamental relationship between effective organizational, departmental, divisional, functional and individual performance, and the prevailing standard of ER. Disputes and grievances arise when the organization or work group is performing badly and are reduced when the organization or work group is performing well. Managerial qualities – especially those of communication and the ability to motivate – reduce the potential of conflict, and enhance total understanding. However, these are of limited value only, where the situation is fundamentally unsound or uncertain. Where this is the case, it is unreasonable to expect continuing high levels of motivation – the adaptation of those involved will have moved on from matters of organizational commitment, to much more fundamental questions about whether they will have a job in the future.

It should also be apparent that ER and the daily operations of the particular organization, department, division or function impact on each other. For example, the professional efforts of those working in a marketing department are enhanced or reduced by the prevailing state of ER in that situation, and the output of nurses, and the quality of patient care, is higher in those hospital wards where the style of ER and staff management is good, and it is lower where there are problems in these areas.

Finally, attention to ER from the point of view of organization and managerial qualities requires the professionalization of this aspect of total managerial performance. Operational success will always be limited if insufficient attention is paid to the effectiveness of the operation of management style, or where, no matter how high the output of the department, there is always an undercurrent of mistrust, conflict, grievance and dispute.

12

THE FUTURE OF ER

INTRODUCTION

At the end of the 20th century, ER is in a state of flux and transformation. There is a fundamental overall shift in the perceptions of what it is, what it constitutes and what it should achieve. There is a questioning of hitherto accepted organizational and managerial approaches to ER. In the UK, there has been a transformation in the status and influence of trade unions and, while in UK terms this has declined, both the EU at large, and different organizations from other parts of the world, ascribe very distinctive directions and objectives to the institutions and practices of ER.

In the past, much of the approach in the UK has been coercive both in nature and operation, based on devising structures and procedures to control the staff and containing conflict inherent in situations.

The transformation is related to, and driven by, a combination of great advances in managerial expertise, advances in the understanding of human behaviour patterns, changes in aspirations and expectations in work situations, and changes in social expectations and aspirations. This transformation has been compounded by technological advance, and the general globalization of activities, together with specific initiatives such as privatization, cost cutting measures, and shake-ups both in the operations of, and the management of, organizations.

Organizations that have promised or implied lifetime employment to their staff have found that there is, inherent in this, a continuing obligation to train, retrain and redevelop staff. This involves the development of alternative patterns of work, a much greater mutual responsibility for training and development, and overall attention to technological advance and developments in organizational behaviour, if this is to be successful in the long term.

There is also the recognition of the position of staff as legitimate and key stakeholders in organizations. This is a long held view in Japan, and parts of western Europe. It is now enshrined by the EU approach of 'social partnership', and embodied in the Social Charter. This means that organizations are increasingly required to adopt positions of openness, honesty, employee participation and effective communication. This in itself becomes the means of focus for the development of the organization, and the generation of harmony and understanding necessary to benefit everybody who works within it.

Above all, however, new and current approaches are concerned to ensure that ER is conducted from a standpoint that is both cost effective and suitable to the needs of the organization. If direct relationships are drawn between the wider and more general aspects of staff identity and motivation, and organizational performance and profitability, it follows that the removal of the barriers of alienation and demotivation, where they exist, is an essential feature. In order to do this effectively, it is necessary to understand what causes these problems in the first place.

Current approaches to ER stem from an organization-wide belief that there is a contribution to be made to organizational performance, customer satisfaction, competitive edge and, above all, profitability if they are adopted. Whichever the precise approach, and from whatever perspective it originates, it is essential that:

■ standards are clearly established and that all staff know and understand them, and are trained in them
■ managers are trained to value the importance of those standards
■ problem-solving, decision-making and the conduct of disputes, grievances and disciplinary issues are conducted both from the standpoint of equity and fairness, and with a view to enhancing (rather than diluting) total departmental performance.

CHANGING ER

If ER is to be transformed into an effective and profitable managerial and organizational activity, the barriers to this have first to be recognized.

Operational barriers

These include the following:

■ **Location** This is a barrier when, for whatever reason, it becomes impossible for the organization to continue to operate in its current premises. Relocation has consequences for the resettlement of families, retraining and development. Even where the new premises are close by, it may affect access, work and attendance patterns. For greater distances, the consequences of widespread disruption have to be addressed. As well as personal consequences, this includes attention to organization culture and structure.

■ **Tradition** This is a problem where there has been a long history of successful work in specific, well-understood and widely accepted ways. This may be underlined where a whole community has grown up around a particular industry or organization and where this is a major provider of employment and prosperity (eg coal mining, iron and steel, shipbuilding and engineering). If this has been steady for long periods, there are strong perceptions of stability and permanence.

■ **Success** (and perceived success) If the organization is known or perceived to be successful in its current ways of doing things then there is a resistance based on 'Why change something that works?' This is especially true if there is a long history of stability and prosperity. It is often very difficult in these circumstances to get workforces to accept that technology, ways of working and the products themselves are coming to the end of their useful life.

■ **Failure** This is a barrier to change where a given state of affairs has been allowed to persist for some time. The view is often taken – by both organizations and the staff concerned – that failure is 'one of those things', a necessary part of being involved in a given set of activities. Resistance occurs when someone determines to do something about it – again, upsetting an overtly comfortable and orderly status quo.

■ **Technology** This is a barrier for many reasons. It is often the driving force behind jobs, tasks, occupations and activities. Their disruption causes trauma to those affected by the consequent need for job and occupation change, retraining, redeployment – and often redundancy. Technological changes may also cause relocation to more suitable premises. Technological changes in turn, cause changes to work patterns and methods. It has been one of the driving forces behind the increase in homeworking where employees can be provided with all the equipment necessary to work without the need to come together at the employer's premises, and part-time working where the demands for maximization on investment in technology and increases in customer bases have led to extended opening and operational hours. Technological change disrupts patterns of identity. It has led to flexible working, away from traditional job titles, restrictive practices and demarcation. Technological change has also disrupted traditions of representation and belonging to trade unions, and professional and occupational bodies. This has occurred as jobs and occupations have become obsolete, causing both the individuals and the bodies concerned to seek new roles.

■ **Vested interests** Needs for organizational change are resisted by those who are, or who perceive themselves to be, at risk. Vested interests are found in all areas. They include senior managers threatened with loss of functional authority, operational staff faced with occupational obsolescence, people in support functions no longer considered necessary, and those on promotional and career paths for whom the current order represents a clear and guaranteed passage to increased prosperity and influence.

■ **Managerial** The managerial barrier is a consequence of the divorce of organization, ownership and control, where there is a divergence between the organization's best interests and need for long-term survival, and the needs of individuals and groups of managers to preserve their own positions. Existing patterns of supervision may again provide both general order and certainty and specific career and promotion paths.

■ **Bureaucracy** The bureaucracy barrier occurs where patterns of order and control have grown up over long periods in the recording and supervision of activities and in the structuring of organizational functions. The problem is worst where the bureaucracy is large and complex, and affects a significant part of the total range of activities.

■ **Redundancy and redeployment** This is referred to above. It is a barrier in its own right because in the current context any proposed change carries redundancy and redeployment as possibilities and because it has so often been a consequence of other changes.

Behavioural barriers

The main barriers are as follows:

■ **'It cannot be done'** This is a barrier both to confidence and understanding and is based on a lack of true, full and accurate information concerning the matters which the organization is proposing.

■ **'There is no alternative'** This comes in two forms. First, it is adopted by the workforce and interest groups in and around it (eg trade unions) that have a vested interest in the maintenance of the status quo either because it is familiar or because any change will result in loss of influence. This is especially true where business has been conducted in an effective and productive steady-state for a long period of time. Second, this may be adopted by directorates and managers as the one and only explanation for a change that is to take place. Conducted in isolation 'there is no alternative' simply becomes a challenge for others to think of alternatives. The matter requires explanation and communication in order to demonstrate to all those affected that alternatives have indeed been considered and that what is now proposed represents the chosen strategic direction.

■ **Lack of clarity** If organizations have not sorted out the basis of the changes that are proposed, neither staff nor customers will go along with them with any degree of confidence or understanding. Aims and objectives must be clearly understood as the prerequisite to successful and effective change, and communicated to those concerned in their own language.

■ **Fear and anxiety** These are human responses to concepts and situations that are unknown or uncertain. They are the initial response (or part of it) to any change that is proposed and, if allowed to get out of hand, can become an exercise in the devising and promulgation of hypothetical scenarios that could, in certain circumstances, become problems on the changing landscape. Not only does this constitute a waste of organizational resources and a diversion from its actual purposes, but such interaction among the staff feeds on itself, generating negativity and unnecessary internal turbulence.

■ **Perfection** At the point at which change is proposed suddenly everything concerning the status quo becomes 'perfect'. Anything that is proposed as an alternative has therefore to address this barrier. It is another manifestation of familiarity and comfort and, faced with the loss of this, such elements become highly worthwhile to retain.

For all barriers, the main issue is to avoid leaving a vacuum. As we have seen in Chapter 6, this allows for the proliferation of over-mighty subjects, vested interests and the propagation of lobbies based on departmental, divisional or sectional interest.

Moreover, all the barriers interact with each other – they cannot be seen in isolation. The potential for conflict and serious ER problems exists, above all, in the interaction of each of the stated areas. It is essential, therefore, that people understand not just that they are changing from something, but also that they are changing to something – and this must be underpinned by clear attention to each of those factors. People will happily accept change if they know, believe or perceive it to be in their interests to do so, and if those interests are not adversely affected. Where those interests are to be adversely affected, early communication at least lets people know where they stand as a prelude to taking action to alleviate the situation as early as possible.

ER and the management of change

When changes are required all methods of communication at the disposal of the organization are to be invoked. This includes statutory obligations to consult with trade unions and other recognized staff representative bodies. Good practice also requires that many different channels of communication are used, paying special attention to those who do not have formal representation. Briefing groups, plenary meetings, individual and group methods, oral and written modes, notice boards, newsletters and circulars will all be used. The content will clearly vary between each organization and each issue; overall, they must address dates and deadlines, effects for staff, ranges of alternatives that may be on offer, retraining, redeployment or redundancy, and a vision and direction for the future that is as clear as possible in the circumstances.

It will also be necessary to address individual staff concerns. If this is not managed properly, disputes and grievances will arise (see Summary box 12.1).

Summary box 12.1   The management of change: the Essex Fire Brigade

In May 1998, the Essex Fire Brigade went on strike. There was no difference between the objectives of the Essex Fire Authority, or the Essex Fire Brigade – each wanted the safest and most responsive service possible.

At issue was how this was to be achieved, and what changes were necessary to improve the service. The Fire Brigade asked for greater investment, guarantees about job security, and enhanced training and development programmes to operate the very latest equipment.

The Fire Authority wanted 16 redundancies and greater flexibility of operation on the part of those who retained their jobs.

Failure to recognize the commonality of interest led to a series of strikes and disputes that simply polarized the issues and entrenched the positions of each party. The Fire Authority, when it became clear that the crews would go on strike, asked the army to provide an emergency service. This caused the staff involved to strengthen their position, and call for the resignation of senior members of the Fire Authority.

The issue was resolved eventually when:

- the Fire Authority agreed to withdraw the redundancies
- the Fire Brigade agreed to go back to work, pending further talks on the future development of the service.

There was therefore no progress. All that had happened was that two contrasting and ultimately antagonistic positions had been adopted by high quality, committed and professional people – in the pursuit of something with which they were both, in principle, in agreement.

When great changes are involved, it is also usual for there to be specific individual and group problems that cannot easily be resolved in the greater scheme of things. It follows from this that it would be necessary to offer individual and group counselling and support methods and mechanisms. These are for the purpose of reassurance, the continued addressing of lingering or persisting uncertainties, and the means of tackling individual cases. They also reinforce organizational concern for, and commitment to, the specific needs of individuals and groups.

Problems are fewer, become apparent earlier, and are easier to tackle, when a general stance of openness and assertiveness is adopted. It also emphasizes the concern that organizations have (or at least should have) for all of their staff. It further underlines the point that organizations need to have sorted out both the required and proposed changes in advance of publishing them, so that when they are published, a priority order of issues to be tackled can easily be agreed.

Change is not a linear process. As the result of one development, it may also be possible to tackle traditional, historic, underlying or fundamental issues that have been allowed to persist for too long. It may also act as a vehicle for management training and development in effective ER, and the need to generate concepts of flexibility, dynamism, creativity and responsiveness among the staff.

Changes in managerial attitudes and expertise

This is a major issue at the end of a period of long-term steady-state operations. Both managers and employees get used to particular patterns and approaches to staff management, problems, and other ER matters over such a period. When at the end of such a period transformation is required, it may be necessary to tackle managerial and supervisory groups, in order to ensure their support for what is proposed. As they will have to implement whatever is necessary with their own staff, this support is essential. Where this part of the change process is not adequately conducted, or not perceived as important, serious conflict and demoralization among staff is certain – and again, this is likely to come out in the form of staff–operational management confrontation, rather than addressing the keys to the resolution of the particular matter. Alongside this, therefore, it may be necessary to engage in an extensive management and supervisory development programme, as a precursor to full implementation. (See Summary box 12.2).

Summary box 12.2   Changes in attitudes

The best organizations have signalled their adoption of positive ER attitudes through the generation of employee involvement, and employee partnership.

Involvement

Employee involvement has its roots in the alternative approaches to production line work first tried by Volvo and Saab in the 1970s. In these approaches, employees were given a wide and varied range of activities to carry out, and they were then divided into work groups. Production targets were established by the organization, and the employees were then given the freedom to allocate the work as they saw fit, provided that targets were met. Employees were thus involved in operational decisions, production line decisions, and production performance. Other organizations, developing these approaches, have involved employees also in the quality of the finished product – Honda for example, now refer customer complaints back to the production line, production shift, and production crew involved in the production of the car in the first place; they have no distinctive quality assurance department with this remit.

Other Japanese companies working in the UK have sought to involve their employees in the future of the company through the dissemination of wide and high-quality information, and through extensive consultation processes. Nissan offers the chance to every employee to take their family to Japan to see how the company works. The Body Shop requires its employees to undertake one day's community service of some sort per month, requiring their people to be involved in out-of-work activities as a condition of employment.

Partnership

Partnership is akin to the EU concept of 'social partners' in ER, and in many organizational cases, trade unions and staff consultation bodies are referred to as social partners.

At its most simple, partnership is the relationship generated between the organization and its staff as the result of extensive consultation and the development of the contribution made by everybody to organizational and operational decision-making processes.

Some organizations espouse the concept of partnership through share ownership schemes and other employee benefits. This is an employee benefit in itself. However, by giving employees a financial stake in the company, as well as a salary, the line of reasoning is that they will be encouraged to take an ever-greater interest in the future prosperity of the company. Especially where employees hold a substantial part of the share capital, a wide range of strategic information is certain to be available to all employees.

Another approach to partnership is that adopted by the John Lewis Partnership. After an initial probationary period, all employees are called partners. All employees have the same basic terms and conditions of employment (other than salary). The company provides extensive information on financial performance and commercial activities. It also produces two staff magazines per month: one on the organization overall, the other on specific activities and achievements of individual members of staff.

Both the partnership and involvement approaches to ER are highly conformist or unitary. At the core of these approaches are the organization's shared values and quality of policy and direction. Each of these must be positive and capable of being shared and adopted. The onus is on organizations and their managers to create the climate and aura in which these can take place; so long as the organization can put its hand on its heart and deliver policy and shared values with integrity, then there is a legitimate requirement, so it is stated, for all those involved to abide by these standards.

Changes in employee attitudes and approaches

Whatever is required here must be underpinned by a fundamental integrity if serious conflict is not to be generated. The most serious problems arise when, for whatever reason, the employees do not believe the message that they are receiving. They may have good reason for this, such as a history of bad employee relations, a history of managerial changes of mind or the knowledge, belief or perceptions that different groups of people get treated with different degrees of favour, understanding and preference. Employees in such circumstances will tend to treat demands for great changes with a lack of trust and value unless, and until, they are given overwhelming reasons to change this attitude.

It may be necessary for organizations in this situation to acknowledge their failings of the past. It may also be necessary to constitute working parties to demonstrate an integrity of purpose in this set of circumstances. This may, for example, include acknowledging the negative aspects of organization realpolitik and the informal ER system, and possibly also taking steps to engage a contingency approach to ER over the period of change.

It is also necessary to recognize that, where there is a history of bad or adversarial ER, the message may need to be repeated time and again, using all means of communication available. As long as the message is consistent, the particular barrier of trust may at least be overcome in the particular set of circumstances (see Summary box 12.3).

Summary box 12.3   Changing employee attitudes: prejudices

In the UK, people exhibit prejudices of all kinds towards ER. ER problems and issues are regularly resolved to the entire satisfaction of everyone at dinner parties and in other social gatherings. Such prejudices gather a measure of great comfort among those who hold them and also reinforce professional attitudes and values. They therefore become very difficult to break down.

Over the past 30 years, moreover, these prejudices have been played on by politicians of all persuasions and extensively reported as such in the UK mass media. The result is that people coming in to work – in all occupations – have done so with a preconceived idea of the attitudes and approaches to ER in particular situations. This reinforces their position as a barrier and helps to make them very difficult to break down.

Where these prejudices have been reinforced through a real history of bad or adversarial or organizational ER, they have to be addressed as a separate issue.

Changes in trade unions and employee representation

As stated elsewhere, UK trade unions have lost most of their political influence. Both trade unions and the Trades Unions Congress (TUC) used to have extensive national influence; this was greatly reduced by the UK Conservative governments of 1979–97, and the Labour government elected in 1997 has not restored this position to any extent.

Trade unions have therefore tended to concentrate their efforts on member benefits, and individual representation. They have also been required to shift their attitudes. One approach has been through single union and single table arrangements and agreements (see Chapter 1), as organizations have sought to streamline their ER procedures and practice, and to reduce the number of different sets of conditions of employment. Another has been to engage trade unions as workplace social partners, very much akin to the macro approach desired by the EU. At the core of this is a fundamental shift in the relationship between employers and trade unions, following the gradual (in some cases) realization that the interests of all are best served through harmonious rather than adversarial ER (see Summary box 12.4).

Summary box 12.4   Trade union attitudes

Most trade unions, and the TUC, have acted as major sponsors for the Labour Party, and especially in the period 1945–75, were seen as the main sponsors of socialism in the UK.

It remains true that some trade unions were used as the vehicle for distinctive political vested interests. However, it should be noted that the record of those who did this is not terribly good. When Arthur Scargill became the leader of the National Union of Mineworkers in 1979, the Union had 459,000 members. Scargill himself was widely presented as a class warrior, who was using the trade union movement to destroy the social fabric of the UK, and to promote a socialist (some said communist) revolution. Twenty years later, his union has 7,500 members. It is possible to measure this in terms of job losses and defections per hour.

At the other end of the political spectrum, trade unions were cited as a barrier to progress, an encumbrance without which managers would find it easy to manage, and they were described by one leading Conservative politician as 'a millstone around the neck of British industry and public services'. Without trade unions, all sectors would be opened up to 'market forces' and they would therefore become successful and profitable in the long-term future.

Quite apart from anything else, this last approach fell down, because nobody ever went so far as to define exactly what 'a market force' actually was.

Changes in organizational structures and activities

Changes in structures and activities have the greatest effect on workplace ER. This means attention to different patterns of work, different hours of work, different skills and attributes – and the human as well as occupational aspirations and expectations that go with these. This is both driven and reinforced by continuing organizational and managerial creativity in the management of employment patterns through the speed of change of technology and therefore occupations, through ever-increasing drives for customer access and satisfaction, and through the resultant demands on staff to re-think the balance between their work and other aspects of life.

It is no longer possible to envisage a 40-year standard working life. In order to continue to work, people have either to change organizations or, by remaining in an organization, to be prepared to be retrained and redeployed. This applies to all occupations, for example, surgeons must be prepared to undergo extensive continuous training and development in the wake of advances in medical technology; administrators may increasingly be required to work from home, or from places other than a designated office, because technology enables them to do this; while many cleaning and security activities are either put out to contract with specialist firms and in any case are subject to ever-greater standards in the use of equipment and following procedures.

A key consequence for this in the management of ER is the ever-greater upwards pressure on wages. Because of this lack of certainty, people are unwilling to settle into steady pay structures. They prefer increased wages when these are available because of the uncertainty of their continuity. Career paths are no longer certain, nor are they clearly designated. Rather than promotion through organizations, the best that may be offered is variety, or the opportunity to work in different locations in the world and, again, it may be necessary to change organizations, rather than to remain in them.

Changes in the law

When the UK government signed the European Union Social Charter in September 1997, it effectively adopted the EU stance on ER. This process had in any case been commenced by the previous government, especially through the Trade Union Reform and Employment Rights Act 1993, which gave statutory rights in terms of maternity, health and safety and employment transfers.

The EU aura of employee relations is one of partnership, rather than adversary. The parties to the traditional UK tripartite system therefore remain very much in place; however, the role, function and attitude of each is required to be fundamentally different. ER is seen as having a positive and enduring contribution to the total prosperity of the European Union.

Implicit in this is the requirement of employing organizations to take a much broader social responsibility for their staff. It is clear that organizations will be required in the very near future to take a much greater responsibility for the provision of adequate pension arrangements for their staff, for ensuring that adequate childcare facilities exist during periods of work, and for enhancing work environment matters such as occupational health and health and safety. At present, many of these aspects are offered as staff benefits to employees in the UK; in future, organizations will be required by law to offer these features to everyone.

More generally, the Social Charter highlights the specific rights of women, the elderly and the disabled at places of work, and specific protection for children and adolescents. It also includes initial and continuing job, vocational and professional training as an employment right for everyone.

The UK is also taking steps to develop ER law. It is proposed that the qualifying period for protection against unfair dismissal be reduced to one year, and this restriction is expected to come into force in 1999. It is anticipated that staff handbooks and other material published, which form a part of the stated or implied terms of contracts of employment, would become legally binding. It is also anticipated that there will be legislation in the area of trade unions, including:

■ a right to union recognition where the majority of the relevant workforce want it
■ the right for all employees – whether union members or not – to be accompanied by a union representative during grievance, disciplinary and disputes procedures
■ greater involvement of trade unions in workplace employment strategies.

Changes in the management of trade unions

If employee interests are to be given the same status and legitimacy as shareholder interests, then employee representatives have to be the subject of a distinctive and defined organizational approach. As we have seen elsewhere (page 67), Japanese companies operating in the UK welcome trade unions as a legitimate and independent employee interest. The EU requires the institutionalization of those in work as a key to both organizational and EU prosperity.

At organizational levels, there is a clear responsibility for this aspect of creating effective ER. There is no reason why organizations should continue to put up with the stifling, bureaucratic and extensive proliferation and duplication of procedures that in many cases hitherto existed. Streamlined approaches to the organization and management of ER have been well understood for some time now, and a key to the continued development of effective ER is the ability to take, develop and implement the strategic and organization-specific approach indicated (see Summary box 12.5).

Summary box 12.5   ER development and the management of trade unions at Broadmoor hospital

Trade unions at Broadmoor special hospital, Berkshire, UK, were required to suggest ways to make consultation procedures more representative, as a key to the development of effective ER.

The human resources director insisted that non-union members also had a voice on the Joint Consultation and Negotiating Committee (JCNC). An internal employee relations seminar initially failed to resolve the issue; however, people representing all interests were required to think further on the matter.

> We all agree that the JCNC is out of date, cumbersome and reactive. The staff side have agreed to work together to make proposals on how the JCNC machinery can be changed for the better

Additionally, more than 300 of Broadmoor's 1,100 staff did not belong to a trade union. The six unions represented on the JCNC expressed their opposition to offering seats to non-union delegates. The Prison Officers' Association (POA) argued most vociferously against such a move. One senior member of the POA said 'I made it clear we would not sit at a joint negotiating body with people who are untrained, unelected and appointed by those who have no interest in being represented.'

A possible compromise would be to allow non-union members to be represented by existing Broadmoor shop stewards and conveners.

The human resources director remained determined to improve this facility. There was also universal agreement that it needed improving. It does illustrate, however, the difficulties encountered when moving from acceptance of an issue to agreeing on the best way forward.

The Japanese approach to ER

Japanese companies operating in the UK, and elsewhere in the EU and North America also, display a fundamentally different approach. At the core is the more simplified direct – unitary and conformist – approach illustrated and summarized in the Sanyo handbook (Appendix B). In order that this works effectively, the organization has certain other obligations as follows.

Conformity

This is the requirement that all staff adopt the high standards of attitude, behaviour and performance required; this is in line with the view taken by Japanese companies at large that they wish their staff to identify with the company itself rather than with a particular occupation ('I work for Sony' as distinct from 'I am marketing manager/ tea person/production worker').

Investment

Investment is seen as a cornerstone of the stated aim of a long-term, enduring and effective business activity. Japanese company investment concentrates especially on the human resource (though also on extensive investment in technology). For example, Nissan spent millions of pounds and dollars training production operatives at Washington, Tyne & Wear, UK, and Smyrna, Georgia, USA, before a single car was produced. The level of investment in technology continues, as does the obligation that is seen to derive from this – of continued investment in staff training.

Alongside this is the attitude to staff training and development that identifies personal, professional, organizational and operational levels and types of training. The standpoint is the development of the individual, as well as that part of the individual that constitutes an employee. Accordingly, some Japanese companies operating in the UK (eg Honda and Sharp) pay for employees to undertake evening classes in whatever activity they see fit, whether work-related or not.

Investment is also apparent in wage levels. Japanese companies undertake to pay the highest wages in their particular sector – for example, Nissan pays substantially more than Vauxhall or Ford for the same category of work. The return on this investment is measured in terms of product, service and sales success. At the core of this is high quality staff. The particular ER pay-off is that this approach goes a long way to removing the causes of conflict and dispute in an organization, and those that historically and traditionally have caused industrial strife in the older industries of the West. The capability to operate speedy, streamlined and effective ER procedures is, therefore, a key return on investment.

Other outputs

Also in return for this form of investment, Japanese employers expect full flexibility of working. There are no demarcation lines, restrictive practices or any attitudes prevalent reflected in the views of 'That is not my job.' People are trained to be able to operate any aspect of the organization process or service and, when necessary, they are expected to do this. Alongside this the view is taken that the creation and maintenance of a high quality workforce, with dedicated and committed staff, is a key to the removal of that part of ER that is concerned with the management of industrial strife (see Summary box 12.6).

Summary box 12.6   High quality staff

High quality staff are either attracted from outside or produced and grown from within.

Outside

The benefit of recruiting from outside is to bring in fresh talent, skills, knowledge and expertise. Attitudes and behaviour are formed and developed at the commencement of employment. Outsiders are also used to bring fresh life or impetus to existing activities.

Once inside, outsiders are trained and developed according to the organization's policies and practices.

The problems normally lie in the length of time the recruitment and selection processes take (several months for some appointments, especially management, technical and professional) and in the length of time it takes to make them fully effective in their new roles (and this is the drive behind all effective induction programmes and activities).

Growing your own

'Growing your own' means that organizations get the staff that they need and want. This extends especially to attitudes and behaviour. It greatly contributes to staff motivation and is a mark of the value placed on the staff and the organization's commitment to them.

The main drawback is the length of time that this takes. Growing your own is a long-term and continuous commitment. It also tends to promote introspection and elitism if it does not include activities away from the organization (eg training and development courses off-site).

The best approach is clearly a mixture of the two. This is based on an understanding and evaluation of the specific benefits of growth and development and where the needs for fresh impetus lie. Emphasis is also needed on the integration of outsiders as quickly and effectively as possible.

Continuous improvement and development

This is a reflection of the required commitment to training and development. It covers improving the ways in which current activities are carried out. It also means reviewing, refining, streamlining and restructuring bureaucracy and administration where necessary. It also includes project work, work improvement activities, attention to quality, secondments and off-site activities, as well as on-the-job training.

Job titles

The great majority of job titles tend to limit and pigeonhole people into restrictive and restricted positions. They create inflexibility. Many job titles also demean the job holder, especially in semi-skilled and unskilled areas. For example, it is not unusual to hear people say 'I'm only a secretary' or 'I'm only a checkout operator' and if individuals themselves think that they are 'only' something, then the organization is likely to regard them in this way also.

This also happens to others elsewhere on organization maps and ladders. There is relative status accorded to, and within, personnel, marketing and finance functions for example, through the use of job titles such as 'Junior Personnel Officer', 'Finance Assistant' or 'Marketing Executive'.

As well as being generally restricting this form of title tends to put a dampener on the enthusiasm of job holders and to indicate boundaries of responsibility, authority and activity that are not to be crossed.

There are also the pigeonholes for the un-pigeonholeable. At their most positive, titles such as 'Project Officer' or 'Manager of Corporate Affairs' tend to be allocated to those whose remits do not sit easily within an organization structure or hierarchy. This tends to reinforce any general lack of flexibility. At its most negative (and much more common), is the tendency to use such titles for those for whom no real job exists. And nobody is fooled – not the rest of the organization, not the work colleagues and certainly not the job holder.

Some organizations have tried to get over this by introducing much more generic and (supposedly) positive titles such as 'crew member', 'cast member' or 'staff member'. Others have gone further still and allowed people to invent their own job titles. In the most extreme cases, this is fanciful and silly, but it does at least indicate that people are not to be bounded by restrictive job titles.

Single workplace status

There is a strong social hierarchy in Japan; this is reflected to an extent at the workplace in that the senior is worthy of respect. However, the workplace requires that this is translated into business needs only. Otherwise, everyone is important in their role whatever that may be. It is quite usual for everyone to wear the same uniform, to go through the same basic induction and orientation programme, to use the same facilities (eg canteen, restaurant and recreation) and to be on the same basic terms and conditions of employment. As an example, the first company to take a major step towards this in the West was Sony. In 1971, the company abolished all clocking on procedures. Rather than taking this inherently adversarial approach, they placed a joint responsibility on the staff for being present when they were required, and on managers to ensure that this indeed took place.

Identity

A strong identity on the part of all staff is both required and insisted upon. In managerial and professional occupations, this may involve working very long hours, taking an active part in corporate hospitality and business related activities outside working hours. Similarly, these activities – whether designated voluntary or not – are not voluntary to such staff in Japanese companies.

It is therefore necessary to note that, in some circumstances, this is seen as coercive and stifling, rather than purely conformist. Above all, the lesson is that such companies cannot possibly be all things to all people, and that it may be necessary, with the best will in the world, to let staff go to more appropriate places of work, rather than diluting the ethos to accommodate them.

Trade unions

In Japanese organizations trade unions are managed. They are set clear boundaries of activity and involvement. In general, they do not conduct collective bargaining, rather they engage in extensive consultation and, where necessary, become involved in resolving problems. Most Japanese companies operating in the UK recognize one union only; where more than one union is recognized, they are required to subscribe to the single status concept, and a single set of main terms and conditions of employment.

The Japanese approach to ER is very distinctive. ER is important, because of the relationship between Japanese approaches to organization management at large, the particular position of ER in this, and the output in terms of product and service quality and success. It is also true that Japanese multinationals – both in Japan, and also their operations in the West – have run into production, service and other operational difficulties. However, the basic approach undertaken seeks to ensure that such difficulties are kept to a minimum, and occur in the short term only. The long-term view is essential if they are to support enduring business principles of:

■ high levels of product and service output and quality
■ long-term existence and profitability based on an ever-increasing range and quality of products and services
■ lifetime employment for all employees who desire it
■ the capacity to transform, if necessary, from one industrial sector to another (eg Mitsubishi transformed their major activity from ships to cars in the late 1960s without a single job loss)
■ the value placed on the individual.

The outcome is a long-term, enduring, profitable and effective business relationship, in which ER plays a key role. It follows from this that managers and supervisors are required to resolve problems. This is achieved, above all, through a fundamental integrity of working relationship, and is supported by quick and easy access, managerial visibility, managerial expertise based on training and development, and underpinned by the existence of simple, direct and effective procedures. The operation of procedures, so the line of reasoning goes, is therefore kept to a minimum. The approach is designed to nip problems in the bud, rather than to avoid facing them in the first place.

The companies are also strong advocates of pendulum arbitration to resolve disputes when they do occur. As a rule, Japanese companies build in 'no strike arrangements' into their ER procedures. Pendulum arbitration – in which the arbitrator hears both sides of the case and then decides wholly in favour of one party or the other – is used when a strike or serious dispute would otherwise occur. This form of arbitration means that one party is known and seen to win, and the other is known and seen to lose. Japanese companies do not like their managers or supervisors to lose disputes and, therefore, train them to ensure that they do not get involved in them, and to resolve problems and issues before they become more serious.

More generally, Japanese companies are open about sharing information, and engage in extensive communication and consultation over all organizational matters – not just ER. This, together with the high levels of investment, commitment to staff development and security, and concentration on organizational performance integrated with ER, helps to build a fundamental integrity of staff relations, which the companies view as central to their continued success (see Summary box 12.7).

Summary box 12.7   The Japanese approach to ER: other outputs

Sanyo

The Sanyo UK plant at Lowestoft has a declared staff absenteeism rate of 0.2 per cent. Whenever someone goes sick, a representative of the company arrives on the individual's doorstep, bringing with them either a box of chocolates or a bunch of flowers and a message from the company to the effect that 'We are very sorry that you are unwell, and are very much looking forward to having you back at work.' Sickness absence is always followed up by interview upon return, and where serious injury or illness is involved, the company takes an active part in ensuring the employee's comfort. It is considered that the approach tends to manage unwarranted absence out of the organization.

Toshiba UK

Upon commencement of employment, all Toshiba employees are greeted, either by the local managing director, or their section head, with a statement to the effect that 'We are looking forward to working with you. You are respected, valued and trusted as a human being and we are employing you because we need you to work for us. If, therefore, you are the kind of employee who tends to have a lot off time off work – for whatever reason, good or bad – then you should consider whether Toshiba is the right company for you. It is essential that you are to work on all the days required – only if you are, are we able to produce the required quality and volume of products and services for our customers.' Toshiba UK has a declared sickness absence rate of 0.5 per cent.

This should be contrasted with the following example:

The UK National Health Service

The NHS has a declared sickness absence rate of 4.9 per cent. The management of sickness costs the NHS £500 million per annum, and this does not include the hiring of temporary or replacement staff. The NHS takes no steps to manage induction, set standards or control absence.

It is clear that attention to this key area can make a major contribution to effective use of resources, provided that the groundwork for effective ER has been carried out and, most importantly, provided that clear, unambiguous standards have first been established.

OTHER ISSUES IN THE MANAGEMENT AND DEVELOPMENT OF EFFECTIVE ER

The main issue remains the continued development of awareness and expertise in the totality of employee relations, and the contribution that it makes to the effective, profitable and enduring management of organizations. Particular attention also needs to be paid to the following:

■ **Technological advance** This brings opportunities in terms of increased opportunities for production, quality and durability, and the derived demand for continued investment in staff training and development.
■ **Investment** This is required in the creation of high quality work environments for all staff, regardless of length of service, hours of work, or occupation carried out. Investment is also required in flexibility, dynamism, creativity and responsiveness, each of which, as they advance employment satisfaction and security, has a direct measurable effect in terms of reduced sickness, absence, turnover, and conflict and grievance.
■ **Culture, attitudes and values** The best organizations develop in 'the way in which things are done' that require their staff to adopt specific attitudes and values, and also to:
  ▪ support the organization's own distinctive and considered view of how it should conduct its affairs
  ▪ be capable of accommodating the differing, and often conflicting, interests of the employees
  ▪ transcend local cultural pressures
  ▪ create a basis of long-term mutual commitment serving the interests of the organization, its customers and the wider community as well as its staff.
Again, the contribution here is in terms of removing the conditions that cause industrial strife, and promoting the conditions that tend towards levels of comfort and security and which, consequently, reduce disputes and grievances.
■ **Business across cultures** This especially applies to organizations operating in global markets and, to a lesser extent, to smaller organizations operating in a variety of localities. Again, this means creating attitudes and values, and supporting these with managerial capability, so that these differences are transcended, and so that, whatever the background or occupation undertaken, the employee is both capable and willing to operate in the ways required.

■ **Strategy** ER strategy is increasingly concerned with developing and reinforcing long-term clarity of employment purpose. This means:
  - reconciling the range of conflict inherent in the mix of staff capabilities and expertise present
  - investing in and committing to the long-term in terms of technology and the derived investment necessary in employees
  - generating staff loyalty and commitment through a corporate determination to have a long-term future.

  Above all, this means attention to attitudes and values, training and development, and to the managerial expertise required for effective ER. It constitutes a mutual and continuous obligation.

■ **Flexible patterns and methods of work** This is based on a combination of the demand to maximize and optimize investment in production and other technology, together with changing patterns of customer requirements. The fundamental shift in staffing patterns and methods of work that has arisen as the result means having the corporate will, and managerial expertise and commitment, to ensure that, whatever the pattern of work or hours worked, all staff are treated with the same fundamental principles of equality and opportunity.

■ **Ethics** There is a realization that there is a much greater propensity for customers to use organizations in which they have confidence and in which they can trust. Outwardly, organizations demonstrate their ethical strength through a variety of means including:
  - concern for the environment
  - concern for suppliers, especially where these come from non-western economies
  - concern for customers, through a commitment to high quality and enduring levels of product and service, supported by an absolute commitment to put right anything that is not satisfactory.

All of this is only possible if there is a fundamental integrity of relationship between the organization and its staff and, arising from this, a mutual commitment to a long-term and enduring staff–management relationship based on openness, honesty and trust. If the organization, for example, promises lifetime job security, then its first duty is to remain in being for that lifetime – and to do this, it must take a view of itself based on integrity rather than expediency or pretence.

CONCLUSIONS

Peter Drucker once said that 'human relations (or ER) management is much too important to be left to personnel functionaries' (1986).

If the view is accepted that management in general concerns achieving things through the efforts of people, and harnessing their talents, capabilities and expertise in order that this takes place, then clearly ER is a key general management function – quite apart from a distinctive sphere of activity.

As organizations and their managers look ever harder at what gives them distinctive competitive and performance edges, so they are studying ever more closely the human side of their activities. Having effective, productive, trained and talented staff is becoming increasingly essential and there is an ever greater demand being placed on organizations to ensure that their people are capable, flexible and willing in as many areas of activity as possible. This in itself, however, is not enough.

For this potential to be maximized, the factors that dilute its full effectiveness have to be removed. When people work in organizations, they come together in specific situations. The behavioural boundaries and constraints, as well as the physical environment, have to be recognized and, whichever perspective is adopted, they have to be managed actively and positively. Corporate inertia in the field of ER is no longer tenable, and if once it was feasible as a distinctive ER strategy, this also no longer remains the case. It is possible for the most bureaucratic, complex and diverse of organizations to have effective ER provided that they take direct positive responsibility for creating institutions, procedures and practices that are going to work in the particular set of circumstances and providing they give their managers and supervisors the necessary training and instil the right attitude to ensure that this is successful.

Above all, the 'ER industry' has to be turned on its head. ER must be seen as a contribution to profitable and effective performance, rather than a function shrouded in its own mystique. The function of ER experts should be to ensure that organization perspectives, strategies, policies and institutions operate in harmony and that these are supported with managerial and supervisory expertise, staff awareness and understanding. In turn, the truly expert manager – in whatever field – must become expert in daily staff management, staff relations – ER – activities, and must recognize that their contribution and expertise in this part of the job is equally as important as in others.

APPENDIX A
THE EUROPEAN
UNION SOCIAL
CHARTER

PREAMBLE

The governments signatory hereto, being members of the Council of Europe,

Considering that the aim of the Council of Europe is the achievement of greater unity between its members for the purpose of safeguarding and realising the ideals and principles which are their common heritage and of facilitating their economic and social progress, in particular by the maintenance and further realisation of human rights and fundamental freedoms;

Considering that in the European Convention for the Protection of Human Rights and Fundamental Freedoms signed at Rome on 4 November 1950, and the Protocols thereto, the Member States of the Council of Europe agreed to secure to their populations the civil and political rights and freedoms therein specified;

Considering that in the European Social Charter opened for signature in Turin on 18 October 1961 and the Protocols thereto, the Member States of the Council of Europe agreed to secure to their populations the social rights specified therein in order to improve their standard of living and their social well-being;

Recalling that the Ministerial Conference on Human Rights held in Rome on 5 November 1990 stressed the need, on the one hand, to preserve the indivisible nature of all human rights, be they civil, political, economic, social or cultural and, on the other hand, to give the European Social Charter fresh impetus;

Resolved, as was decided during the Ministerial Conference held in Turin on 21 and 22 October 1991, to update and adapt the substantive contents of the Charter in order to take account in particular of the fundamental social changes which have occurred since the text was adopted;

Recognising the advantage of embodying in a Revised Charter, designed progressively to take the place of the European Social Charter, the rights guaranteed by the Charter as amended, the rights guaranteed by the Additional Protocol of 1988 and to add new rights,

Have agreed as follows:

PART I

The Parties accept as the aim of their policy, to be pursued by all appropriate means both national and international in character, the attainment of conditions in which the following rights and principles may be effectively realised:

1. Everyone shall have the opportunity to earn his living in an occupation freely entered upon.
2. All workers have the right to just conditions of work.
3. All workers have the right to safe and healthy working conditions.
4. All workers have the right to a fair remuneration sufficient for a decent standard of living for themselves and their families.
5. All workers and employers have the right to freedom of association in national or international organisations for the protection of their economic and social interests.
6. All workers and employers have the right to bargain collectively.
7. Children and young persons have the right to a special protection against the physical and moral hazards to which they are exposed.
8. Employed women, in case of maternity, have the right to a special protection.
9. Everyone has the right to appropriate facilities for vocational guidance with a view to helping him choose an occupation suited to his personal aptitude and interests.
10. Everyone has the right to appropriate facilities for vocational training.
11. Everyone has the right to benefit from any measures enabling him to enjoy the highest possible standard of health attainable.

12. All workers and their dependants have the right to social security.

13. Anyone without adequate resources has the right to social and medical assistance.

14. Everyone has the right to benefit from social welfare services.

15. Disabled persons have the right to independence, social integration and participation in the life of the community.

16. The family as a fundamental unit of society has the right to appropriate social, legal and economic protection to ensure its full development.

17. Children and young persons have the right to appropriate social, legal and economic protection.

18. The nationals of any one of the Parties have the right to engage in any gainful occupation in the territory of any one of the others on a footing of equality with the nationals of the latter, subject to restrictions based on cogent economic or social reasons.

19. Migrant workers who are nationals of a Party and their families have the right to protection and assistance in the territory of any other Party.

20. All workers have the right to equal opportunities and equal treatment in matters of employment and occupation without discrimination on the grounds of sex.

21. Workers have the right to be informed and to be consulted within the undertaking.

22. Workers have the right to take part in the determination and improvement of the working conditions and working environment in the undertaking.

23. Every elderly person has the right to social protection.

24. All workers have the right to protection in cases of termination of employment.

25. All workers have the right to protection of their claims in the event of the insolvency of their employer.

26. All workers have the right to dignity at work.

27. All persons with family responsibilities and who are engaged or wish to engage in employment have a right to do so without being subject to discrimination and as far as possible without conflict between their employment and family responsibilities.

28. Workers' representatives in undertakings have the right to protection against acts prejudicial to them and should be afforded appropriate facilities to carry out their functions.

29. All workers have the right to be informed and consulted in collective redundancy procedures.
30. Everyone has the right to protection against poverty and social exclusion.
31. Everyone has the right to housing.

PART II

The Parties undertake, as provided for in Part III, to consider themselves bound by the obligations laid down in the following articles and paragraphs.

Article 1 – The right to work

With a view to ensuring the effective exercise of the right to work, the Parties undertake:

1. to accept as one of their primary aims and responsibilities the achievement and maintenance of as high and stable a level of employment as possible, with a view to the attainment of full employment;
2. to protect effectively the right of the worker to earn his living in an occupation freely entered upon;
3. to establish or maintain free employment services for all workers;
4. to provide or promote appropriate vocational guidance, training and rehabilitation.

Article 2 – The right to just conditions of work

With a view to ensuring the effective exercise of the right to just conditions of work, the Parties undertake:

1. to provide for reasonable daily and weekly working hours, the working week to be progressively reduced to the extent that the increase of productivity and other relevant factors permit;
2. to provide for public holidays with pay;
3. to provide for a minimum of four weeks' annual holiday with pay;

4. to eliminate risks in inherently dangerous or unhealthy occupations, and where it has not yet been possible to eliminate or reduce sufficiently these risks, to provide for either a reduction of working hours or additional paid holidays for workers engaged in such occupations;

5. to ensure a weekly rest period which shall, as far as possible, coincide with the day recognised by tradition or custom in the country or region concerned as a day of rest;

6. to ensure that workers are informed in written form, as soon as possible, and in any event not later than two months after the date of commencing their employment, of the essential aspects of the contract or employment relationship;

7. to ensure that workers performing night work benefit from measures which take account of the special nature of the work.

Article 3 – The right to safe and healthy working conditions

With a view to ensuring the effective exercise of the right to safe and healthy working conditions, the Parties undertake, in consultation with employers' and workers' organisations:

1. to formulate, implement and periodically review a coherent national policy on occupational safety, occupational health and the working environment. The primary aim of this policy shall be to improve occupational safety and health and to prevent accidents and injury to health arising out of, linked with or occurring in the course of work, particularly by minimising the causes of hazards inherent in the working environment;

2. to issue safety and health regulations;

3. to provide for the enforcement of such regulations by measures of supervision;

4. to promote the progressive development of occupational health services for all workers with essentially preventative and advisory functions.

Article 4 – The right to a fair remuneration

With a view to ensuring the effective exercise of the right to a fair remuneration, the Parties undertake:

1. to recognise the right of workers to a remuneration such as will give them and their families a decent standard of living;

2. to recognise the right of workers to an increased rate of remuneration for overtime work, subject to exceptions in particular cases;

3. to recognise the right of men and women workers to equal pay for work of equal value;

4. to recognise the right of all workers to a reasonable period of notice for termination of employment;

5. to permit deductions from wages only under conditions and to the extent prescribed by national laws or regulations or fixed by collective agreements or arbitration awards.

The exercise of these rights shall be achieved by freely concluded collective agreements, by statutory wage-fixing machinery, or by other means appropriate to national conditions.

Article 5 – The right to organise

With a view to ensuring or promoting the freedom of workers and employers to formal local, national or international organisations for the protection of their economic and social interests and to join those organisations, the Parties undertake that national law shall not be such as to impair, nor shall it be so applied as to impair, this freedom. The extent to which the guarantees provided for in this article shall apply to the police shall be determined by national laws or regulations. The principles governing the application to the members of the armed forces of these guarantees and the extent to which they shall apply to persons in this category shall equally be determined by national laws or regulations.

Article 6 – The right to bargain collectively

With a view to ensuring the effective exercise of the right to bargain collectively, the Parties undertake:

1. to promote joint consultation between workers and employers;

2. to promote, where necessary and appropriate, machinery for voluntary negotiations between employers or employers' organisations and workers' organisations, with a view to the regulation of terms and conditions of employment by means of collective agreements;

3. to promote the establishment and use of appropriate machinery for conciliation and voluntary arbitration for the settlement of labour disputes;

and recognise:

4. the right of workers and employers to collective action in cases of conflicts of interest, including the right to strike, subject to obligations that might arise out of collective agreements previously entered into.

Article 7 – The right of children and young persons to protection

With a view to ensuring the effective exercise of the right of children and young persons to protection, the Parties undertake:

1. to provide that the minimum age of admission to employment shall be fifteen years, subject to exceptions for children employed in prescribed light work without harm to their health, morals or education;
2. to provide that the minimum age of admission to employment shall be eighteen years with respect to prescribed occupations regarded as dangerous or unhealthy;
3. to provide that persons who are still subject to compulsory education shall not be employed in such work as would deprive them of the full benefit of their education;
4. to provide that the working hours of persons under eighteen years of age shall be limited in accordance with the needs of their development, and particularly with their need for vocational training;
5. to recognise the right of young workers and apprentices to a fair wage or other appropriate allowances;
6. to provide that the time spent by young persons in vocational training during the normal working hours with the consent of the employer shall be treated as forming part of the working day;
7. to provide that employed persons of under eighteen years of age shall be entitled to a minimum of four weeks' annual holiday with pay;

8. to provide that persons under eighteen years of age shall not be employed in night work with the exception of certain occupations provided for by national laws or regulations;

9. to provide that persons under eighteen years of age employed in occupations prescribed by national laws or regulations shall be subject to regular medical control;

10. to ensure special protection against physical and moral dangers to which children and young persons are exposed, and particularly against those resulting directly or indirectly from their work.

Article 8 – The right of employed women to protection of maternity

With a view to ensuring the effective exercise of the right of employed women to the protection of maternity, the Parties undertake:

1. to provide either by paid leave, by adequate social security benefits or by benefits from public funds for employed women to take leave before and after childbirth up to a total of at least fourteen weeks;

2. to consider it as unlawful for an employer to give a woman notice of dismissal during that period from the time she notifies her employer that she is pregnant until the end of her maternity leave, or to give her notice of dismissal at such a time that the notice would expire during such a period;

3. to provide that mothers who are nursing their infants shall be entitled to sufficient time off for this purpose;

4. to regulate the employment in night work of pregnant women, women who have recently given birth and women nursing their infants;

5. to prohibit the employment of pregnant women, women who have recently given birth or who are nursing their infants in underground mining and all other work which is unsuitable by reason of its dangerous, unhealthy or arduous nature and to take appropriate measures to protect the employment rights of these women.

Article 9 – The right to vocational guidance

With a view to ensuring the effective exercise of the right to vocational guidance, the Parties undertake to provide or promote, as necessary, a service which will assist all persons, including the handicapped, to solve problems related to occupational choice and progress, with due regard to the individual's characteristics and their relation to occupational opportunity: this assistance should be available free of charge, both to young persons, including schoolchildren, and to adults.

Article 10 – The right to vocational training

With a view to ensuring the effective exercise of the right to vocational training, the Parties undertake:

1. to provide or promote, as necessary, the technical and vocational training of all persons, including the handicapped, in consultation with employers' and workers' organisations, and to grant facilities for access to higher technical and university education, based solely on individual aptitude;

2. to provide or promote a system of apprenticeship and other systematic arrangements for training young boys and girls in their various employments;

3. to provide or promote, as necessary:
   a   adequate and readily available training facilities for adult workers;
   b   special facilities for the retraining of adult workers needed as a result of technological development or new trends in employment;

4. to provide or promote, as necessary, special measures for the retraining and reintegration of the long-term unemployed;

5. to encourage the full utilisation of the facilities provided by appropriate measures such as:
   a   reducing or abolishing any fees or charges;
   b   granting financial assistance in appropriate cases;
   c   including in the normal working hours time spent on supplementary training taken by the worker, at the request of his employer, during employment;
   d   ensuring, through adequate supervision, in consultation with the employers' and workers' organisations, the efficiency of

apprenticeship and other training arrangements for young workers, and the adequate protection of young workers generally.

Article 11 – The right to protection of health

With a view to ensuring the effective exercise of the right to protection of health, the Parties undertake, either directly or in cooperation with public or private organisations, to take appropriate measures designed inter alia:

1. to remove as far as possible the causes of ill health;
2. to provide advisory and educational facilities for the promotion of health and the encouragement of individual responsibility in matters of health;
3. to prevent as far as possible epidemic, endemic and other diseases, as well as accidents.

Article 12 – The right to social security

With a view to ensuring the effective exercise of the right to social security, the Parties undertake:

1. to establish or maintain a system of social security;
2. to maintain the social security system at a satisfactory level at least equal to that necessary for the ratification of the European Code of Social Security;
3. to endeavour to raise progressively the system of social security to a higher level;
4. to take steps, by the conclusion of appropriate bilateral and multilateral agreements or by other means, and subject to the conditions laid down in such agreements, in order to ensure:
    a   equal treatment with their own nationals of the nationals of other Parties in respect of social security rights, including the retention of benefits arising out of social security legislation, whatever movements the persons protected may undertake between the territories of the Parties;
    b   the granting, maintenance and resumption of social security rights by such means as the accumulation of insurance or

employment periods completed under the legislation of each of the Parties.

Article 13 – The right to social and medical assistance

With a view to ensuring the effective exercise of the right to social and medical assistance, the Parties undertake:

1. to ensure that any person who is without adequate resources and who is unable to secure such resources either by his own efforts or from other sources, in particular by benefits under a social security scheme, be granted adequate assistance, and, in case of sickness, the care necessitated by his condition;
2. to ensure that persons receiving such assistance shall not, for that reason, suffer from a diminution of their political or social rights;
3. to provide that everyone may receive by appropriate public or private services such advice and personal help as may be required to prevent, to remove, or to alleviate personal or family want;
4. to apply the provisions referred to in paragraphs 1, 2 and 3 of this article on an equal footing with their nationals to nationals of other Parties lawfully within their territories, in accordance with their obligations under the European Convention on Social and Medical Assistance, signed at Paris on 11 December 1953.

Article 14 – The right to benefit from social welfare services

With a view to ensuring the effective exercise of the right to benefit from social welfare services, the Parties undertake:

1. to promote or provide services which, by using methods of social work, would contribute to the welfare and development of both individuals and groups in the community, and to their adjustment to the social environment;
2. to encourage the participation of individuals and voluntary or other organisations in the establishment and maintenance of such services.

Article 15 – The right of persons with disabilities to independence, social integration and participation in the life of the community

With a view to ensuring to persons with disabilities, irrespective of age and the nature and origin of their disabilities, the effective exercise of the right to independence, social integration and participation in the life of the community, the Parties undertake, in particular:

1. to take the necessary measures to provide persons with disabilities with guidance, education and vocational training in the framework of general schemes wherever possible or, where this is not possible, through specialised bodies, public or private;

2. to promote their access to employment through all measures tending to encourage employers to hire and keep in employment persons with disabilities in the ordinary working environment and to adjust the working conditions to the needs of the disabled or, where this is not possible by reason of the disability, by arranging for or creating sheltered employment according to the level of disability. In certain cases, such measures may require recourse to specialised placement and support services;

3. to promote their full social integration and participation in the life of the community in particular through measures, including technical aids, aiming to overcome barriers to communication and mobility and enabling access to transport, housing, cultural activities and leisure.

Article 16 – The right of the family to social, legal and economic protection

With a view to ensuring the necessary conditions for the full development of the family, which is a fundamental unit of society, the Parties undertake to promote the economic, legal and social protection of family life by such means as social and family benefits, fiscal arrangements, provision of family housing, benefits for the newly married and other appropriate means.

Article 17 – The right of children and young persons to social, legal and economic protection

With a view to ensuring the effective exercise of the right of children and young persons to grow up in an environment which encourages the full development of their personality and of their physical and mental capacities, the Parties undertake, either directly or in cooperation with public and private organisations, to take all appropriate and necessary measures designed:

1. a to ensure that children and young persons, taking account of the rights and duties of their parents, have the care, the assistance, the education and the training they need, in particular by providing for the establishment or maintenance of institutions and services sufficient and adequate for this purpose;
    b to protect children and young persons against negligence, violence and exploitation;
    c to provide protection and special aid from the state for children and young persons temporarily or definitively deprived of their family's support;
2. to provide to children and young persons a free primary and secondary education as well as to encourage regular attendance at schools.

Article 18 – The right to engage in a gainful occupation in the territory of other Parties

With a view to ensuring the effective exercise of the right to engage in a gainful occupation in the territory of any other Party, the Parties undertake:

1. to apply existing regulations in a spirit of liberality;
2. to simplify existing formalities and to reduce or abolish chancery dues and other charges payable by foreign workers or their employers;
3. to liberalise, individually or collectively, regulations governing the employment of foreign workers;

and recognise:

4. the right of their nationals to leave the country to engage in a gainful occupation in the territories of the other Parties.

Article 19 – The right of migrant workers and their families to protection and assistance

With a view to ensuring the effective exercise of the right of migrant workers and their families to protection and assistance in the territory of any other Party, the Parties undertake:

1. to maintain or to satisfy themselves that there are maintained adequate and free services to assist such workers, particularly in obtaining accurate information, and to take all appropriate steps, so far as national laws and regulations permit, against misleading propaganda relating to emigration and immigration;

2. to adopt appropriate measures within their own jurisdiction to facilitate the departure, journey and reception of such workers and their families, and to provide, within their own jurisdiction, appropriate services for health, medical attention and good hygienic conditions during the journey;

3. to promote cooperation, as appropriate, between social services, public and private, in emigration and immigration countries;

4. to secure for such workers lawfully within their territories, insofar as such matters are regulated by law or regulations or are subject to the control of administrative authorities, treatment not less favourable than that of their own nationals in respect of the following matters:
   a remuneration and other employment and working conditions;
   b membership of trade unions and enjoyment of the benefits of collective bargaining;
   c Accommodation;

5. to secure for such workers lawfully within their territories treatment not less favourable than that of their own nationals with regard to employment taxes, dues or contributions payable in respect of employed persons;

6. to facilitate as far as possible the reunion of the family of a foreign worker permitted to establish himself in the territory;

7. to secure for such workers lawfully within their territories treatment not less favourable than that of their own nationals in respect of legal proceedings relating to matters referred to in this article;

8.   to secure that such workers lawfully residing within their territories are not expelled unless they endanger national security or offend against public interest or morality;

9.   to permit, within legal limits, the transfer of such parts of the earnings and savings of such workers as they may desire;

10. to extend the protection and assistance provided for in this article to self-employed migrants insofar as such measures apply;

11. to promote and facilitate the teaching of the national language of the receiving state or, if there are several, one of these languages, to migrant workers and members of their families;

12. to provide and facilitate, as far as practicable, the teaching of the migrant worker's mother tongue to the children of the migrant worker.

Article 20 – The right to equal opportunities and equal treatment in matters of employment and occupation without discrimination on the grounds of sex

With a view to ensuring the effective exercise of the right to equal opportunities and equal treatment in matters of employment and occupation without discrimination on the grounds of sex, the Parties undertake to recognise that right and to take appropriate measures to ensure or promote its application in the following fields:

a   access to employment, protection against dismissal and occupational reintegration;

b   vocational guidance, training, retraining and rehabilitation;

c   terms of employment and working conditions, including remuneration;

d   career development, including promotion.

Article 21 – The right to information and consultation

With a view to ensuring the effective exercise of the right of workers to be informed and consulted within the undertaking, the Parties undertake to adopt or encourage measures enabling workers or their representatives, in accordance with national legislation and practice:

a   to be informed regularly or at the appropriate time and in a comprehensible way about the economic and financial situation of the undertaking employing them, on the understanding that the disclosure of certain information which could be prejudicial to the undertaking may be refused or subject to confidentiality; and

b   to be consulted in good time on proposed decisions which could substantially affect the interests of workers, particularly on those decisions which could have an important impact on the employment situation in the undertaking.

Article 22 – The right to take part in the determination and improvement of the working conditions and working environment

With a view to ensuring the effective exercise of the right of workers to take part in the determination and improvement of the working conditions and working environment in the undertaking, the Parties undertake to adopt or encourage measures enabling workers or their representatives, in accordance with national legislation and practice, to contribute:

a   to the determination and the improvement of the working conditions, work organisation and working environment;

b   to the protection of health and safety within the undertaking;

c   to the organisation of social and socio-cultural services and facilities within the undertaking;

d   to the supervision of the observance of regulations on these matters.

Article 23 – The right of elderly persons to social protection

With a view to ensuring the effective exercise of the right of elderly persons to social protection, the Parties undertake to adopt or encourage, either directly or in cooperation with public or private organisations, appropriate measures designed in particular:

1. to enable elderly persons to remain full members of society for as long as possible, by means of:

    a   adequate resources enabling them to lead a decent life and play an active part in public, social and cultural life;

    b   provision of information about services and facilities available for elderly persons and their opportunities to make use of them;

2.   to enable elderly persons to choose their life-style freely and to lead independent lives in their familiar surroundings for as long as they wish and are able, by means of:

    a   provision of housing suited to their need and their state of health or of adequate support for adapting their housing;

    b   the health care and the services necessitated by their state;

3.   to guarantee elderly persons living in institutions appropriate support, while respecting their privacy, and participation in decisions concerning living conditions in the institution.

Article 24 – The right to protection in cases of termination of employment

With a view to ensuring the effective exercise of the right of workers to protection in cases of termination of employment, the Parties undertake to recognise:

    a   the right of all workers not to have their employment terminated without valid reasons for such termination connected with their capacity or conduct or based on the operational requirements of the undertaking, establishment or service;

    b   the right of workers whose employment is terminated without a valid reason to adequate compensation or other appropriate relief.

To this end the Parties undertake to ensure that a worker who considers that his employment has been terminated without a valid reason shall have the right to appeal to an impartial body.

Article 25 – The right of workers to the protection of their claims in the event of insolvency of their employer

With a view to ensuring the effective exercise of the right of workers to the protection of their claims in the event of the insolvency of their employer, the Parties undertake to provide that workers' claims arising from contracts of employment or employment relationships be guaranteed by a guarantee institution or by any other effective form of protection.

Article 26 – The right to dignity at work

With a view to ensuring the effective exercise of the right of all workers to protection of their dignity at work, the Parties undertake, in consultation with employers' and workers' organisations:

1. to promote awareness, information and prevention of sexual harassment in the workplace or in relation to work and to take all appropriate measures to protect workers from such conduct;
2. to promote awareness, information and prevention of recurrent reprehensible or distinctly negative and offensive actions directed against individual workers in the workplace or in relation to work and to take all appropriate measures to protect workers from such conduct.

Article 27 – The right of workers with family responsibilities to equal opportunities and equal treatment

With a view to ensuring the exercise of the right to equality of opportunity and treatment for men and women workers with family responsibilities and between such workers and other workers, the Parties undertake:

1. to take appropriate measures:
    a   to enable workers with family responsibilities to enter and remain in employment, as well as to re-enter employment after an absence due to those responsibilities, including measures in the field of vocational guidance and training;
    b   to take account of their needs in terms of conditions of employment and social security;
    c   to develop or promote services, public or private, in particular child daycare services and other childcare arrangements;
2. to provide a possibility for either parent to obtain, during a period after maternity leave, parental leave to take care of a child, the

duration and conditions of which should be determined by national legislation, collective agreements or practice;

3. to ensure that family responsibilities shall not, as such, constitute a valid reason for termination of employment.

Article 28 – The right of workers' representatives to protection in the undertaking and facilities to be accorded to them

With a view to ensuring the effective exercise of the right of workers' representatives to carry out their functions, the Parties undertake to ensure that in the undertaking:

a   they enjoy effective protection against acts prejudicial to them, including dismissal, based on their status or activities as workers' representatives within the undertaking;

b   they are afforded such facilities as may be appropriate in order to enable them to carry out their functions promptly and efficiently, account being taken of the industrial relations system of the country and the needs, size and capabilities of the undertaking concerned.

Article 29 – The right to information and consultation in collective redundancy procedures

With a view to ensuring the effective exercise of the right of workers to be informed and consulted in situations of collective redundancies, the Parties undertake to ensure that employers shall inform and consult workers' representatives, in good time prior to such collective redundancies, on ways and means of avoiding collective redundancies or limiting their occurrence and mitigating their consequences, for example by recourse to accompanying social measures aimed, in particular, at aid for the redeployment or retraining of the workers concerned.

Article 30 – The right to protection against poverty and social exclusion

With a view to ensuring the effective exercise of the right to protection against poverty and social exclusion, the Parties undertake:

a   to take measures within the framework of an overall and coordinated approach to promote the effective access of persons who live or risk living in a situation of social exclusion or poverty, as well as their families, to, in particular, employment, housing, training, education, culture and social and medical assistance;

b   to review these measures with a view to their adaptation if necessary.

Article 31 – The right to housing

With a view to ensuring the effective exercise of the right to housing, the Parties undertake to take measures designed:

1.   to promote access to housing of an adequate standard;
2.   to prevent and reduce homelessness with a view to its gradual elimination;
3.   to make the price of housing accessible to those without adequate resources.

PART III

Article A – Undertakings

1.   Subject to the provisions of Article B below, each of the Parties undertakes:
    a   to consider Part I of this Charter as a declaration of the aims which it will pursue by all appropriate means, as stated in the introductory paragraph of that part;
    b   to consider itself bound by at least six of the following nine articles of Part II of this Charter: Articles 1, 5, 6, 7, 12, 13, 16, 19 and 20;

c   to consider itself bound by an additional number of articles or numbered paragraphs of Part II of the Charter which it may select, provided that the total number of articles or numbered paragraphs by which it is bound is not less than sixteen articles or sixty-three numbered paragraphs.

2.   The articles or paragraphs selected in accordance with sub-paragraphs b and c of paragraph 1 of this article shall be notified to the Secretary General of the Council of Europe at the time when the instrument of ratification, acceptance or approval is deposited.

3.   Any Party may, at a later date, declare by notification addressed to the Secretary General that it considers itself bound by any articles or any numbered paragraphs of Part II of the Charter which it has not already accepted under the terms of paragraph 1 of this article. Such undertakings subsequently given shall be deemed to be an integral part of the ratification, acceptance or approval and shall have the same effect as from the first day of the month following the expiration of a period of one month after the date of the notification.

4.   Each Party shall maintain a system of labour inspection appropriate to national conditions.

Article B – Links with the European Social Charter and the 1988 Additional Protocol

1.   No Contracting Party to the European Social Charter or Party to the Additional Protocol of 5 May 1988 may ratify, accept or approve this Charter without considering itself bound by at least the provisions corresponding to the provisions of the European Social Charter and, where appropriate, of the Additional Protocol, to which it was bound.

2.   Acceptance of the obligations of any provision of this Charter shall, from the date of entry into force of those obligations for the Party concerned, result in the corresponding provision of the European Social Charter and, where appropriate, of its Additional Protocol of 1988 ceasing to apply to the Party concerned in the event of that Party being bound by the first of those instruments or by both instruments.

PART IV

Article C – Supervision of the implementation of the undertakings contained in this Charter

The implementation of the legal obligations contained in this Charter shall be submitted to the same supervision as the European Social Charter.

Article D – Collective complaints

1. The provisions of the Additional Protocol to the European Social Charter providing for a system of collective complaints shall apply to the undertakings given in this Charter for the States which have ratified the said Protocol.

2. Any State which is not bound by the Additional Protocol to the European Social Charter providing for a system of collective complaints may when depositing its instrument of ratification, acceptance or approval of this Charter or at any time thereafter, declare by notification addressed to the Secretary General of the Council of Europe, that it accepts the supervision of its obligations under this Charter following the procedure provided for in the said Protocol.

PART V

Article E – Non-discrimination

The enjoyment of the rights set forth in this Charter shall be secured without discrimination on any ground such as race, colour, sex, language, religion, political or other opinion, national extraction or social origin, health, association with a national minority, birth or other status.

Article F – Derogations in time of war or public emergency

1. In time of war or other public emergency threatening the life of the nation any Party may take measures derogating from its obligations under this Charter to the extent strictly required by the exigencies of the situation, provided that such measures are not inconsistent with its other obligations under international law.

2. Any Party which has availed itself of this right of derogation shall, within a reasonable lapse of time, keep the Secretary General of the Council of Europe fully informed of the measures taken and of the reasons therefor. It shall likewise inform the Secretary General when such measures have ceased to operate and the provisions of the Charter which it has accepted are again being fully executed.

Article G – Restrictions

1. The rights and principles set forth in Part I when effectively realised, and their effective exercise as provided for in Part II, shall not be subject to any restrictions or limitations not specified in those parts, except such as are prescribed by law and are necessary in a democratic society for the protection of the rights and freedoms of others or for the protection of public interest, national security, public health, or morals.

2. The restrictions permitted under this Charter to the rights and obligations set forth herein shall not be applied for any purpose other than that for which they have been prescribed.

Article H – Relations between the Charter and domestic law or international agreements

The provisions of this Charter shall not prejudice the provisions of domestic law or of any bilateral or multilateral treaties, conventions or agreements which are already in force, or may come into force, under which more favourable treatment would be accorded to the persons protected.

Article I – Implementation of the undertakings given

1. Without prejudice to the methods of implementation foreseen in these articles the relevant provisions of Articles 1 to 31 of Part II of this Charter shall be implemented by:
    a   laws or regulations;
    b   agreements between employers or employers' organisations and workers' organisations;
    c   a combination of those two methods;
    d   other appropriate means.
2. Compliance with the undertakings deriving from the provisions of paragraphs 1, 2, 3, 4, 5, and 7 of Article 2, paragraphs 4, 6 and 7 of Article 7, paragraphs 1, 2, 3 and 5 of Article 10 and Articles 21 and 22 of Part II of this Charter shall be regarded as effective if the provisions are applied, in accordance with paragraph 1 of this article, to the great majority of the workers concerned.

Article J – Amendments

1. Any amendment to Parts I and II of this Charter with the purpose of extending the rights guaranteed in this Charter as well as any amendment to Parts III to VI, proposed by a Party or by the Governmental Committee, shall be communicated to the Secretary General of the Council of Europe and forwarded by the Secretary General to the Parties to this Charter.
2. Any amendment proposed in accordance with the provisions of the preceding paragraph shall be examined by the Governmental Committee which shall submit the text adopted to the Committee of Ministers for approval after consultation with the Parliamentary Assembly. After its approval by the Committee of Ministers this text shall be forwarded to the Parties for acceptance.
3. Any amendment to Part I and to Part II of this Charter shall enter into force, in respect of those Parties which have accepted it, on the first day of the month following the expiration of a period of one month after the date on which three Parties have informed the Secretary General that they have accepted it.

In respect of any Party which subsequently accepts it, the amendment shall enter into force on the first day of the month following the expiration of a period of one month after the date on which that Party has informed the Secretary General of its acceptance.

4. Any amendment to Parts III to VI of this Charter shall enter into force on the first day of the month following the expiration of a period of one month after the date on which all Parties have informed the Secretary General that they have accepted it.

PART VI

Article K – Signature, ratification and entry into force

1. This Charter shall be open for signature by the Member States of the Council of Europe. It shall be subject to ratification, acceptance or approval. Instruments of ratification, acceptance or approval shall be deposited with the Secretary General of the Council of Europe.
2. This Charter shall enter into force on the first day of the month following the expiration of a period of one month after the date on which three Member States of the Council of Europe have expressed their consent to be bound by this Charter in accordance with the preceding paragraph.
3. In respect of any Member State which subsequently expresses its consent to be bound by this Charter, it shall enter into force on the first day of the month following the expiration of a period of one month after the date of the deposit of the instrument of ratification, acceptance or approval.

Article L – Territorial application

1. This Charter shall apply to the metropolitan territory of each Party. Each signatory may, at the time of signature or of the deposit of its instrument of ratification, acceptance or approval, specify, by declaration addressed to the Secretary General of the Council of Europe, the territory which shall be considered to be its metropolitan territory for this purpose.
2. Any signatory may, at the time of signature or of the deposit of its instrument of ratification, acceptance or approval, or at any time thereafter, declare by notification addressed to the Secretary

General of the Council of Europe, that the Charter shall extend in whole or in part to a non-metropolitan territory or territories specified in the said declaration for whose international relations it is responsible or for which it assumed international responsibility. It shall specify in the declaration the articles or paragraphs of Part II of the Charter which it accepts as binding in respect of the territories named in the declaration.

3. The Charter shall extend its application to the territory or territories named in the aforesaid declaration as from the first day of the month following the expiration of a period of one month after the date of receipt of the notification of such declaration by the Secretary General.

4. Any Party may declare at a later date by notification addressed to the Secretary General of the Council of Europe that, in respect of one or more of the territories to which the Charter has been applied in accordance with paragraph 2 of this article, it accepts as binding any articles or any numbered paragraphs which it has not already accepted in respect of that territory or territories. Such undertakings subsequently given shall be deemed to be an integral part of the original declaration in respect of the territory concerned, and shall have the same effect as from the first day of the month following the expiration of a period of one month after the date of receipt of such notification by the Secretary General.

Article M – Denunciation

1. Any Party may denounce this Charter only at the end of a period of five years from the date on which the Charter entered into force for it, or at the end of any subsequent period of two years, and in either case after giving six months' notice to the Secretary General of the Council of Europe who shall inform the other Parties accordingly.

2. Any Party may, in accordance with the provisions set out in the preceding paragraph, denounce any article or paragraph of Part II of the Charter accepted by it provided that the number of articles or paragraphs by which this Party is bound shall never be less than sixteen in the former case and sixty-three in the latter and that this number of articles or paragraphs shall continue to include the articles selected by the Party among those to which special reference is made in Article A, paragraph 1, sub-paragraph b.

3. Any Party may denounce the present Charter or any of the articles or paragraphs of Part II of the Charter under the conditions specified in paragraph 1 of this article in respect of any territory to

which the said Charter is applicable, by virtue of a declaration made in accordance with paragraph 2 of Article L.

Article N – Appendix

The appendix to this Charter shall form an integral part of it.

Article O – Notifications

The Secretary General of the Council of Europe shall notify the Member States of the Council and the Director General of the International Labour Office of:

a   any signature;

b   the deposit of any instrument of ratification, acceptance or approval;

c   any date of entry into force of this Charter in accordance with Article K;

d   any declaration made in application of Articles A, paragraphs 2 and 3, D, paragraphs 1 and 2, F, paragraph 2, L, paragraphs 1, 2, 3 and 4;

e   any amendment in accordance with Article J;

f   any denunciation in accordance with Article M;

g   any other act, notification or communication relating to this Charter.

APPENDIX TO THE REVISED EUROPEAN SOCIAL CHARTER

Scope of the revised European Social Charter in terms of persons protected

1.   Without prejudice to Article 12, paragraph 4, and Article 13, paragraph 4, the persons covered by Articles 1 to 17 and 20 to 31 include foreigners only in so far as they are nationals of other Parties lawfully resident or working regularly within the territory of the

party concerned, subject to the understanding that these articles are to be interpreted in the light of the provisions of Articles 18 and 19. This interpretation would not prejudice the extension of similar facilities to other persons by any of the Parties.

2. Each Party will grant to refugees as defined in the Convention relating to the Status of Refugees, signed in Geneva on 28 July 1951 and in the Protocol of 31 January 1967, and lawfully staying in its territory, treatment as favourable as possible, and in any case not less favourable than under the obligations accepted by the Party under the said convention and under any other existing international instruments applicable to those refugees.

3. Each Party will grant to stateless persons as defined in the Convention on the Status of Stateless Persons done in New York on 28 September 1954 and lawfully staying in its territory, treatment as favourable as possible and in any case not less favourable than under the obligations accepted by the Party under the said instrument and under any other existing international instruments applicable to those stateless persons.

Part I, paragraph 18, and Part II, Article 18, paragraph 1

It is understood that these provisions are not concerned with the question of entry into the territories of the Parties and do not prejudice the provisions of the European Convention on Establishment, signed in Paris on 13 December 1955.

Part II

Article 1, paragraph 2

This provision shall not be interpreted as prohibiting or authorising any union security clause or practice.

Article 2, paragraph 6

Parties may provide that this provision shall not apply:

a   to workers having a contract or employment relationship with a total duration not exceeding one month and/or with a working week not exceeding eight hours;

b   where the contract or employment relationship is of a casual and/or specific nature, provided, in these cases, that its non-application is justified by objective considerations.

Article 3, paragraph 4

It is understood that for the purposes of this provision the functions, organisation and conditions of operation of these services shall be determined by national laws or regulations, collective agreements or other means appropriate to national conditions.

Article 4, paragraph 4

This provision shall be so understood as not to prohibit immediate dismissal for any serious offence.

Article 4, paragraph 5

It is understood that a Party may give the undertaking required in this paragraph if the great majority of workers are not permitted to suffer deductions from wages either by law or through collective agreements or arbitration awards, the exceptions being those persons not so covered.

Article 6, paragraph 4

It is understood that each Party may, insofar as it is concerned, regulate the exercise of the right to strike by law, provided that any further restriction that this might place on the right can be justified under the terms of Article G.

Article 7, paragraph 2

This provision does not prevent Parties from providing in their legislation that young persons not having reached the minimum age laid down may perform work in so far as it is absolutely necessary for their vocational training where such work is carried out in accordance with conditions prescribed by the competent authority and measures are taken to protect the health and safety of these young persons.

Article 7, paragraph 8

It is understood that a Party may give the undertaking required in this paragraph if it fulfils the spirit of the undertaking by providing by law that the great majority of persons under eighteen years of age shall not be employed in night work.

Article 8, paragraph 2

This provision shall not be interpreted as laying down an absolute prohibition. Exceptions could be made, for instance, in the following cases:

a   if an employed woman has been guilty of misconduct which justifies breaking off the employment relationship;

b   if the undertaking concerned ceases to operate;

c   if the period prescribed in the employment contract has expired.

Article 12, paragraph 4

The words 'and subject to the conditions laid down in such agreements' in the introduction to this paragraph are taken to imply inter alia that with regard to benefits which are available independently of any insurance contribution, a Party may require the completion of a prescribed period of residence before granting such benefits to nationals of other Parties.

Article 13, paragraph 4

Governments not Parties to the European Convention on Social and Medical Assistance may ratify the Charter in respect of this paragraph provided that they grant to nationals of other Parties a treatment which is in conformity with the provisions of the said convention.

Article 16

It is understood that the protection afforded in this provision covers single-parent families.

Article 17

It is understood that this provision covers all persons below the age of eighteen years, unless under the law applicable to the child majority is attained earlier, without prejudice to the other specific provisions provided by the Charter, particularly Article 7.

This does not imply an obligation to provide compulsory education up to the above-mentioned age.

Article 19, paragraph 6

For the purpose of applying this provision, the term 'family of a foreign worker' is understood to mean at least the worker's spouse and unmarried children, as long as the latter are considered to be minors by the receiving State and are dependent on the migrant worker.

Article 20

1. It is understood that social security matters, as well as other provisions relating to unemployment benefit, old age benefit and survivor's benefit, may be excluded from the scope of this article.
2. Provisions concerning the protection of women, particularly as regards pregnancy, confinement and the post-natal period, shall not be deemed to be discrimination as referred to in this article.
3. This article shall not prevent the adoption of specific measures aimed at removing de facto inequalities.
4. Occupational activities which, by reason of their nature or the context in which they are carried out, can be entrusted only to persons of a particular sex may be excluded from the scope of this article or some of its provisions. This provision is not to be interpreted as requiring the Parties to embody in laws or regulations a list of occupations which, by reason of their nature or the context in which they are carried out, may be reserved to persons of a particular sex.

Articles 21 and 22

1. For the purpose of the application of these articles, the term 'workers' representatives' means persons who are recognised as such under national legislation or practice.

2. The terms 'national legislation and practice' embrace as the case may be, in addition to laws and regulations, collective agreements, other agreements between employers and workers' representatives, customs as well as relevant case law.

3. For the purpose of the application of these articles, the term 'undertaking' is understood as referring to a set of tangible and intangible components, with or without legal personality, formed to produce goods or provide services for financial gain and with power to determine its own market policy.

4. It is understood that religious communities and their institutions may be excluded from the application of these articles, even if these institutions are 'undertakings' within the meaning of paragraph 3. Establishments pursuing activities which are inspired by certain ideals or guided by certain moral concepts, ideals and concepts which are protected by national legislation, may be excluded from the application of these articles to such an extent as is necessary to protect the orientation of the undertaking.

5. It is understood that where in a State the rights set out in these articles are exercised in the various establishments of the undertaking, the Party concerned is to be considered as fulfilling the obligations deriving from these provisions.

6. The Parties may exclude from the field of application of these articles, those undertakings employing less than a certain number of workers, to be determined by national legislation or practice.

Article 22

1. This provision affects neither the powers and obligations of States as regards the adoption of health and safety regulations for workplaces, nor the powers and responsibilities of the bodies in charge of monitoring their application.

2. The terms 'social and socio-cultural services and facilities' are understood as referring to the social and/or cultural facilities for workers provided by some undertakings such as welfare assistance, sports fields, rooms for nursing mothers, libraries, children's holiday camps, etc.

Article 23, paragraph 1

For the purpose of the application of this paragraph, the term 'for as long as possible' refers to the elderly person's physical, psychological and intellectual capacities.

Article 24

1. It is understood that for the purposes of this article the terms 'termination of employment' and 'terminated' mean termination of employment at the initiative of the employer.

2. It is understood that this article covers all workers but that a Party may exclude from some or all of its protection the following categories of employed persons:
   a workers engaged under a contract of employment for a specified period of time or a specified task;
   b workers undergoing a period of probation or a qualifying period of employment, provided that this is determined in advance and is of a reasonable duration;
   c workers engaged on a casual basis for a short period.

3. For the purpose of this article the following, in particular, shall not constitute valid reasons for termination of employment:
   a trade union membership or participation in union activities outside working hours, or, with the consent of the employer, within working hours;
   b seeking office as, acting or having acted in the capacity of a workers' representative;
   c the filing of a complaint or the participation in proceedings against an employer involving alleged violation of laws or regulations or recourse to competent administrative authorities;
   d race, colour, sex, marital status, family responsibilities, pregnancy, religion, political opinion, national extraction or social origin;
   e maternity or parental leave;
   f temporary absence from work due to illness or injury.

4. It is understood that compensation or other appropriate relief in case of termination of employment without valid reasons shall be determined by national laws or regulations, collective agreements or other means appropriate to national conditions.

Article 25

1. It is understood that the competent national authority may, by way of exemption and after consulting organisations of employers and workers, exclude certain categories of workers from the protection provided in this provision by reason of the special nature of their employment relationship.
2. It is understood that the definition of the term 'insolvency' must be determined by national law and practice.
3. The workers' claims covered by this provision shall include at least:
    a   the workers' claims for wages relating to a prescribed period, which shall not be less than three months under a privilege system and eight weeks under a guarantee system, prior to the insolvency or to the termination of employment;
    b   the workers' claims for holiday pay due as a result of work performed during the year in which the insolvency or the termination of employment occurred;
    c   the workers' claims for amounts due in respect of other types of paid absence relating to a prescribed period, which shall not be less than three months under a privilege system and eight weeks under a guarantee system, prior to the insolvency or the termination of the employment.
4. National laws or regulations may limit the protection of workers' claims to a prescribed amount, which shall be of a socially acceptable level.

Article 26

It is understood that this article does not require that legislation be enacted by the Parties.

It is understood that paragraph 2 does not cover sexual harassment.

Article 27

It is understood that this article applies to men and women workers with family responsibilities in relation to their dependent children as well as in relation to other members of their immediate family who clearly need their care or support where such responsibilities restrict their possibilities of preparing for, entering, participating in or advancing in economic activity. The terms 'dependent children' and 'other members of their immediate family who clearly need their care and support' mean persons defined as such by the national legislation of the Party concerned.

Articles 28 and 29

For the purpose of the application of this article, the term 'workers' representatives' means persons who are recognised as such under national legislation or practice.

Part III

It is understood that the Charter contains legal obligations of an international character, the application of which is submitted solely to the supervision provided for in Part IV thereof.

Article A, paragraph 1

It is understood that the numbered paragraphs may include articles consisting of only one paragraph.

Article B, paragraph 2

For the purpose of paragraph 2 of Article B, the provisions of the revised Charter correspond to the provisions of the Charter with the same article or paragraph number with the exception of:

a   Article 3, paragraph 2, of the revised Charter which corresponds to Article 3, paragraphs 1 and 3, of the Charter;

b   Article 3, paragraph 3, of the revised Charter which corresponds to Article 3, paragraphs 2 and 3, of the Charter;

c   Article 10, paragraph 5, of the revised Charter which corresponds to Article 10, paragraph 4, of the Charter;

d   Article 17, paragraph 1, of the revised Charter which corresponds to Article 17 of the Charter.

Part V

Article E

A differential treatment based on an objective and reasonable justification shall not be deemed discriminatory.

Article F

The terms 'in time of war or other public emergency' shall be so understood as to cover also the threat of war.

Article I

It is understood that workers excluded in accordance with the appendix to Articles 21 and 22 are not taken into account in establishing the number of workers concerned.

Article J

The term 'amendment' shall be extended so as to cover also the addition of new articles to the Charter.

APPENDIX B
SANYO INDUSTRIES
(UK) LTD: STAFF HANDBOOK

AGREEMENT

THIS AGREEMENT is made the tenth day of June 1982 BETWEEN:

(1) SANYO INDUSTRIES (UK) LIMITED
     of Oulton Works, School Road,
     Lowestoft, Suffolk NR33 9NA

(hereinafter referred to as 'the Company')

(2) THE ELECTRICAL ELECTRONIC TELECOMMUNICATIONS
     AND PLUMBING UNION
     of Hayes Court, West Common Road,
     Hayes, Bromley, Kent BR2 7AH

(hereinafter referred to as 'the Union').

The Company and the Union have agreed to enter this Agreement for the purpose of recognising various mutual and other objectives which is in the interests of both parties and of the employees of the Company to achieve and accordingly the Company and the Union have agreed the following matters:

1. (1) The independence of the practices and procedures laid down in the respect of the factory premises at Oulton Works, School Road, Lowestoft ('the Establishment') from time to time

    (2) The non-federated status of the Establishment established by this Agreement

(3) Each of the terms and provisions of this Agreement is dependent upon the observance of all the other terms and provisions, individual provisions cannot be acted upon without consideration of all other relevant provisions in the Agreement

(4) For the duration of this Agreement the Union shall have sole recognition and bargaining rights for all employees covered by this Agreement

2. In order to achieve the above objectives it is agreed that:

(1) All aspects of the Establishment and its operations will be so organised as to achieve the highest possible level of efficiency performance and job satisfaction so that the Company shall:
  (i) be competitive and thus remain in business
  (ii) provide continuity and security of employment for an effective work force
  (iii) establish and maintain good working conditions
  (iv) establish and maintain good employee relations and communications by supporting the agreed consultative negotiating grievance and disciplinary procedures set out in this Agreement

(2) Both parties accept an obligation to ensure that the Establishment will operate with effective working methods with the best utilisation of manpower and without the introduction of wasteful and restrictive working practices and this objective will be achieved by:
  (i) the selection, training, retraining and supplementary training of employees, wherever necessary, to enable such employees to carry out any job
  (ii) the maximum co-operation with and support from all employees for measures and techniques used in any area to improve organisation and individual efficiency and to provide objective information with which to control and appraise the performance of individual employees and the Establishment
  (iii) the maximum co-operation and support from all employees in achieving a completely flexible well motivated work force capable of transferring on a temporary or permanent basis into work of any nature that is within the capability of such employee having

due regard to the provision of adequate training and safety arrangements

(3) Both parties recognise that the well-being of the employees is dependent upon the Company's success and that the high standards of product quality and reliability are essential if the products produced at the Establishment are to become and remain competitive and that therefore the maximum co-operation and support must be given to measures designed to achieve maintain and improve quality and reliability standards.

3. The following matters have been agreed in connection with the Union:

(1) Employees will not be required to become union members but the Company will encourage all employees covered by this Agreement to become a member of the Union and participate in Union affairs and in this connection the Company will provide a check off arrangement for the deduction of union subscriptions

(2) Union representation will be established in the following manner:

(i) The number of representatives of the Union together with the constituencies which they will represent will be agreed between the Union and the Company

(ii) The representatives will be elected in accordance with the Union Rules by union members in each constituency

(iii) Each such representative ('the Constituency Representative') will be accredited by the Union and the Union will then send details of the credentials of such representative for approval to the Head of Personnel who will confirm such approval with the Union and thereafter inform the appropriate line management concerned of the appointment

(3) The elected representatives will elect from amongst themselves a senior representative ('the Senior Representative') in accordance with the Union Rules

(4) The Senior Representative will be responsible for controlling and co-ordinating the activities of the Union in accordance with the terms and conditions of this Agreement and within

the Union Rules and Regulations and will ensure that each elected representative shall have a working knowledge of the Union Rules and Regulations and in this connection in conjunction with the Personnel Department of the Company the Senior Representative shall ensure that the representatives shall have a comprehensive understanding of the employee relations procedures and practices of the Establishment and of general employee relations procedures and practices and it is agreed that all communication between the representatives and the full-time official(s) of the Union will be made through the Senior Representative

(5) Each elected representative must be employed in the constituency which he represents

(6) The Company will provide adequate facilities to ensure that all Union elections and ballots of members shall be carried out in secret and by the use of voting papers and not by way of a show of hands

4. It is agreed by the Company and the Union that all matters of difference should wherever possible be resolved at the source of such difference as speedily as practicable and it is the intention of the parties that all such matters will be dealt with in accordance with the agreed procedure and in this connection:

(1) Where a matter relates to an individual employee covered by this Agreement such employee must in the first instance raise the same with the supervisor who will then be given the appropriate time necessary to resolve the situation PROVIDED ALWAYS that:

(i) if the employee is not satisfied with the solution proposed by the supervisor then the employee may request the services of the constituency representative to reach a solution with the supervisor

(ii) if the constituency representative and the supervisor shall fail to reach agreement then the constituency representative will discuss the matter with the Department Manager or his representative

(iii) if after careful deliberation a satisfactory solution cannot be found then the constituency representative shall be entitled to raise the issue with the Senior Representative who will then decide if the grievance should be discussed at a higher level of management within the

Company and the services of the Personnel Officer may then be called upon if it is considered that this will help to resolve the matter

(iv)   failing such resolution discussions will then take place between the Senior Representatives of the Company normally including the Head of Personnel together with the Senior Union Representative and the constituency representatives on the Joint Negotiation Council ('JNC') referred to in Clause (5) below

(v)   in exceptional circumstances the services of the National Officer of the Union may be requested to assist in the matter either by the Union or by the Company and in such circumstances the Company will arrange an appropriate meeting to be attended by senior representatives of the Company and the Union as well as the National Officer or the Full-time Official

(2)   Insofar as differences shall arise in connection with issues of a Departmental nature then the procedure shall commence with a meeting between the constituency representative and the Department Manager or his representative

(3)   In the case of an issue concerning the Establishment or the Company as a whole the matter will commence on the same basis as is set out in Sub-Clause (iii) above

5.   The Company and the Union will establish a Joint Negotiation Council ('JNC') for the purpose of providing a forum through which discussions regarding improvements to employment conditions and other major matters can be discussed and in this connection:

(1)   The JNC will consist of representatives from the Company including the Head of Personnel and Senior Company Representatives and on behalf of the Union the Senior Representative from Production/Warehousing one constituency representative from Administration

(2)   Discussions regarding substantive improvements to employment conditions will normally be held on an annual basis during December in each year and such discussions will not include changes arising as a result of promotions transfers or changes to job content which can be implemented at any time as agreed

(3)   Matters agreed by the JNC will constitute one of the terms and conditions of employment for each employee covered by this Agreement

(4)   The Senior Representative will be given appropriate facilities to consult with Union Members Constituency Representatives and the Full-time Official or National Officer of the Union to enable the Senior Representative to conduct a meaningful collective bargaining exercise

(5)   All claims on behalf of Union Members must be made in writing by the Senior Representative to the Head of Personnel who will convene the appropriate meeting of the JNC

(6)   It is recognised by both parties that whilst discussions are taking place all business and negotiations discussed at the JNC will remain confidential to its members and the Company recognises its responsibility to ensure clear communication to employees of the results of such discussions and negotiations and in this connection the Head of Personnel will be responsible in consultation with the members of the JNC for announcing the details of any offer to be made to employees following such discussions and negotiations as aforesaid

(7)   In exceptional circumstances the services of the National Officer or the Full-time Official of the Union may be requested by the JNC and in such circumstances the Company will arrange an appropriate meeting to be attended by representatives of the Company and the Union and the National Officer

6.   In addition to the JNC the Company will establish a Joint Consultative Council ('JCC') and the following provisions shall apply thereto:

(1)   The membership of the JCC shall consist of the Head of Personnel (as Chairman) and appropriate members of the Company's Senior Executives and the Senior Representative together with one constituency representative from each of Production, Engineering and Administration and a further constituency representative on a rotating basis as a co-opted member and in addition the Managing Director of the Company shall act as President of the JCC and shall attend meetings from time to time

(2) The JCC shall meet on a monthly basis for the purposes of discussing issues of a mutual nature and one week prior to each JCC meeting the Personnel Officer will publish an Agenda agreed with the Senior Representative who will be responsible for submitting items for discussion on behalf of the Union in time for such items to be included on the Agenda

(3) Items to be included for discussion at JCC meetings will include:

(i)   manufacturing performance
(ii)   operating efficiency
(iii)   manufacturing planning
(iv)   employment levels
(v)   market information
(vi)   establishment environment
(vii)   employment legislation
(viii) union policies and procedure
(ix)   level of union membership

(4) Following each meeting of the JCC the Head of Personnel will be responsible for communicating to all employees the nature and content of the discussions and in this connection the Company and the Union recognise the need to conduct meetings of the JCC in constructive manner for the benefit of the Company and all its employees

7. In the event that the Company and the Union shall be unable ultimately to resolve between themselves any discussions or disputes they may jointly agree to appoint an arbitrator and in this connection:

(1) The Arbitrator will consider evidence presented to him by the Company and the Union and any factors that he believes to be appropriate

(2) The Arbitrator will decide in favour of one party

(3) The decision of the Arbitrator will be final and binding and will represent the final solution to the issue

8. DISCIPLINARY MEASURES

It is in the interest of the Company and its employees to maintain fair and consistent standards of conduct and performance. This procedure is designed to clarify the rights and responsibilities of the Company, the Union and employees with regard to disciplinary measures

Principles

The following principles will be followed in applying this procedure:

8.1 In the normal course of their duties, the Company will make employees aware of any shortcomings in performance or conduct. This counselling stage is separate from the disciplinary procedure as such

8.2 When the disciplinary procedure is invoked, the intention is to make the employee aware that the Company is concerned with their conduct or performance and to assist the person to improve to a satisfactory level

8.3 When any disciplinary case is being considered, the Company will be responsible for fully investigating the facts and circumstances of the case

8.4 The procedure will operate as quickly as possible, consistent with the thorough investigation of the case

8.5 The employee will always be informed of any disciplinary action to be taken and the reasons for it, indicating the specific areas for improvement

8.6 Normally the formal procedure will commence with the issuing of the first formal warning, however, the disciplinary procedure may be invoked at any stage depending on the seriousness of the case

8.7 Each formal warning will apply for 12 months. Should the employee improve their conduct or performance to an acceptable level and maintain the improvement for the duration of the warning, this will result in the deletion of the warning from their record

9. DISCIPLINARY PROCEDURE

The stages of the disciplinary procedure are as follows:

9.1 First Formal Warning

A formal warning at this stage represents the outcome of investigation and discussion into an employee's conduct or performance. If a first formal warning is issued, the individual concerned will be advised to this effect both verbally and in writing by the Company representative conducting the hearing, indicating the duration of the warning (which will be 12 months), the reasons for the warning and the specific areas for improvement

9.2 Final Warning

If there is no significant and sustained improvement in the employee's conduct or performance, then the next stage of the procedure is the final warning. If a final warning is issued, the individual concerned will be advised to this effect by the Company representative conducting the hearing, both verbally and in writing, indicating the duration of the warning (which will be 12 months), the grounds for the warning and the specific areas for improvement

9.3 Dismissal

If there is no significant and sustained improvement in the employee's conduct or performance during the period of the final warning, then following thorough investigation by the Company, the next stage of the procedure will be the dismissal stage. This stage will also be invoked in cases of gross misconduct (see Establishment Regulations). If an employee is dismissed he will be advised in writing of the principal reasons for the dismissal, and the notice periods which will apply to him

9.4 Union Representation

At all stages of this procedure and consistent with the circumstances of the issue the Company will ensure the involvement of the appropriate constituency representative. When, following careful investigation, disciplinary action is contemplated by the Company, the union members concerned will be afforded the services of the Union constituency representative

10. APPEALS

Appeals against disciplinary action will follow the procedure as outlined below

10.1 All appeals will be in writing by the Senior Representative within two working days after the disciplinary action shall have been taken by the Company

10.2 The appeal will be made to the Personnel Officer who will arrange the formal appeal hearing within two working days of the appeal

10.3 The appeal will be heard by a Senior Personnel representative and a Senior Manager of the Department concerned who has not been involved in the case

10.4 The appeal will be conducted on the employee's behalf by the Senior Representative accompanied by the Department representative

10.5 The employee appealing, his Supervisor and other appropriate employees may be called to give evidence if is thought their involvement is essential to the outcome of the hearing

10.6 The decision of the hearing is final. It is recognised that the Union may wish to discuss the matter as a collective issue

11. INDUSTRIAL ACTION

The Company and the Union undertake to follow the procedures agreed to and recognise that this Agreement provides adequate and speedy procedures for the discussion of Company related affairs and the resolution of problems and as such precludes the necessity for recourse to any form of industrial action by either the Company the Union or the Employees.

Signed by

M. SADA

N.T. SALMON

duly authorised for and on behalf of

SANYO INDUSTRIES (UK) LIMITED
Signed by

R. SANDERSON
L. CHITTOCK
duly authorised for and on behalf of

THE ELECTRICAL ELECTRONIC TELECOMMUNICATIONS AND PLUMBING UNION

Dated this 10th day of June 1982.

Source: Sanyo (UK) Ltd (1982). Reproduced with permission of Sanyo Industries (UK) Limited, Oulton Works, School Road, Lowestoft, Suffolk NR33 9NA

REFERENCES

Adair, J (1975) *Effective Leadership*, Kogan Page, London.

Argyris, C (1990) *Understanding Organizational Behaviour*, John Wiley, New York.

Baddeley, J (1981) *Understanding Industry*, Butterworths/Industrial Society, London.

Blake, R and Mouton, J (1986) *The New Managerial Grid*, Gulf, New York.

Cartwright, D (ed.) (1959) *Studies in Social Power*, University of Michigan Press, Ann Arbor.

Donovan, D (1968) Report of the Royal Commission on Trades Unions and Employers Associations, HMSO, London.

Drucker, P F (1986) *The Practice of Management*, Heinemann, London.

Etzioni, A (1964) *Power and Organisations*, McGraw-Hill, London.

French, J and Raven, B (1959) 'The bases of social power', in D Cartwright (ed.) *Studies in Social Power*, University of Michigan Press, Ann Arbor.

Furnham, A (1997) *The Psychology of Managerial Incompetence*, Whurr, London.

Goldthorpe, J *et al.* (1968) *The Affluent Worker*, Vols 1, 2 and 3, Cambridge University Press, Cambridge.

Handy, C B (1994) *The Age of Unreason*, Macmillan, London.

Handy, C B (1994) *Understanding Organizations*, Penguin, Harmondsworth.

Harrison, R (1987) *Organization and Culture*, Prentice Hall, Hemel Hempstead.

Herzberg, F (1962) *Work and the Nature of Man*, Pelican, London.

Likert, R (1961) *New Patterns of Management*, McGraw-Hill, London.

Livy, B (1989) *Corporate Personnel Management*, Pitman, London.

Maslow, A (1960) *Motivation and Personality*, Harper & Row, New York.

Mayo, E (1943) *The Hawthorne Studies: The human problems of an industrial civilization*, MacMillan, New York.

McGregor, D (1980) *The Human Side of Enterprise*, McGraw-Hill, London.

Reddin, W (1970) *Managerial Effectiveness*, McGraw-Hill, Maidenhead.

Schein, E (1990) *Organizational Psychology*, Prentice Hall, Hemel Hempstead.

Semler, R (1992) *Maverick*, Free Press, New York.

Taylor, F W (1947) *Scientific Management*, Harper & Row, New York.

Trice, H M and Beyer, J M (1985) 'Using six organisational rites to change culture' in R H Kilman *et al.* (eds) *Gaining Control of the Corporate Culture*, Jossey-Bass, San Francisco, pp 374–5.

Walton, D and McKersie, A (1965) *A Behavioural Theory of Labour Negotiations*, McGraw-Hill, Maidenhead.

Weber, M (1986) *Social and Economic Organization*, Free Press, New York.

FURTHER READING

Armstrong, M (1996) *Personnel Management*, Kogan Page, London.

Ash, M K (1985) *On People Management*, McDonald, New York.

Bennett, R (1996) *European Management*, Pitman, London.

Bercusson, B (1997) *European Labour Law*, Butterworths, London.

Brewster, C (1990) *Industrial Relations*, Pan, London.

Brewster, C (1991) *Management of Ex-Patriots*, Kogan Page, London.

Cartwright, R (1995) *In Charge of Human Resource Management*, Blackwell, Oxford.

Cheatle, K (1996) *Human Resource Management*, NCVCCO, London.

Commission of the European Union (1997) *The European Union Social Charter*, EU, Brussels.

Commission of the European Union (1997) *The Treaty of Amsterdam*, EU, Brussels.

Evenden, A and Biddle, D (1992) *The Human Side of Enterprise*, Routledge, London.

Farnham, D (1994) *Employee Relations*, IPD, London.

Farnham, D and Pimlott, J (1992) *Industrial Relations*, Prentice Hall, Hemel Hempstead.

Furner, A and Hyman, R (eds) (1992) *Industrial Relations in the New Europe*, Blackwell, Oxford.

Griseri, P (1998) *Managing Values*, Macmillan, London.

Handy, C B (1984) *The Future of Work*, Penguin, Harmondsworth.

Hantrais, L (1996) *European Social Policy*, Macmillan, London.

Herzberg, F (1970) *Work and the Nature of Man*, Free Press, New York.

Kessler, S and Bayliss, F (1996) *Contemporary British Industrial Relations*, Macmillan, Basingstoke.

Legge, K (1992) *Human Resource Management*, Macmillan, London.

Lessem, R S (1987) *Intrapreneurship*, Wildwood House, London.

Lessem, R S (1989) *Managing Corporate Culture*, Gower, London.

Morita, A (1987) *Made in Japan: The Sony story*, Fontana, London.

Mumford, A (1989) *Management Development*, IPD, London.

Pascale, R and Athos, A (1983) *The Art of Japanese Management*, Fontana, London.

Peters, T and Austin, N (1985) *A Passion for Excellence*, Collins, London.

Pettinger, R (1997) *Introduction to Management*, Macmillan, London.

Pettinger, R (1998) *Managing the Flexible Workforce*, Cassell, London.

Pettinger, R (1998) *The European Social Charter: A manager's guide*, Kogan Page, London.

Pettinger, R and Frith, R (1996) *Preparing and Handling Industrial Tribunal Cases*, Technical Communications Ltd, Oxford.

Pettinger, R and Frith, R (1996) *The Management of Discipline and Grievances*, Technical Communications Ltd, Oxford.

Rice, J (1995) *Doing Business in Japan*, Penguin, Harmondsworth.

Roddick, A (1992) *Body and Soul: The Body Shop story*, Ebury, York.

Salamon, M (1992) *Industrial Relations*, Prentice Hall International, Hemel Hempstead.

Salomon, G (1992) *Human Resource Strategies*, Open University Press, Milton Keynes.

Sieff, M (1990) *Humanity and Management: The Marks and Spencer approach*, McGraw-Hill, Maidenhead.

Sisson, K (1991) *Personnel Management in Britain*, Blackwell, Oxford.

Sternberg, E (1995) *Just Business*, Warner, London.

Storey, J (1996) *New Perspectives on Human Resource Management*, Blackwell, Oxford.

Thomason, G (1986) *A Textbook of Human Resource Management*, IPD, London.

Thomason, G (1987) *A Textbook of Industrial Relations*, IPD, London.

Torrington, D and Hall, L (1992) *Personnel Management: A New Approach*, Prentice Hall International, Hemel Hempstead.

Trevor, M (1992) *Toshiba's New British Company*, Policy Studies Institute, London.

Vroom, V (1964) *Work and Motivation*, John Wiley, Chichester.

Vroom, V and Deci, E L (1992) *Management and Motivation*, Penguin, Harmondsworth.

Warr, P (1987) *Psychology at Work*, Penguin, Harmondsworth.

Wickens, P (1996) *The Road to Nissan*, Macmillan, London.

Williams, A and Dobson, P (1995) *Changing Culture*, IPD, London.

Woodward, J (1970) *Industrial Organisation: Behaviour and Control*, Oxford University Press, Oxford.

INDEX

References in *italic* indicate figures or tables

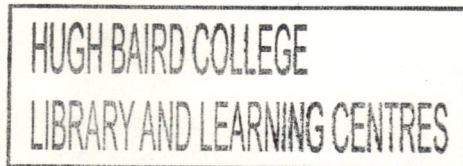